# SIX Under EIGHT

## MADELEINE WEST

VIKING
*an imprint of*
PENGUIN BOOKS

VIKING

UK | USA | Canada | Ireland | Australia
India | New Zealand | South Africa | China

Penguin Books is part of the Penguin Random House group of companies
whose addresses can be found at global.penguinrandomhouse.com.

Penguin
Random House
Australia

First published by Penguin Random House Australia Pty Ltd, 2016

Cover and text design by Alissa Dinallo © Penguin Group (Australia)
Author and twins photographed by Earl Carter
Older children photographed by Rob Palmer
Typeset in 12.5/16.5pt Fairfield Light by Alissa Dinallo
Printed and bound in Australia by Griffin Press, an accredited ISO AS/NZS 140001
Environmental Management Systems printer.

National Library of Australia
Cataloguing-in-Publication data:

West, Madeleine, author.
Six under eight / Madeleine West.
9780670078929 (paperback)
West, Madeleine--Diaries.
West, Madeleine--Family.
Parenting.
Television actors and actresses--Australia--Biography.
791. 45028092

**penguin.com.au**

To all my little people ... and to he who is helping them grow.

# CONTENTS

# INTRODUCTION

Hi! I am Madeleine and I am a mum. Not a tiger mum or a helicopter mum; occasionally a soccer mum but not a sporty mum. Definitely a busy mum. I am a happy mum, a sleepy mum, a grumpy mum (and all the other dwarves), a funny mum, striving to be a yummy mum but more frequently a crummy mum. I am not always a great mum; sometimes I question if I am even a good mum, but I am, first and foremost, Mum. Mother of many: blessed six times over with the pitter, splatter and clatter of tiny feet. I am no expert and never try to be, but I have run the parenthood gauntlet a few times now, and can say I have experienced a fair slice of what it has to offer. I have made plenty of mistakes; that's part of being human. But I have tried my hardest to learn from them: that is being clever.

The most important thing to remember is this: You . . . Are . . . The . . . Grown-up . . . and you are a parent. Navel gazing, a few tears, a bit of griping, a good, cleansing whinge over a chamomile at mothers' group – these things are part and parcel with parenthood, they are our birthright, in that from the moment we give birth to our child, it's our right to whinge about our child. Provided, that is, we limit it to letting off a little steam now and then. Because at the end of the day, we are adults, they are children, and the two roles should not be confused.

Yes, we will all flip out a little at times, but our children rely upon us to provide a stable foundation, day in, day out. Yes, it is mundane, it is limiting. Yes, it curtails our freedom and demands every decision we make and choice we take be made through the prism of our children's wellbeing first and foremost. But this is parenthood. It is a role we take on voluntarily and one that must be carried out with selflessness, care and consideration. There is no place for selfishness on this merry-go-round.

Our little ones need to know we will be there to wipe their noses, clean their bums, feed them, clothe them, soothe their fears, sit with them through the night when they're sick, watch them play sports, help them with their homework, laugh and cry with them, all without thanks, just the occasional card and homemade macaroni necklace.

So, contemplating parenthood? Well, before you worry about pre-natal classes and nursery colour schemes, first be prepared to swallow your pride, put your ambition in the backseat, rev up your courage, and strap yourself in for what will be the most terrifying, exhilarating, devastating, rewarding, eye-opening, wonderful ride of your life. Gird your loins and lock down your ego, because there are no medals and no backslaps; their gratitude will be signified by mere grunts more often than not, and their affection for you may prove as changeable as underwear, especially as they approach those tumultuous teens.

Others will be full of good advice, generally well-meaning, frequently useful, occasionally misguided, sometimes utterly useless. And competition in the mothers' group relay (graduating to the school gate) can prove so fierce, it's a wonder parenting has not yet qualified as an Olympic event!

You will question your choices, your motives, your destiny and your sanity. However, if you can accept parenthood for what it is: essentially an obstacle course designed to be unwinnable, unrelenting, and without end – same challenges, different day – then you are a good parent. If you can accept that you don't have all the answers, never have, never will, and that every other parent out there, no matter how calm and collected they appear, is really just another mother duck, paddling away furiously while trying to look like they have it all together, then you are a good parent. If, when your child throws themselves on the supermarket floor because you selected the wrong brand of cereal, or tells you they hate you because you announce it is bed time, or use your favourite dress as an art smock to fiddle with the oil paints you thought you had locked away, or they arrive home with a tattoo/piercing/ boyfriend and when you voice your displeasure they promptly disappear into their cave, err, bedroom for the next six months, surfacing only for fridge raids and oxygen – if you can still smile, remember that they were, are, and always will be your baby, inextricably tied to you by blood, love and perhaps a court order, then YOU ARE A GOOD PARENT!

So take time to enjoy it, to smell the roses, treasure each stage and phase they pass through en route to the next. The most common declaration among parents is just how fast their children grow. They are ours for such a brief moment; revel in it before the great big world claims them for itself.

So please read on, not with pity or envy, or seeking enlightenment, but in solidarity. We are all parents, know parents, have had parents, or are thinking about becoming parents, whichever side of the tracks we come from or where we are headed. I cannot promise you will find gold between these pages, but there might be the odd cookie to be found under the sofa that is my life, and some loose change stuffed down between the cushions. If you can glean some little nugget of wisdom along the way then all of my trials and tribulations have been worth it. So glean away, read away, try not to look away, and please contain the urge to run away – because THIS IS PARENTHOOD folks, when it becomes an extreme sport.

# CHAPTER

# 26 JULY 2014

*4.50 a.m.* It's the wee hours of my thirty-seventh birthday. Since 1:15 a.m. I've tossed and turned, rearranged the pillows umpteen times, polished off last night's chicken breast, ironed a shirt, watched an inane Canadian cooking show (not to cast aspersions – one day some of my best friends may be Canadian), downed a chocolate milk and a banana, emptied the dishwasher, attacked a muesli bar, and made a valiant attempt to complete one of those 'whopper' crosswords from a glossy mag.

Hmm, whopper. What an appropriate noun, given that my rapidly expanding girth has, in the past week, precluded me not just from wearing heels and being able to see my feet when upright, but also from bending over, or getting up from the floor once down.

'Serves you right', I can imagine you smirking, dearest diary. 'That's where post-midnight chocolate milk gets you.' But rest assured, my extremities remain scrawny as ever, my buttocks a mere afterthought in the wake of the enormous, vein-addled, white balloon that is my twin-cradling belly. (Though, in a mystery deserving of the Twilight Zone, while my bum remains runty, this duo has blessed me with cellulite!?! The rear view of my hindquarters is reminiscent of freshly fallen snow dimpling the sad sacks that were my butt cheeks.) Yep, I'm up the duff with a troublesome twosome, a quite maniacally apt way to wrap up the progeny production which already features four drunk midgets, eight years old and under, currently snoozing at the end of the hall. Admittedly, they are all still in last night's clothes. Technically fresh, but still last night's. After school there was the usual slap-dash bath routine then, as I'd planned to take them out for a frenzy of nasty take-away, a new outfit was called for. Come bedtime, PJs were at hand but, excluding the odd smear of tomato sauce, the attire was still in good nick so I figured why not put them to bed as is? They wake ready-dressed, no fussing and fuming by Mum. I get fifteen more minutes of tossing and turning. Everyone wins.

I blame my insomnia on the hubby, The Chef, currently having a week away in Brazil, ahem, 'working'. Oh, all right, I shouldn't 'ahem' his seemingly endless work trips. He is knee-deep in a book about travel (convenient, I know) and works exceptionally hard building an empire on his own blood, sweat and tears. It would just be nice if I got to see him a little more often, or he had time to change the odd nappy. Mind you, if I was forced to step in and juggle 400-odd employees, man the pass at any one of his heaving restaurants, oversee financials, build a resort, or mentor budding cooks and celebrity wannabes on *MasterChef*, I'd be buying a fake passport and jumping on the next flight to Zurich. I dare say he has a similar impulse when faced with a loaded Huggies, so I guess that makes us even. Anyhoo, my beloved sent me a 1:15 a.m. text to alert me to the fact he had made his connection in Auckland, and, oh yeah, 'Happy birthday'. Bless his cotton socks. Plus, it's such a comfort,

SHOPPING LIST

Tim Tams
Prunes
250 g pack self-pity

at 1.15 a.m., to know his chosen airline has fulfilled its fundamental duty of dropping him at said destination within the specified timeframe. Phew!

And so the 'bip bip' of the message tone dragged me from the tender arms of sleep. Assuming a text at that hour could only mean one of two things: a family tragedy/emergency, or that I'd won a Botswanian lottery and just needed to provide my banking details to the nominated email address and watch the millions roll in, I had to get up and check it. Now I sit, wide awake, before nary a sparrow has farted.

So how on earth did we reach this point? This nexus, this prelude to utter insanity?

The Chef and I met at a dinner for an internationally acclaimed celebrity chef. Apparently The Chef admired the cut of my catsuit, I liked his shaggy mane and withering take on vegetarianism, and we shared a cab on the way home. It would be convenient here to invoke the 'rest is history' cliche, not to mention saving on word count, but in those halcyon days of early twentydom, my head was still too far up my own backside to see the wood for the trees and thus, it took a few years and a failed engagement elsewhere first. Finally, I gathered the courage to meekly ask The Chef to the tennis. Suffice to say he gave me his house key the next day . . . the fool. In a small concession to my former blindness, we would name our first daughter after the restaurant where we met. (Insert collective 'awwwwww'! here.) And no, her name is not Wendy, Jade Dragon or Subway.

Mini-Me (or Minnie) is, at eight, a Godiva-maned, impish-grinned beauty of fierce determination and horse-obsession. Number One Son Buddy, at the grand old age of six, is a sensitive soul with a withering tantrum on him, and a vocal range that will never require amplification of any kind. He came into this world bellowing fit to rival a Boeing 747 and hasn't really ceased since, unless, of course, you put an iPad in front of him. The Princess is the personification of golden-haired 'butter wouldn't melt in her mouth' four-year-old fairy princess sweetness with the sky-blue eyes of an angel – till she lets rip the tantrum power she shares with her brother, and her propensity for cutting the cheese at whim regardless of place or company present. Yep, all style, no class. And that brings us to our darling Tinker. At two, Tink is by far the most petite, a delicate little flower, but she's a rough-and-tumble grumpy-pants who eschews the fully fitted-out cubby in the Ikea food hall in favour of wandering about fastening and unfastening the buckles on all the high chairs. That's my girl. She's destined to be a fabulous locksmith, or a thief.

On that note, I hear the little madam calling 'mama' while simultaneously trying to activate the side-drop bar on her cot. It's 5:03 a.m. and the day has begun. Happy birthday to me . . .

## THURSDAY 9 OCTOBER

*5:24 a.m.* My sincerest apologies for interrupting your slumber with another pre-dawn entry but it's clearly when I do my best thinking and my battered sense of humour is perhaps most intact.

My apologies also for failing to write over these past two-and-a-half months, but I discovered this fabulous herbal formula which miraculously gave me back the gift of sleep – till it stopped bloody working. My middle-of-the-night malady these days seems to be not so much insomnia, but inability-to-get-comfy-induced wakefulness. There is no escaping the stark reality now, I'm well and truly up the duff and my uterus represents a prime bit of turf these two *in utero* trapeze artists spend most of the day and night wrangling over. They experiment with positions that would put

SHOPPING LIST

Gargantuan-sized value pack of infant nappies

Tim Tams

Novelty children's toothpaste

Womb renovation: extension with an ensuite

4

a pretzel to shame, and frequently assume a full-length stretch at the narrowest possible point to ensure they inflict the ultimate discomfort, usually at about 2 a.m. when such behaviour is guaranteed to drag me from the deepest sleep.

Twins . . . oh dear. How the heck have we come to this particular juncture? I want to blame faulty genealogy but there's been nary a whisper of multiples on The Chef's side and the last report of doubles tennis was on my mother's father's side over ninety years ago. I guess when you run this whole reproduction gauntlet enough times you start playing Russian Roulette.

With delivery imminent, I can now prepare an itinerary for each evening. Knowing I'll not sleep a wink overnight, I assemble small piles of snacks, reading matter and warm clothing and scatter them throughout the house at points where I think my wandering will least disturb the rest of the family. Heaven forbid the tiny toddler should be awoken by my presence and set up a squall which, domino-like, will see them all wide awake seeking food and entertainment while the world remains steadfastly dark outside. It's tough enough amusing myself, let alone the whole tribe. The Chef's pulling his hair out daily as it is. I'd hate to be accused of causing kiddy-acquired baldness.

## GET HELP, REAL HELP – THE PAID KIND

Many people have asked me how I manage with four munchkins, let alone having two on the way. I think it's critical to manage your life, your time and your schedules so you aren't merely managing, but actually living, with all the joy and fulfilment that entails.

For many years, I managed to juggle the equation of children, work and social life with the help of grandparents and occasional sitters, until I discovered number four was on the way. It took a lot of prompting but I finally succumbed and got help: the paid kind. Best decision I've ever made. Our little miracle worker, Sally Salvation, is lovely, loving and, critically, is a mother herself, so she just gets it. What I require of her is clearly negotiated and she is remunerated appropriately, though I regard much of what she has brought to our family as priceless. This has effectively removed the awkward dance of requesting help from grandparents. Now their time with the kids is about love and pleasure, not obligation. Don't get me wrong, they still mind the kids on occasion, but those occasions are now anticipated with excitement, not stress.

It is also imperative, when seeking to employ another set of hands, to ensure they fit seamlessly into the unique dynamic of your home. Remember that what you are looking for is not a friend or a third parent, but someone to assist you in ensuring all of your children's needs are met. Simple as that. A positive demeanour, an engaging manner balanced with the ability to maintain a professional distance, and prioritising your children's welfare are all crucial. A heavy presence which commands your attention or makes you feel uncertain of your parenting abilities and uncomfortable in your own home will only end in disaster.

Whomever you bring into your nest must also be able to adapt to your unique parenting style. I, for example, am a dyed-in-the-wool control freak. The girl who slavishly deconstructed, annotated and plotted her scripts has morphed into the mother who cannot sleep at night if she hasn't pressed a week's worth of uniforms and planned out a fortnight's-worth of evening meals, each tailored so they can be re-invented as a nutritious lunchbox-filler the next day. As the brood has grown, so too have my OCD parenting tendencies. I am a great believer in the Butterfly Effect: one bed left unmade before breakfast could see nations fall by dinnertime. Hence my habit of rushing around like a rabid ferret — one who is comatose on the couch by 9 p.m.

The Chef is more likely to engage in a serious tickle session with the munchkins than enforce the brushing of teeth. If he seems somewhat absent from my rants, dearest diary, trust me, he is very much present, but probably wading through his daily instalment of 300-odd critical emails rather than bathing the brood. I know which task I prefer; hand me the bubble bath! The Chef is here, but has an uncanny ability to disappear while sitting right in front of you, blending seamlessly into his environment, be it the kitchen table, his study or the couch. I put this chameleon-like skill down to him being able to tune out the white noise of parenting (the thrashing tantrums, the uncontrollable weeping, the gnashing and bashing and howling . . . and the kids can be quite noisy too) much more successfully than I can. The Chef is the most tender and playful of fathers, but he doesn't suffer fools and is the stricter disciplinarian. Our distinct roles evolved quite rapidly. I run the home, The Chef runs the business. It may sound archaic but there is nothing 1950s about the astronomical hours he works, just as there is nothing remotely barefoot and pregnant about my attempts to keep a foot in both worlds: mother and actor. The stark reality is, however, my industry and parenthood do not a merry partnership make. They are two pieces of a whole that simply will not fit. I revisit my profession as one would a beloved holiday home: for occasional, much-anticipated stays, yearning to stay longer but acutely aware that lingering too long will destroy the magic.

The Chef has been burning the midnight oil since he was fifteen. His career has become a crucial part of who he is, and the empire he has built crumbles in his absence. It is equal parts rewarding and exhausting. Just as I at times yearn to throw off the domestic yoke and run scream-ing into the toned, tanned, couture-clad embrace of the entertainment industry, so too does The Chef dream of staying home crafting play-doh creatures with the kiddies. The reality is, though, that without my fren-zied fulfilment of the daily to-do list, and without his hours slaving over stoves, contracts, rosters and plans for expansion, this boat would not stay afloat. The sacrifices The Chef makes to bring home the bacon also make my brief flirtations with acting possible. My gratitude translates as happily cranking up the washing machine five times a day, dividing the evening meal into G and AO sittings, and traipsing off to school twice a day loaded up like a packhorse. We both still have individual BIG DREAMS, we have just found that the best way to achieve them is together. Accordingly, anyone we bring into the home has to fit into that equation. Otherwise the formula simply does not work.

As for offers of help from friends and family: take 'em. Whom do you impress by being a martyr? Precisely no-one; well, perhaps a very small percentage of the population. That same percentage whose claim to fame is that they had a 'natural' delivery, and insist on rolling out a blow-by-blow account of the experience over dinner. Look, all power to those women; it's ace, truly, but at the end of the day, I've had multiple root canals and been physically hit by a speeding bus and I know how damn much both of those hurt. If I insisted on recounting them to complete strangers with great pride, or actually did them again, my friends and family would have me institutionalised with just cause.

## SUNDAY 12 OCTOBER

*5:30 p.m.* I'm wrapping up bath time. The floor is saturated, I'm saturated, the dog is saturated – and he spent the entire period downstairs, so it just goes to show what a Herculean task getting four kids hygienically sealed truly is, only for them to start rolling in dirt and sprouting lint again.

I have never been one to gild the lily when it comes to the whole mothering palaver. I am a staunch advocate of the philosophy that you cannot polish a number two, hence, many might justifiably wonder why I've had children at all. Not just that but why so many? Let me preface my answer by saying I adore my babies and, with the exception of a little more sleep and a little less endless tidying (I'm anal about a tidy, not necessarily clean, but tidy, house) I wouldn't change a thing. Children were never on my radar, however. Sure, they were cute, but so are some rodents, and rodents rarely require nappy changes. Besides, I was incredibly busy stroking my own ego, and it was enough of an effort battering my own inflated sense of self against glass ceilings without entertaining the thought of being responsible for a whole other being.

Now, I'm what some doctors like to dub 'the one per cent': that tiny, terrifying percentage of the population for whom contraceptives do not work. Short of using prophylactics or having major surgery, I might as well have saved my dollars and gone *au naturel* for the fat lot of good all those varied potions over the years have done me. We have tried everything over the years: pills, potions, rings, implants, jumping up and down, wishful thinking . . . suffice to say if the contraceptive contains a synthesised hormone, my reproductive system points, laughs and continues on its merry way.

Now, before you can interject with that most cliched of questions: 'You do know what's causing this, don't you?', let me say, 'Yes; we do own a television. And I've finally worked out how to operate the remote control.' The whole malarkey is really utterly unfair when you consider that with so many kids, there is no time to dabble in that causative factor – certainly not often enough to be so frequently slipping one through to the keeper!

SHOPPING LIST

*Bubble bath*

*Maternity pads*

*My sanity*

## WEDNESDAY 15 OCTOBER

*12:15 a.m.* After two hours' sleep I wake, panicked, drenched in the cold sweat of a lingering nightmare in which I have insufficient infant bedding. Could it be true? I thought I had baby linen aplenty, but have I stuffed up the sums? I'm gonna need two lots of everything! I begin to prowl the house and run a stock check of the neat piles of folded stuff I've stacked in the 'nursery'.

In preparation for the twins, my first 'Shock! Horror!' moment was when I realised I had run out of bedrooms. Putting newborns in with older children simply does not work for either party, as the twins will invariably be deprived of sleep and the older child will feel their personal space is being encroached upon.

As a temporary measure, I have set up my teensy tiny office (2 m by 4 m on a good day) as the nursery, with two bassinets (I plan on sleeping them together initially but not for too long; inevitably their sleeping patterns will shift and it's important to be able to separate them so one isn't waking or disturbing the other), a comfy feeding chair, and changing facilities on my desk.

> SHOPPING LIST
>
> White goods catalogues
>
> Professional mugger (please, steal my credit card so I can cancel it! I'm doing far more damage with it than any petty thief ever will!)

# BATTEN DOWN THE HATCHES, THE INFANTS ARE COMING! SOME PERSONAL OBSERVATIONS ON SETTING UP YOUR NURSERY

One word: minimal. Keep it simple. The temptation, on your first nursery shopping spree, when you launch yourself at some mega suburban baby warehouse, will be to panic and buy everything.

The manufacturers know this and love it! Everything is so beautiful, so functional, so practical, according to the advertising on the box. Truth is, you won't use half of it. And the half that is truly useful tends to stand the test of time, so a friend or relative may already have it and be willing to pass it on. Ask around before you pull out your wallet.

Most baby stuff seems to be built in inverse proportions to the size of the baby using it: the smaller the baby, the bigger and clunkier the item (read change table, elaborate mechanised bouncer, foofy cradle assembly) and most are useful for a very limited time. They also tend to be very expensive. Those baby superstores know they have a captive audience, so rather than sage advice on what you really will need, you will be given the hard sell on what makes them the most money, and has you coming back for more when it becomes redundant or the baby grows out of it.

## Some purchases which have proved pointless

• Baby bath: used it precisely twice, then discovered it was quicker, cleaner and simpler to wash the baby in the bathroom sink, graduating to the kitchen sink, then finally a shallow bath.
• Change table: unless you are not able to bend or kneel down, this is nothing more than a glorified storage unit. What a waste of money, and that most precious commodity, space! A simple foam insert changing mat on a bench or table, inside a wardrobe or on the floor, does just as well at about 1/30th of the price.
• Mechanised bouncers: all well and good till the batteries run out or the thing has a meltdown, then we are back to square one.
• Cradles: so much fluffy, lacy, cutesy frippery, so little growth space.

And such a short shelf life! Speaking of shelving, if desperate for a snug, cradle-like environment, a sturdy, padded dresser drawer ticks all the boxes.

- Walkers: don't even think about it.

## Some 'recommended' purchases and additions that just make no sense

- Installation of a dimmer switch – why? Last time I popped out a kid, as much as it looked and behaved like an alien life form, I felt no compulsion to provide it with a light and sound show to mimic life on Mars. Whatever happened to a lamp with a low wattage bulb?
- Lay down linoleum in the nursery, or strip back to floorboards for easy cleaning. Oh, for goodness' sake! Yes, babies can be messy, and sometimes their number threes (explosive poo) and projectile vomiting can be reminiscent of both the *Alien* and *Exorcist* movie franchises (see above . . . hmm . . . maybe should get a dimmer switch after all) but surely the reality of carpet occasionally copping a bit of baby puke is not justification enough to begin renovating the house. Just arm yourself with a towel whenever approaching said alien, err, baby, and if all else fails, put down a tarpaulin.
- A small sink and tap assembly installed in the nursery. Well, of course! Must get one for the yacht and the helicopter as well! Puh-lease! If the effort of walking to the nearest bathroom or the kitchen is beyond you, then parenthood has some rude shocks in store for you. If you are actually contemplating this addition, let's pause for a moment to consider your home's resale value and have pity on any future real estate agent trying to capture you a decent sale price, trying to explain to potential buyers the presence of linoleum and a sink in the middle of an otherwise normal bedroom.

## What you do need

- A fully approved and accredited cot (minus side padding or buffers – they are suffocation hazards).
- Kinetic bouncer; the type where the baby's own movements create the motion. Keeps them occupied for hours.
- Microwaveable steriliser bags. Cheap and compact, so very portable, and much more kitchen-friendly than bulky conventional sterilisers.

Most are not particularly environmentally friendly but there are some biodegradable versions available and all offer 20+ uses.

- A compact, lightweight pram. The lightweight component is utterly critical: you will be surprised at how often you will be folding, lifting and packing the damn thing.
- Approved and accredited car seats: for pure functionality, the removable capsules are tricky to lug around, unless you have the pram base accessory, which is fabulous but the baby will grow out of it quickly, requiring a whole new pram assembly.
- Breast pump, if you're intending to feed with breast milk. These little gems allow some modicum of freedom for Mum, and allows Dad or other family members to help with feeds, especially the night feeds, giving new mums a chance to catch up on some Zs. Also, milk can be collected and stored in the freezer for emergencies or when (shock, horror) Mum is contemplating a night out!
- For best results, you want a hospital-grade pump, but these are prohibitively expensive. A better option is to hire one just for as long as you need it. Most pharmacies, hospitals and maternal health centres offer a breast-pump hire program, or can direct you to somewhere that does.
- A 'child magnet', designed so that at the press of a discreet button, your errant children are instantly propelled back to your side, regardless of where they've wandered off to, or where you've left them. Sadly, this brilliant innovation has not yet been invented.

Setting up a nursery for twins, I have discovered, is much the same as for singletons, just doubled. My first purchase for this room, where I intend to hide myself and the twins away from the world until I get them into a routine, is a twin feeding cushion. You wrap this little number about your midsection like some mildly demented item of catwalk couture, and lay a bub along each side of your body, under your arms. All being well, their tiny faces will line up precisely with your breasts and before you can say 'two for the price of one' you are feeding simultaneously. It will be a juggling act, yes, but also an enormous time-saver (given there are four other children in the household to service) and hopefully get them into a co-ordinated feeding routine and thus sleeping in simpatico. Also, your arms are free to knit, read, land aircraft using semaphore, or just fiddle on the iPad. Genius!

Next up, I went a little crazy, and having spotted a mini bar fridge on sale online, I picked it up, along with an electric kettle. My perhaps warped thinking ran along these lines: all the bedrooms, including my study-cum-nursery, are up two flights of stairs. The kitchen is downstairs. Past experience tells me that snacks and drinks are a must for Mum while breastfeeding, and there is no way I will be hauling two squalling babies downstairs to secure some calories, then back up to feed them. Also, the downstairs area, like in most modern homes, is open plan. A baby's piercing cry carries a long way in such environments, and it just isn't worth waking the entire household. I figure, with a fridge and kettle on hand, I will be able to boil up a cup of tea (and one day prepare bottles) while changing nappies. I can grab a snack from the fridge, all within the four moderately sound-proofed walls of my office. Hopefully this will keep disruption to the rest of the family to a minimum, and my mini-fridge will prove the perfect storage unit for expressed milk, separate from the smells and potential contaminants of the kitchen refrigerator. At the end of the day, I can easily on-sell the lot thanks to the wonders of the internet.

This little set-up may sound ludicrous to anyone else, but having battled out four rounds of this particular game before, I know how disruptive a new baby can be in a family unit, especially one with small children, and where one parent has no option but to work long hours through those early weeks. I also know how groggy and disoriented pure exhaustion can leave you. Jiggling one grizzly bub about the house on your hip is challenge enough, let alone two, and if I can avoid tumbling down the stairs with both tiny tots in tow, I will. Finally, I must admit I am not going out of my way to amend my broken sleep, knowing what is coming. With any luck, being accustomed to functioning at half to a quarter of usual brain capacity will take the edge off when they finally arrive.

Ladies, I know the prevailing advice is to rest before the baby comes, as you will need your strength and to be well rested once they arrive. Baloney! I call BS on that! The hardest part is adjusting to going from a sound eight-hour sleep to having barely three, broken down into minuscule instalments, so, contrary to all you've read and heard, embrace broken sleep now, because no amount of rest at this point will be enough to charge you up for the twenty-odd years of shattered nights you have coming.

Back to the bedding situation, I'm still not sure I have enough. But one tip generously passed on to me that I'm more than happy to pass on to you is this: in setting up the bassinet and cot, buy three inexpensive fitted sheets, preferably linen or cotton, and three cheap, fitted waterproof sheets for both. Now put them all on the bed, interchanging layers: waterproof, fitted sheet, waterproof, fitted sheet and so on. Now, in the event of an accident at either end during the night, just whip a layer off each and you have a fresh bed without scrambling around for fresh linen in the middle of the night while juggling a hungry, soiled baby. It's a rare night that the baby will soil all three layers, so you will always have a functional bed while washing the other linen. On that note, I've almost finished my peanut butter protein bar so it's time to try to catch forty winks (read: read some salacious online gossip until I nod off, drooling on to my own shoulder). Nite!

*3:06 a.m.* This is no longer merely inconvenient, it's become downright annoying. No matter what position I assume, I cannot get comfortable . . . you thought I was going somewhere else with this 'position' talk, didn't you? Please! I'm 36 weeks up the duff with twins, drag your mind out of the gutter. On my back, the circulation to my extremities is cut off; roll to the left, my spine is pulled one way, to the right it's the other. My front isn't even an option. I try sleeping sitting up, invariably slip into one of the above-mentioned poses and immediately wake, aching and rendered unable to shift. My list of aches and small physical irritations is growing by the day. Haemorrhoids? Check. Sore back and legs, check, check. Varicose veins coursing, ropey and rugged, down one leg? Check! Itchy skin? Ooh yeah, check! My poor stomach might have escaped stretch marks by some miracle, but it is still covered in a network of angry red squiggly lines, inflicted by my constant scratching.

With The Chef away on an overnighter to Sydney and the kids all sleeping soundly, I've opted to run a bath. Oooh, I know, extravagant! Lights off, two candles lit, relaxation awaits. I'd love to be luxuriating in the gentle twang of chimes and chants but it is three o'clock in the morning and sometimes you just have to know your limits. I've just lain back, eyes closed, and dreamily open them a moment later to spot a huge bloody spider directly above me on the ceiling. I leap up and immediately wrench some muscle in my nether regions. That's invariably going to bother me for longer than is necessary. Yep, cheers, local flora and fauna. Oh well, at least I've managed a rinse-off. Undressing for bed this evening I had found both cups of my bra were stained with dried colostrum. Puh-lease. Could I become any more horrendous?

# THURSDAY 16 OCTOBER

*5:42 p.m.* It was 31 degrees celsius today, and for some unknown reason I sat outside for a moment and promptly fell asleep, only rousing two hours later to Tink rousing in her crib. I've been feeling slightly off ever since, and while an enormous slice of me screams 'Yes! Yes! Get 'em out!', the slightly more rational side reminds me, in a firm whisper, that my beloved obstetrician has inconveniently taken his family to Hawaii (rude) and doesn't return till the weekend. His replacement is not coming anywhere near me. I'm sure he is perfectly lovely, but any doctor who, having made me wait over an hour, then pronounces, 'No no no, I'm not scanning you today, I simply haven't time,' before unceremoniously shoving me out the door with a proclamation of 'You are doing great!' ain't winning in my book. To be honest, his whole demeanour reminds me of the white rabbit of *Alice in Wonderland* fame, and that isn't a compliment. Would you trust that bumbling bunny with sharp instruments around seven crucial layers of your subcutaneous abdominal region? Me neither.

Anyway, it's verging on dinner time/bath time/where's a stiff drink when you need one, might as well get on to it so I can go to bed ASAP and watch that pre-recorded special on delivering and raising twins. If I'm going to lie there awake I might as well be terrified out of my wits too!

### SHOPPING LIST

Aloe vera

Ice

Functioning brain

Ticking time bomb (scratch that, forgot I'm already carrying two)

# FRIDAY 17 OCTOBER

*6:22 p.m.* Oh, just realised today is the day . . . sorta. I'm thirty-seven weeks, which means I'm more or less at term for twins. What does that mean, really? At term? That I've come to terms with having twins? Lotta baloney that, and utterly

### SHOPPING LIST

Small wheel of Camembert, just to admire

Half bottle Cristal (wonder if they do it in the 100ml minis you get in hotel bar fridges? Just want half a glass . . . desperately. Need to celebrate)

Large platter of sushi to fling at passers-by for judging my Cristal quaffing false advertising. I'm still well and truly in denial city with no intention of moving on. Does it mean I've made fundamental, non-negotiable terms regarding the imminent arrival of twins? Hmm: if it includes daily massages, a hospital suite decked out in flowers, soft cheeses, sushi and champagne, well, I'm much more comfortable with that interpretation.

## MONDAY 20 OCTOBER

*12 NOON* Like sands through the hourglass, time is rapidly running out. My body aches with the smallest movement. Most of my organs now seem to reside either up around my shoulders or down in my toes. Every twinge, every lurch, every minor leak, sends me into flurries of terror with a touch of dread. Dread seems to be a common theme to most of my days, as I've developed a tendency to wet myself when laughing, coughing, sneezing or just breathing deeply. It would seem my bladder just has no place in my new body structure composition.

Frankly, I feel like I have no idea what I am doing and what is about to come.

Accordingly, I finally succumb and attend a class on having twins. From the start, I try to be open and receptive, but immediately feel like the elephant in the room when, while introducing ourselves, it is revealed I'm the only expectant mum there who already has other children. When prompted to reveal how many, jaws crash to the floor at my response. It takes some serious work by the instructor to recapture the class's attention, and even an hour later at tea break, I feel the weight of the stares directed my way, loaded with pity, perhaps a hint of admiration, but mostly just bewilderment. I feel like addressing all assembled just to say, 'Trust me, I'm as shocked as all of you that I've ended up here – probably more so.'

SHOPPING LIST

*BS detector*

*Gag. Note to self: no-one likes a know-it-all spouting their homegrown wisdom unasked.*

The advice dished out on feeding, sleeping arrangements and ensuring you take time for yourself is all sound, with some really handy little nuggets in there. However, I cannot stop the little voice in my head that interjects at every juncture, querying: 'But what happens to your strict feeding timetable if it clashes with school drop-off? Or if Minnie has netball at that time? Or Buddy has to attend a play date? Or Tink fills her nappy then proceeds to unload its contents about the house?' Hmm, it would seem even the most useful hints will require tweaking to fit into our family schedule, or lack thereof.

## THE GIFT THAT IS ADVICE FROM OUTSIDERS

I think a healthy way to take such advice is to take what you know will work for you, what you feel will be helpful and what you can manage, and discard the rest. Strict scheduling is a fantastic concept, and works for some. BUT we are all unique, hence there is no one-size-fits-all solution to how best to get through the day, whether you have one child or fourteen. Some families, regardless of their size, will need to bring in help to function optimally. Others, whether they are big or small, won't. Some will find a more regimented approach, dotting every 'i' and crossing every 't', is the only way to get things done. Some families will flourish under a more relaxed, free-form style of parenting. Whichever, experiment a little to discover what works best for you, but as always, only take on those opinions and titbits of advice that best suit you and how you want to parent. The judgement of others has no place in your day. Judgements are the product of opinions, and like the products of bums, are best left unseen and disposed of ASAP. If you genuinely respect and admire someone's approach, then by all means take on their suggestions, but only when it is well-meaning and given in the spirit of sharing. Parenthood brings enough guilt and fear without the unwanted words of others adding to it.

## TUESDAY 21 OCTOBER

*12:17 a.m.* Just cut the cheese with such force I actually woke myself up. Apparently this is completely normal and nothing to be ashamed of.

*8 a.m.* I am nesting. Something's gotta give, and soon. I have the urge to start wrapping up some outstanding tasks while I still have time, and mindful of the fact I will be having a caesarean with the requisite six-week abstinence from driving it entails, now is the time to get things done. First up, Buddy needs a haircut, I'm in desperate need of a colour, we need an indoor irrigation system for the plants from Bunnings, I have an outstanding lay-by consisting of tiny suits and muslin wraps to collect, and finally, at the school, I've requested to come in early to make Buddy's production costume with him, as I won't be available in two weeks when it's scheduled to be done.

> SHOPPING LIST
>
> *Adult nappies (WTF?????)*
>
> *Discretion and manners. I'm so knackered, both are in short supply. Ahhh, screw it: the world can go bite me.*

I am strongly tempted to pick up the phone and order The Chef's PA to clear his schedule due to an 'errands that need to be run emergency', while I assume a prostrate position on the couch with an emergency Tim Tam infusion, but can't imagine that would go down well. Alternatively, I have a wonderful, amazing, fabulous nanny, starting with me full-time once the twins arrive. Maybe I could bring forward our employment arrangement by a few weeks? Hmm, that would mean stiffing the family she works with on the days she isn't slaving it out with me already. Bugger.

Ah well, best get to it. *Sigh*.

**2:05 a.m.** Okay, note to self: at this late stage of twin pregnancy, REST. Best intentions, best insmentions. The endless and insistent chatter about babies, pregnancy and delivery from utter strangers at the hairdresser, along with the tummy touching that accompanied it, left me grumpy. Traipsing from store to store in 31°C heat left me exhausted and puffy and I clearly didn't drink enough fluids. By the time I arrived at the school I didn't have time to eat lunch, and inhaling craft glue fumes left me giddy and nauseous, so even when I did get home I couldn't eat. I did get everything done, even successfully gluing two fingers together with the hot glue gun, and Buddy, my precious little man, loved the one-on-one time making his costume, but I haven't felt right all evening and am now beset with cramps and feeling sick. I call the hospital, and the lovely midwife who picks up assures me all will be fine but suggests I come in for a twenty-minute monitoring session while the family sleeps. Feeling guilty and overly dramatic, I go regardless.

Forty minutes later, with a hot chocolate and a slice of cake in my belly, and a very normal monitoring result in my hands, I'm back home and in bed. False alarm this time, but a sensation of impending doom (whoops, I mean impending motherhood) is upon me, and I know that at any moment now, four will become six, all under eight years old. Never was any bloody good at maths.

Despite this, I must admit that, as I toss and turn, rearranging the pillows in a desperate attempt to get comfortable, I am quietly accepting the inevitable, and with that comes a quiet inner peace. Even if I can't bloody sleep.

## TAKE CARE OF YOU, AND THE WORLD WILL FOLLOW SUIT

Despite my feeling a fool and a drama queen, yet again my midnight dash to the hospital has underlined that this pregnancy malarkey is serious business and mums should always follow their instincts.

My third pregnancy, with Princess, ended abruptly at thirty-seven weeks when my waters broke. There was no gush, just a barely detectable trickle. Many around me opined that it was nothing, I was fine, but my instincts screamed otherwise. I insisted on being examined and sure enough, our little buttercup was on her way. Had I ignored what my body was trying to tell me, there was a very real chance I could have contracted an infection, with dire consequences for my baby still in utero.

Similarly, before you are talked out of pursuing your favoured approach regarding birth, don't be afraid to ask questions, and if you are uncomfortable with the answers, ask for a second opinion. It is critical that you are comfortable with each step being taken, and feel fully informed of all your options.

However, it is also important to remember that advice, be it from obstetrician, midwife or doula, is being given with your best interests, and those of your baby in mind. Life doesn't always go according to the script we have written ourselves, and if you find yourself at a point where the reality of the situation departs from your birth plan, then you really must be prepared to give yourself over to the experts. Certainly, ask for a second opinion, but at the end of the day, these people are here to secure the safe delivery of babies, not pamper to our vanity. Once you have that precious little bundle in your arms, the means by which they got there will and should be irrelevant.

As mothers and mothers-to-be, we are very good at putting everyone else's needs ahead of our own, constantly pushing down our instinctive concerns for ourselves when it might inconvenience someone else. This is no way to start the journey of motherhood. To my mind, a decent dose of self-love and self-respect rubs off on our children and those around us in the healthiest way imaginable, as it teaches them the importance of taking care of yourself. How can we effectively care for others, in our home and the world at large, if we cannot care for ourselves?

In terms of big-picture thinking, if we consistently regard our needs as secondary to those of others, we show our children that what we want and need is not important, and make excuses for not pursuing our own goals. As they follow everything we do, this sets the seed in their minds that ego is a bad thing, and self-respect to be dismissed.

As a family, my little circus troupe actively exercise self-concern, adhering to the motto: Don't make excuses, make it happen. I try to teach my children that the only thing making excuses guarantees is a front-row seat to watching the world pass you by, and that is something no parent wants for their child.

Listen to your instincts and respect them. When you instinctively feel something's not quite right, and you want it checked out, do it, without apology. There is no embarrassment in seeking peace of mind.

Pregnancy can entail the contradictory experience of feeling deeply powerful and yet deeply vulnerable. It affects every aspect of your being: physical, emotional and psychological, so never apologise for wanting all your concerns explored. Good friends, family, midwives and medical personnel understand this. The concern and care shown me by the midwives at my hospital, and the gentle understanding my obstetrician has shown me from day one, even over something as simple as talking me back down from the ledge over some trivial issue, using the right mixture of humour and concern, have assured me I have the right people in my corner on this, one of the most important journeys of my life. It's one I've been on four times already, but as I've come to understand, it is constantly changing. The people who help you achieve your goals along the way remain forever in your heart and memory, and teach you to practise the same care and concern with others – qualities I hope to pass on to my progeny, and hope they pass on to their own.

# CHAPTER

# WEDNESDAY 22 OCTOBER

*10:20 a.m.* I've noticed a trend in our family: that whenever I am heavily pregnant, The Chef has a brainwave that invariably requires me to do things I don't wanna do (drag your mind out of the gutter).

I've just received a call from The Chef announcing we will be babysitting two miniature pigs. Isn't that . . . fanTASTic?!

Oh, and a major renovation and remodelling of the house which we have been wrangling with Heritage over for some months now has suddenly been given the green light and will begin . . . the week after the twins are due. FANtasTIC!!!

When The Chef arrives home, I can tell from the look on his face that all has not gone to plan. The two porkers emerge from the back seat of his beautiful new car, thrice the size we expected them to be – apparently they aren't so miniature after all.

They immediately start squealing at a volume designed to induce madness. Speechless, The Chef just points to his back seat. I poke my head in to see every available square of upholstery embellished with excrement. And the smell! He complains about Tink's nappies. Ha!

It takes some hours to finally entice them into the backyard, which naturally involves a tour of the house. Although brief, it is just long enough for them to announce their arrival with liberal toilet breaks here, there and everywhere. Once they're cajoled from the kitchen into the yard, the real fun begins. They immediately start rooting up our lawn for the tasty treats beneath. And I thought we were welcoming two teacup-sized bundles that required bottle-feeding and tender love! 'Practise for the coming twins,' I'd consoled myself!

Despite a good feed and a bowl of eagerly lapped-up milk in the evening, the two pigs, promptly christened 'Squeak' and 'Squealer' by Minnie, proceed to justify their new names by doing just that . . . all night. Finally the fracas ceases at around 3 a.m., which is when I invariably awake anyway.

SHOPPING LIST

Gumboots/wellies/galoshes

Waterproof overalls

Careworn Akubra hat and sprig of wheat to clench between my teeth

Lessons in speaking fluent 'Strine', so all the other farmers understand me when we compare notes on breeds, breeding and drought, and shake our collective fists at the government.

At daybreak we discover why they fell quiet so suddenly. In a surprisingly coordinated team effort they have uprooted a large section of the garden and eaten through the watering system. Around a quarter of the backyard is now flooded. The Chef finishes off his espresso before proclaiming, 'We'll just keep them the week, then?' I merely smile. Sweet victory . . .

## FRIDAY 24 OCTOBER

*5:02 a.m.* In a shock development, the pigs put themselves to bed in the garden at 7 p.m. and we have not heard a peep since. They are still not staying, though. The kids have succeeded in what we stopped the pigs from doing by traipsing pig crap throughout the house, and the bloody oinkers have developed a truly fetching habit of peeing right in front of all the doors leading out to the garden, greeting us with yet another undesirable odour every time we leave the house.

I'm putting my sleeplessness to good use this morning, going over the renovation plans with a fine-tooth comb and drawing up an interior plan for the desperately needed new spaces.

Including excavation, building and re-landscaping, we are looking at a three-month stretch of tradespeople, mud, noisy heavy machinery, and no access to the front of the house. As luck

> **SHOPPING LIST**
>
> *Cancel the compost order for the next few months, the pigs have generously provided plenty . . . would just be nice if more of it was on the garden, not in the house.*

would most definitely not have it, my study-cum-nursery is directly above the area of major works. The thought of trying to establish newborn twins into some semblance of a sleeping/feeding routine in such conditions is giving me nightmares, and so I have made a decision. Two weeks after they are born, I will be moving the twins, all their siblings and my irreplaceable nanny to a little hideaway which, as luck would most definitely have it, we have just finished building after eight years of saving, planning and dreaming. Oh, I will be going too; I'm not yet brave enough to attempt to palm all six kids off while I skip the country for more tropical climes. I'm certain that day will come, but it's not here yet.

The hideaway will eventually be an investment property but is still vacant, and I am very aware of how lucky we are to be in this position. Timing works well, with the Christmas holidays on the near horizon, so the kids will only miss three weeks of school, which we can wrangle with a semi-correspondence arrangement. As the kids are currently in grade three, prep and three-year-old kinder, we will never be able to do this again, so the time is ripe. The Chef will get down when he can (hmm, I wonder if that's a gleam of merriment in his eye, contemplating an escape from those first difficult new-baby weeks), and we will return on occasion when I am again allowed to drive. Sorted.

Dearest diary, should you ever find yourself contemplating a touch of home improvement with a baby pending, and without a retreat to escape to, my advice would be: Don't. Put it off for a few months. We don't have an option in this case, as our permit will expire following some serious planning permission prevarication. I've lived through a renovation with a new baby twice now and it's simply not worth the stress and anxiety. This is a period fraught with physical and emotional upheaval as it is. Don't exacerbate it by bringing strangers, machinery and mess into your nest. A few months can make the world of difference.

If it cannot be avoided, consider renting elsewhere on a short-term basis. If you are determined to live in, block off your living quarters so they are inaccessible to any tradespeople, soundproof with blankets or even egg cartons, and manoeuvre furniture to best suit your needs. It may mean setting up kitchen equipment in a section of your lounge or bedroom, but anything is better than trying to make a cup of tea in the kitchen after a sleepless night with tradespeople traipsing through to the tune of jackhammers and drills.

## SATURDAY 25 OCTOBER

*5:35 p.m.* Damn nesting! As time runs out, I have been incessantly 'wrapping up' those last few jobs, and striving to spend quality time with the kids, rather than just blowing a gasket at them.

Accordingly, I chaperoned Buddy to an ice-skating party in the city, and out of typical parental guilt, brought along the two littlies for lunch and a run around at an adjacent indoor play centre.

It's a Saturday, so naturally parking is nigh on impossible, and locating Buddy's party group among the throngs of folk striding about with razorblades attached to their feet, wrapped up for Siberia just when Melbourne is finally getting its heat on, is also nearly impossible, and then navigating our way back to the shopping centre without scout-like orienteering skills IS impossible.

Destination finally reached amid the crowds of Saturday morning shoppers, I spend the next two hours tightly assuring myself this is quite relaxing, sitting over coffee and a paper then bounding up every five minutes to frantically lap the periphery of the play equipment attempting to locate an errant child. It's a carefully choreographed dance, and one being played out by nearly every other parent there, except for those smiling encouragingly at their child who, being a little more shy and retiring, refuses to budge from their plastic chair while Mum or Dad or both ape how much fun it will be ricocheting themselves off inflatable castles or hurtling down the mega slide and colliding with that kid who insists on climbing backwards up the slide despite all the signs sternly advising not to. Of course, that kid's parents won't be scouting the periphery either. This is 'their time', they have paid good money and as far as they are concerned Little Ricky and Little Annabelle are Children of the World for the next hour and forty-five minutes or at least until Dad has read every article in the sports section and done the Saturday super crossword.

SHOPPING LIST

Nothing, just a quiet, restful weekend to ponder life, love, and the many wonders of parenthood

(Yep, wrote shopping list after 3 hours inhaling the newest essential oil on the market: 'Peace, delusion and denial'.)

Thankfully, there are no injuries and minimal sharing of snot, and Buddy has had his first taste of ice skating without losing a finger, so it's a blessedly quiet and contented carload as we head home.

The Chef and I have organised to attend a football match tonight with friends (why? WHY?) so rather than round the evening out with a nap, I down a shot of espresso (which, given the limited caffeine I've been imbibing in the past few months, shoots me straight to Mars), order pizza, get the grotty tribe cleaned up, PJ-ed and happily playing with play-doh, before hoisting myself upstairs for a make-over. I've given up on trying to conceal the shadows under my eyes, and like anything that touches my skin lately, the sensation of foundation is highly irritating, so a lick of lippy and mascara has to suffice. Now, the frock: anything that is tailored, layered or stretchy doesn't even get a look in. Pieces that once gracefully displayed a hint of décolletage now look like a plastic shopping bag overstuffed with doughnuts, so they don't make the cut, and anything with a chance of making it must be able to conceal an industrial-strength maternity bra. As for pants — schmants! No way!

The pitiful few garments that have survived are, in a word, comical. They are, to a dress, Lycra-based, and while clinging to all the right places in the leg, thigh, hip and bum departments, they are forced to balloon out over my ridiculous gut, stretched taut like my own poor skin, threatening to twang off me like a broken guitar string at any moment. The absence of flowing folds of material actually exacerbates the huge gulf between the size of my belly and the rest of me. I look like the Magic Pudding: all dense, fruity barrel in the middle, with spindly arms and legs jutting out like a child's drawing.

The frock I finally settle on features a black-and-white geometric pattern which, I tell myself, will soften my clunky silhouette. Truth be told, it just looks like I've attached a soccer ball to the front of my body in homage to the game we are about to watch. I succumb to dumb vanity and don a pair of high heels – regardless of my condition, old habits die hard.

All in all, it turns out to be a great night of chatting, catching up with old acquaintances, and being regaled by complete strangers with quips about how devoted I must be to the sport, dressing my bump as a soccer ball. Hawdy haw haw . . .

Still, our team romps home with a stunning victory, and all is going well until that final siren sounds and, as if in response, the wind is knocked out of me by a massive Braxton Hicks contraction. 'I've had 'em before, I'll have 'em again', I assure myself, but a second one strikes as I'm ascending the stairs, causing a stumble noticed by The Chef and our friends. I brush off their concerns and we all joke that if the twins come tonight I will have to call them Mel and Vic, regardless of sex, in honour of Melbourne Victory, but the contractions continue, albeit irregularly, throughout the drive home, and well into the night, keeping sleep at bay even more than usual. Finally, aided by a couple of Panadol, they subside in the early hours and I drift off into a fitful sleep.

## SUNDAY 26 OCTOBER

*6 a.m.* I wake feeling stiff but relatively cramp-free. Minnie and The Chef are headed up to the hills for her riding lesson and a few hours hands-on at two of his venues, so I throw some sandwiches together for them, then let the other kids rouse before getting them dressed and starting the day.

Aware that this will be my last 'free' Sunday for a while, and that Sunday is always my most fruitful day, I get all domestic goddess in nesting mode.

Princess had an accident of the usual four-year-old variety overnight so it's as good a time as any to strip all the beds and get that linen out on the line in the fresh spring air. Next, I attack the uniforms with gusto, giving every item from blazer to sport sock a press. Once lunchboxes have been prepared for the next day, I clear out their school bags, clean up as much of the pig poo from the yard as my bump allows, and give the pots and lawn a water. The fridge needs a wipe out, then I decide to go *Masterchef* 'mystery box' on the contents and whip up a white chocolate, coconut and fresh raspberry cake and pound out a Singaporean marinade paste while it cools. This is slathered over a chicken and shoved in the slow cooker with vegetables and broth. A bit of basmati rice is quickly pan-tossed with sesame oil and added to the chicken, and dinner is practically served.

SHOPPING LIST

*Oh bugger off, if you think I am dragging myself down to the local shopping centre just to chase parks around an overcrowded car park only to be abused by some wanker in his hotted-up Holden, probably get stuck in a lift pumping inane Muzak, then finally trudge back to the car to find I've left my groceries at the checkout because I'm so overloaded with babies it feels like I'm lugging around 20 kg canned goods, then you have another think coming!!!*

What the heck is wrong with me? Seriously, am I insane? Who am I trying to impress? Nigella?

I've boiled the kettle for a well-deserved cuppa and am pulling the last load of linen from the line when a grade A contraction doubles me over. I narrowly miss dropping Minnie's freshly laundered sheets into a pile of pig's business, so I wait for it to subside before pulling down the pillowcases and doona cover. 'Bloody Braxton Hicks,' I mutter to no-one in particular as I head in to prepare the kids some afternoon tea. Another swiftly follows, however, then another. I take a Panadol but can't help acknowledging that these ones are coming a bit more regularly than BHs usually do, and lasting longer. Also, the pain seems to start in my sternum, coursing through my stomach and my back on a downwards trajectory – again, a bit different to the usual.

## BRAXTON HICKS

What or who are Braxton Hicks? A member of a new boy band? A member of the Senate? A member of one of those religious cults in the deep South where they talk in tongues and gyrate wildly? Nup. Braxton Hicks are a tightening of the abdominal wall. Also known as prodromal labour or practice contractions, Braxton Hicks are sporadic uterine contractions that can start as early as six weeks into a pregnancy but generally begin well into the second or third trimester. Named for the nineteenth-century English doctor who 'discovered' them, John Braxton Hicks, they:

• last for 30 seconds to 1 minute
• are uncomfortable, not painful
• come irregularly
• occur no more than once or twice an hour, a few times a day
• usually stop if you change position or activity. They differ from actual labour in that they:
• don't become closer together
• don't last longer or become more intense after time
• don't become longer or stronger when you walk.

   If you feel contractions but the discomfort eases off, they are probably Braxton Hicks. They will come more frequently late in pregnancy as your body revs up for the big event. If you are not sure if it's pre-labour or actual labour you are experiencing, however, never hesitate to call your doctor.

The Chef and Minnie return soon after, to my grumbles of being walloped by pain. Don't think he doesn't try to force me to sit down and put my feet up; he does, but do I listen? No, instead, I continue preparing dinner, and the pains continue apace. The Chef emerges from his study thirty minutes later to find me mid-squeeze and unable to speak. 'Hospital?'

   I'm dismissive. 'Look, if they keep happening I'll call the delivery suite and get their opinion, but I'm not rushing in there like a drama queen.' Three contractions later, I'm on the phone. The lovely midwife who picks up is nonplussed, convinced they are just Braxton Hicks, but given it is to be my fifth caesarean and I'm technically full-term with large twins, she feels it would not hurt for me to swing by for a quick monitoring session to see if there are any irregularities. Personally, I'm not keen on setting a foot in the place just yet so go into negotiation mode: Can I get the kids fed, then come in? It's not a problem, so I set about wrangling my little entourage into jammies and serve up dinner. Naturally, the moon must be in the seventh house or some such rubbish because all four have turned feral, the table and floor soon smeared with sticky Hainanese rice and spilt broth. I manage to shovel a respectable portion of chicken into each of them, and clear away as much of the debris as my screaming belly will allow, then let MJ the dog in to essentially vacuum the scraps while I serve up cake. Our devoted Australian shepherd and truffle-dog-in-training, MJ is without a doubt my fifth 'child'. Sadly, to date, he is far more adept at sniffing out the children's dropped food scraps than he is fungi. The Chef hovers around me, trying again to get me to sit, attempting to wrangle the dustpan and brush from me. Instead, I grab my keys and tell him I'll be back shortly so to save me some dinner. I opt to drive myself (stupid, stupid, foolish woman that I am), utterly convinced I will be making the return journey within the hour.

I sit awkwardly behind the wheel, twisting myself into an odd yogi-like position so as to best ride out the squeezes. I make a game of counting down the length of each contraction, hovering on around thirty seconds each. I've grinned and borne my way through another three by the time I've reached the hospital, located a park and tottered inside. Their force lifts me up on my tippy toes so I'm sure I look a right loon as I enter the maternity department like some corpulent ballerina.

Once in and strapped to the monitor with multiple wires, wraps and pads, it is as though my body just lets loose and slams me with a barrage of toe-curling uterine wrenches. I can only describe it as being akin to your body attempting to turn itself inside out like a jumper pulled fresh from the dryer. The midwife looks over the paper trail of squiggly lines after ten minutes, a-ha-ing to herself before efficiently scampering off to call my obstetrician. Talk about timing: she informed me as I arrived that my guy had arrived back from Hawaii that morning. Relief floods my body till another whopper starts up. I fight back by focusing on what I still need to buy from Big W. I've pulled my phone out to Google lambskin rugs when she returns, props herself up on the bed and pats my knee.

'Those babies are coming out tonight,' she smiles.

I wait for an alarm or something to sound on the monitor, as surely my heart has stopped.

'But, but, but—' is about all I can manage before she launches into an explanation.

Apparently, one of my tsunami-sized contractions distressed one of the twins, and given I'm technically 'at term' there is no reason why we shouldn't be cautious and bring those bubs into the world on this appropriately dark and stormy night. Personally, I have a few very good reasons why, not least that I haven't made it back to Big W yet.

I ask to speak to Doc, my obstetrician, and finally broker a deal. He will come in and examine me, and if in the interim the contractions cease, or the distressed bub improves, or upon examination he finds I'm not dilated, he won't immediately call in the troops but will rather play it by ear.

I gush my thanks but can't help dropping into organisational mode. The Chef is scheduled to head to Perth in the morning and will not return till midnight Wednesday. The Chef immediately begins a round of desperate calls trying to extricate himself from all commitments, but unfortunately he can't pull a sickie on this one as it is the launch of his newest book, and apparently it is too late to organise a fill-in. Funny that.

Images of other commitments I'm supposed to be keeping fill my head. My perfect timeline is being mangled before my very eyes and, without me there to supervise, I have a sinking feeling I will return home to find that in my absence the pigs have been allowed to move into the children's bedrooms.

By the time poor Doc arrives, jetlagged to the hilt but still dapper in his uniform of pristine, freshly pressed suit, the once-distressed baby is happy as Larry, the two little noodles rebounding off each other with much enthusiasm. One hurdle overcome. The midwife confides that the baby might have been sleeping when we began the trace and it read as distress. Doc's subsequent examination shows I'm not dilated. Phew! He is not, however, happy to send me home as, at this late stage, I could go from cervix closed to waters broken within an hour. At least in a hospital environment I can be monitored regularly and quickly, and if something were to happen there's some chance the medical staff could put the brakes on long enough for The Chef to return.

My options as spelt out by Doc are: stay, at least until The Chef returns.

Go, and risk complications. Or . . . get them critters out now.

Two hours later, Sal has generously agreed to spend the next two nights at the house, I have informed all concerned, and been installed on the ward.

The comedy extravaganza continues when Doc tells me it would be great if I could get my hands on the compounded progesterone he had prescribed me, as this may soften the cramps, but there is not currently any at the hospital and, it being a Sunday night, no compounding pharmacies are open to make up a batch. One glance at the clock tells me all the kids will be tucked up in bed (they better be) so I organise a taxi to swing by the house and collect it from The Chef, giving the operator detailed instructions about where to go to collect it and my precise location to drop it off. Naturally a comedy of errors ensues: an hour later the meds still have not been collected, as the driver had been waiting at the neighbour's house. The taxi driver then calls me to ask not just where the hospital is, but how to get to the street it is on. Finally he is out the front and despite the operator having told him I was a maternity patient in the labour ward, he has the temerity to ask me to come downstairs in the rain, locate him, collect the meds, and add a $15 surcharge to the fee, thank you very much. I actually laugh and after the day I've had, boy, does it feel good! I finally coax him upstairs and he calls again fifteen minutes later as he wanders the labour ward, intermittently sticking his head into rooms and asking new mums in various stages of wiping, feeding or undress, if they know where Madeleine is before ending up back at the lifts. I advise him to turn around, where of course he is confronted with the reception desk. Apparently it wasn't there when he arrived.

Meds secured, I am hit by a wave of exhaustion so profound I can barely keep an eye open. The gorgeous midwives try to tempt me with a bowl of minestrone soup (is that what it is?) and a bundle of mixed sandwiches, but I'm too trapped between the realms of fatigue and anxiety to even contemplate a bite. Distraction comes in the form of writing a detailed list of overnight-bag contents I feel I may need. I send it to The Chef, and then with the aid of a blessed prescription for Temazepam from Doc, I nod off. For two whole hours.

## MONDAY 27 OCTOBER

*7:15 a.m.* The cycle begins again. I chow down on a muesli bar and nod off . . . for an hour. One of the twins starts hiccupping and I'm awake again.

The pattern continues until around 3 a.m. By 3:30 a.m. I've showered and deign to watch some highly relevant, very topical infomercials. I doze off again and only wake when a midwife enters. My attempts to greet her reveal my voice has disappeared somewhere between the Ab Pro King and the Bullet Vitamizer. It's probably stress-induced. That, or my body knows I have a few days off from the kids and so won't be needing my vocal cords to screech at them like a fishwife who's run out of her anti-depressants.

Voice box unplugged forthwith.

What do I do with myself?

It's been a very long time since I've had so much time on my hands with which to do so little. More to the point, it's been a very long time since I've had so much time on my hands in which I'm not allowed to do anything . . .

Whatever, who cares? All I know is I can hear the breakfast trolley rattling this way, and I suddenly realise I'm so hungry I could actually fathom gnawing my red-painted fingernails for a quick cocktail of calories and chemicals. Time to put the brakes on a little, and if not let go of the steering wheel, at least loosen my vice-like grip on it.

---

### SHOPPING LIST

'War and peace'

Webster's complete encyclopaedic dictionary

The complete works of Shakespeare

The complete collection of Miele appliances operational handbooks

(Jeez . . . how do I fill all this free time?)

---

## STOP TRYING TO BE SUPERWOMAN

It might make you feel better, but no-one will be handing you any awards for having ironed all the sheets before heading for the delivery ward. Don't overdo it.

Your doctor or obstetrician doesn't recommend things like rest, diet changes or avoiding certain activities for the fun of it. Their advice is more of a prescription than an option; it's given because it's good for you! Unfortunately, mums are excellent at securing the health of others to a T, while ignoring or underestimating their own needs.

If your doctor gives specific instructions, especially when you're pregnant, follow them. Dismiss the wise words of the medical profession at not just your own peril, but that of your unborn baby. Or in my case, babies. Alternative medicine most certainly adds a valuable stream to the avenues available when it comes to ensuring optimum health, it's just a little harder to guarantee consistency of training. In some cases the same claim can be levelled at the medical profession, but Australia's universities, hospitals and general practices are subject to stricter checks and balances than alternative practitioners and the homeopathic industry. Just be cautious, follow your instincts, and get recommendations from medical practitioners whose knowledge you trust and respect. Our health is number one in this life, and we owe it to our loved ones to ensure its longevity.

## TUESDAY 28 OCTOBER

*5.50 a.m.* Time idles by very slowly on a hospital ward. By turns too cold and too warm, I get all OCD over small details like the arrangement of towels in the bathroom and how many English breakfast tea bags are left in the caddy.

I miss the kids.

I miss being at home.

The enforced rest, however, must be good for me, and after the hullabaloo of the weekend, I can't quite believe it is Wednesday and we are still truckin'. The two little tots are now 3 kg each! That, along with the fact that tomorrow marks thirty-eight weeks suggests that they shouldn't need to go into the special care nursery at all. Passing these small milestones seems like a miracle.

SHOPPING LIST

*Some wet paint I can watch dry . . . .*

The sore throat has inevitably become a full-blown cold with blocked sinuses, clicky ears, loss of taste and smell (the ultimate bummer when you are obliged to eat up) and a fetchingly pus-y eye infection. I'm looking and feeling a bit like a scarecrow, so my doctor requests some IV fluids for tonight, but otherwise all is well and I should by rights be at home playing Mum – bar the fact I have two passengers on board threatening to set the water slide in motion and slip out any time now.

One luxury of being in hospital is that it does put you in a position to request certain things you never usually would. Case in point: I have organised to have my eyelashes tinted here in my room this morning. I hate worrying about having to wear make-up at the best of times, but don't want to look like I've been dragged backwards through a bush either. So a bit of tint is a perfect concession to both.

Upon arriving, the poor girl looks at the equipment she has to work with and scratches her head. I contort my body along the bed enough to allow her easy access to my eyes and am soon asleep, only rousing when I begin snoring. Embarrassing! By the time she has finished I've stiffened up to the point that it takes me a considerable amount of time to get up again. And when I'm almost there, I pass wind. Charming!

As I bid her a hasty farewell in the hallway, a couple with an extra-wide mobile crib stagger past. Twins!!! I can't help begging a look at them, forgetting I've still got masking tape attached to my forehead, yanking my lids up as the lash dye dries. What a sight I must be – with my bright red eye, I'm sure I look like an escapee from the infectious-diseases unit. They oblige me, however, the darlings, and I get to coo over their tiny little girls to my heart's content. The new mum tells me she feels so comfortable now that they're out and she can eat again, having been restricted to a liquid diet up until the birth. Ah! Her words are like manna from heaven!

In the afternoon, my tribe descends on the hospital. Oh dear . . . I don't think the maternity unit knows what hit it. I feel a compulsion to take them from room to room, duck my head in and exclaim to any new parents within, 'This is what you have just signed up for!'

They are reasonably well behaved until talk turns to Halloween and what costumes they will be donning. Minnie has not had a new dress-up in quite some time so I let her know I've bought her a zombie frock with black inflatable wings, now hidden in the laundry, and Princess, whose dress-up collection only extends to fairies and mermaids, a Spider Princess number. Tink can recycle last year's Witchipoo dress (seeing as she wasn't able to walk properly at the time – amazing to think how much she has developed in such a short period – it hasn't technically fulfilled its trick-or-treating duty yet) while Buddy, having quite a selection of evil pirates and superheroes, can choose from his existing wardrobe. Naturally a meltdown ensues. He wants a new outfit and pronto. I point to my belly.

'I'm not getting out of here and hitting the costume shops any time soon, so it's make do or miss out, Buddy.'

Oh, the tears that follow that statement! I finally talk him down from the roof by suggesting we paint a spooky rib cage on a white shirt, then mix and match a few other pieces to create a ragtag skeleton-cum-zombie pirate. He seems mollified until Minnie looks at him quizzically and points out that I'm in hospital, so I can't help him paint a shirt. This is enough to tip him over the edge and the tears flow again. Finally, I pull out the big guns and offer to take them downstairs for milkshakes. Hooray!!!

As we pass the maternity reception, one of the midwives pulls me up to say I must not go far as Doc has, unbeknownst to me, ordered a bag of fluids just to 'freshen me up' and an anaesthetist is on her way to slip a drip in. Delightful. What is this, a deodorant commercial? I look at my children's faces and take a hard line.

'If I don't get some sugar and fat into this lot, they are very likely going to dismantle the whole unit, room by room, so how about I slip downstairs to the coffee shop, grab some shakes, then return?' She looks at them and clearly senses how tenuous the situation is, quickly agreeing to cover for me and stall the anaesthetist as we scramble to the elevator quick smart.

After a wrangle over the more obscure flavours on offer, all four are soon sucking away contentedly and it's time to say goodbye. There's a moment when all of them kiss me and then my belly, saying 'Night-night' to the twins, when I have to bite my lip to halt threatening tears. Off they go, another argument brewing between Minnie and Buddy over swapping the dregs of their shakes. Ahh, it's good to see that despite my absence in the past few days nothing has changed on the home front.

Back upstairs, it takes another forty-five minutes for the anaesthetist to arrive and I'm feeling a little emotional, cheated of that time with my rowdy kids, but again, I'm supposed to be resting, so fair enough.

When she arrives we chat about vein competency and other such fascinating subjects while she examines my arms. Having been in and out of hospital for hydration throughout this pregnancy, I have as intimate a knowledge of my veins as any self-respecting drug abuser, and point out that the one she has selected is probably next to a valve as we have had trouble with it before. She opts to give it a go regardless and immediately there is swelling and much pain as the valve inflates. Hmm. Second attempt is a winner and we are away.

For the next eight hours I will feel like a genuine invalid, basically bound to the bed or tottering about, pushing the beeping contraption on a pole that is the modern-day drip.

Oh well, shouldn't complain: in just three days' time my arms will be overloaded not with medical machinery but with two squeaking newborns.

*7 p.m.* Contraction. Hard, fast, wallops me with such force I'm slammed out of my dozing and into stark wakefulness. Nononono! Not yet! The Chef is still in Perth. Just a few more hours, please! I resolve to stay in bed and have a stern word with the girls about their poor timing. I'm a stickler for punctuality and this is not a good start! Two more toe-curlers swiftly follow, then nothing . . .

When the nurse drifts in to check my drip, I let her know, and she gives me a thorough going-over before concluding it was probably just a response to having all the kiddies here that afternoon. That would be right – clearly the twins heard their siblings going bananas and decided they wanted to get out and join in the fun.

## PREPARING SIBLINGS FOR THE ARRIVAL OF NEW SIBLINGS

I have frequently read about giving older siblings a gift 'from the baby' upon their arrival, as a means of soothing any concerns, anxieties or rivalry the older sibling may feel. I've tried it, more than once, and have to say in my experience, it did squat diddly in terms of achieving those lofty goals.

Older siblings might feel jealous and put out by a new arrival, but this is an important part of growing up and a valuable life lesson. Older kids are pretty savvy to the whole situation and young toddlers will not comprehend the meaning of such a gift anyway – it's just more coloured paper to rip to shreds and toys to break ASAP.

I have found a slightly more effective method is to actually give older siblings the very important role of teacher, rather than bribing them. Each time, I've emphasised with any of mine old enough to understand that they now have the very important job of teaching the new one or ones how things are done in our family: whose toys are whose, how to share, how to ask for what you want, how to be polite and respectful, how to love and protect each other, how to sit quietly and eat dinner etc – pretty much anything that currently causes you strife behaviourally with the older sibling(s).

I have found this technique most useful because when charged with teaching these behaviours to another sibling, the older sibling will suddenly feel obliged to model these behaviours themselves (win win!). It might take a few reminders along the lines of how very important their job is, but for me it has consistently worked, despite varying age gaps, and huge variations in personality type. It's not unlike the 'buddy system' in primary schools, which generally has lots of success in integrating prep-level students into the school curriculum, but without anyone needing to wear a uniform or bake cakes for a fundraiser. Again: Win win!!!

# WEDNESDAY 29 OCTOBER

*3:02 a.m.* It's been a restless night. I've avoided any sleep aids, sick of spending my days trying to navigate around the heavy fog in my head, and I'm still anxious about a return visit from Mr Crampy, however, I now have to face the prospect of no sleep ever again. Yes, enough with the dramatics, Madeleine, but it's hard not to go a bit Shakespearean when your body is crying out for rest but your head simply will not comply.

The Chef arrived back from Perth on the red eye just after midnight. I guess that means I can uncross my legs now, which should make walking and using the bathroom so much easier!

I realise with a happy little jolt that we've made it. I rub my belly and can feel the twins lying there – in breech of course: I'd expect nothing less from

> SHOPPING LIST
>
> *An uneventful birth*
>
> *Two healthy babies*
>
> *An OFF switch, for my ovaries*

two of my tribe, but with their heads together, as though stealing a few private moments while it's still just the two of them, snug in their little hidey-hole, perhaps conscious that soon, nothing will ever be the same again.

My skin feels exceptionally smooth under my palms, and I wrangle my way into the bathroom, drip bag attached to its pole in hand, to look myself over before the mirror. I can detect slight changes already: my belly seems to be lower today, my breasts fuller and rounder, the nipples smooth and dark. There are many small lumps beneath the skin, suggesting that my body is gearing up to feed these little suckers from the outside now rather than from within. For the first time in a long time, I gaze at my body in admiration for the amazing job it has done, to have come so far despite being so sickly and thin. I hope the tide is turning in a good way and that my system is transitioning, preparing itself for the next phase of this journey. I'm feeling surprisingly positive and suddenly a little bit excited, my apprehension temporarily alleviated by happy thoughts of the little miracles soon to arrive. I remind myself that natural twins are a rare and special event, and that at the end of the day, all children, no matter how they are conceived, are miracles.

When I get back to bed, it is with these happy thoughts, sweet and bright as sugar plums, dancing through my head, that I drift off – admittedly fitfully, given the orchestra that is the beeping, buzzing, slurping drip feeder in the background, for a grand total of forty minutes. Miracles!

## THURSDAY 30 OCTOBER

*1:28 a.m.* I dozed off at 8:30 p.m. last night, woke again at 10:30 p.m., quickly nodded off again, and am now on my second round of waking. A distinct pattern is emerging. After an hour of tossing and turning, snacking, reading and plucking my eyebrows, I finally give in and go for a wander around the maternity ward. I'm immediately drawn to the nursery, with its rows of teeny tiny tots assigned to night-time supervision. My boobs start to tingle. Yep, there's no denying it. After four kids, my constant waking is my body's way of preparing me for the broken sleep of newborn feeding. This is clearly my system's way of ensuring I remain functional during the day while being up and about feeding at night: sleep deprivation. Either that or I'm training for a stint at Guantanamo Bay.

Suddenly I don't feel quite so resentful about being so restless. There is a purpose. After all, it can only improve. Hopefully, as they learn to sleep, it's a skill I too will regain.

During the day I ran into one of the women I met during my one and only 'Preparing for Twins' class, Danielle. She is sitting in the nursery, dazedly gazing at two tiny, perfect pink dolls. I gently say hello and she remembers me straight away. Born last night at thirty-five weeks, they will be in the Special Care unit for a week or two yet, but otherwise they don't need any assistance breathing, and she is clearly utterly smitten.

The same nurse who was in charge of the nursery then is still in charge now. Does she ever sleep? When I met her earlier she revealed she had five children of her own, so perhaps not!

She sees me gazing through the glass and kindly asks me in for a closer look at the snoozing bundles. I explain my theory on my sleeplessness and she agrees 100 per cent. As she points out, the only absurdity is that this is prime time for getting some rest and here I am crawling the walls.

So what scares me?

I suppose my great fear is that my poor body, stretched to its very limits, will collapse in a heap once its incubatory duties are complete and refuse to recover. That is when my double-trouble tots will need me most, let alone the rest of the tribe. Dear diary, wish me strength and luck – I'm gonna need it.

After two slow strolls around the trolleys, acquainting myself with those tiny faces in repose and falling a bit in love with all of them, I've had my fill and return to my room. Am I ready for another two to join the fray? 'Yes,' I say, with a quivering lip. Absolutely terrified, but absolutely ready . . .

## YOUR HOSPITAL STAY AND THE NIGHT-TIME NURSERY

All private hospitals now offer a program in which, following a few days' stay, you will be transferred to a nearby hotel for a night or two, giving new mums and dads a little bit of luxury and clearing hospital beds for incoming patients.

If you are fit and healthy post-birth, this is a wonderful offer for many parents. However, one thing to think about is that the hotel experience is much more hands-off than being in hospital when it comes to doctors and nursing staff availability. The hotel program offers only one midwife between four or five new mums and no doctors unless they are specially called in. If you are nervous or have concerns, you are essentially on your own, and certainly can't expect the same level of one-on-one care that you enjoyed in hospital.

And an even more noticeable difference is in the nursery options. Private hospitals and many public hospitals all offer night nurseries where the baby can be wheeled away after the last feed and settled till the next feed is absolutely necessary. This allows you optimal rest time. No such service is available at the hotel, so you have to function as if you were at home and if you are exhausted and sleep deprived, you just have to slug it out.

I went the hotel route with my second and third babies and really enjoyed it. By number four, however, I opted to stay at the hospital and rest up for as long as possible, because I knew I certainly wouldn't get any rest at home.

If you need the rest, particularly if you are going home to other children, I would recommend eschewing the hotel offer, staying on at the hospital and getting some serious sleep. Trust me, you will need it! As much as I support accepting the fine art of functioning on broken sleep, the post-birth recovery period is a different proposition, especially if you have undergone a caesarean section or experienced complications. If this is you, take advantage of your hospital's facilities and let the wonderful staff take care of your baby and you. Then get your partner to take you and only you to a swanky hotel for a special occasion, and enjoy the whole experience in the right context!

---

*6:06 a.m.* I'm up early for a quick shower, then I'm out and across the road for strong decaf coffee and a few chocolate bars. It's my last day and I'm determined to make the most of it. Back in my poky little room I'm greeted by a symphony of crying tots. Tomorrow two more voices will join the chorus and I will be attending to them, not sipping coffee while trying to churn through a few emails. I'm trying to compose requests to the kids' teachers for some comprehensive assignments and class notes for while they are absent, having scoured the newsletter diary for precisely what activities they will individually miss, but my head keeps nodding. That would be right – I'm right at the end of the pregnancy and now my body is ready for sleep. Not fair! Today has to be a day of last minute i-dotting and t-crossing, and I simply won't achieve anything if I'm on the nod.

As chance would have it, it is The Chef's mum Nanny Spaghetti's (so called because the kids love her bolognaise above and beyond every other foodstuff, much to The Chef's chagrin) birthday tomorrow, on the twins' due date. I'm scratching my head trying to figure out what I can get her from my hospital bed. Sadly, shopping sprees have been rather low on my list of priorities of late, and I thought I'd have another week at my disposal in which to get things done.

I scratch around downstairs, and all I can say is thank goodness for well-stocked pharmacies. Sometimes, usually when you don't even know what you are looking for, providence just drops something in your lap. So it was with the gorgeous beauty case, matching make-up case, candle, body wash and moisturising cream I picked up for Nanny Spaghetti.

Phew! Last task ticked off: now I just have to have those babies.

## SATURDAY 1 NOVEMBER

**2:19 a.m.** Despite exhaustion, best intentions and wishful thinking, I've been waking every two hours since 10 p.m. and finally give up. I'm not allowed to eat or drink so start wandering the maternity ward, invariably ending up at the nursery again. It is packed as usual, with all three nurses on duty juggling babies, and still more little mites crying in their cribs. I'm certainly not about to pick up anyone else's newborn (tempted as I am) but do offer to rock a few cribs while talking to the nurses. We talk about a variety of subjects, anything to stave off the fatigue for them, I suppose, and anything to distract me from this bloody insomnia. Again, I do a few laps, taking in every tiny face, smitten with each and every one.

> SHOPPING LIST
>
> *Sorry, shutting up shop today – now and forever.*

Satisfied, I bid the ladies good night, and am heading for the door when one points out: 'Tomorrow we should have yours in here, and hopefully you will be getting some sleep!'

Suddenly, it well and truly dawns on me: tomorrow, my skin will house only me, and I'll be mother to six. Bring it on!

## EXPRESS YOURSELF

To lactate or not to lactate, that is the question. Perhaps I'm not quoting *Hamlet* verbatim, but if there is one issue that divides the mummy-blogger masses it is whether to breastfeed your baby or opt for formula. At the end of the day, it's a pretty basic dilemma: if you can (and I'm not just talking about physical ability here, but also psychologically, if it works within your career, home life and beliefs) then great! Go for it! If you can't, don't! And blow a big raspberry at anyone who challenges your decision.

For me, I've always gone for it, and it has certainly presented its own challenges. Like the time I was forced by a screaming baby to pull over and feed on a major road, and having just returned the baby to her car seat, noticed a vehicle had slowed coming the other way, its driver staring at me, mouth agape. I waved, thinking it must be an acquaintance . . . nothing. Nonplussed, I returned to the driver's seat, and it was only as I was pulling my seat belt across that I noticed not only was my maternity bra 'unhinged', so to speak, but my breast was still hanging out in all its glory. Hmm . . .

On a whole other level of weird is the conundrum that is 'expressing' – unavoidable when you return to work but want to continue breast-feeding. The amount of paraphernalia that comes with this exercise verges on the ridiculous. We are talking a pump (of which the hospital-grade models are frequently the size and shape of a small inner-city apartment) breast cups, tubing, bottles, storage bottles, chiller bag, milk storage bags, ice packs, sterilisation packs and a nifty carry case the size of a removalist truck in which to lug it all around.

The return to work itself, while liberating and often necessary, is fraught with potential mishaps. My pinnacle of embarrassment occurred during my time on Foxtel drama *Satisfaction*.

Playing a high-end escort on national television comes with its own peaks and troughs, particularly when you are contractually obliged to get your bits out just five weeks after popping your second kid.

This was the case for me. Second week in I thought I'd hit my stride. The combination of long days filming from 5 a.m. after being up throughout the night with my son seemed possible on a strict diet of lollies and caffeine. I should have been making a greater effort to implement a routine which ensured Buddy was starting to sleep through the night, but frankly, I missed him desperately and so was happy to feed him through the dark hours, at the cost of my sanity during the day.

As I said, by week two I thought I had it in the bag, until I was obliged to film a rather sensual scene with a Very Lovely Actor who was, unfortunately, sprouting a veritable crop of lint in his belly button which looked about ready to harvest. Ask me not how or why, but this set off a let-down response in me. I gushed, and gushed, and gushed. Thankfully, by that point in the scene, my character was lying on her stomach. The scene eventually ended, but after 'cut' had been called, I refused to get up and remained stubbornly prone. The assistant director noticed and asked if I was okay. 'Fine, fine! Just having a quick rest . . .'

You see, the release had mixed with the liberal coating of fake tan slathered over my entire body, mingling to create a chocolate-milk effect which pooled on the white satin sheets beneath my torso. With the wardrobe department screaming blue murder for me to come and don my next almost-costume, I crab-shuffled off the bed, apologising profusely to the poor props department who were left to remove my stains. Note to self: breastfeeding and fake tan do not mix. It took me a while to realise that the seemingly unbudging brown ring permanently tattooed around my sweet little man's mouth was not some exotic allergic reaction but more a WorkCover claim waiting to happen. Ah well, he's been a breast man ever since – thank goodness I demanded organic fake tan, like any good diva!

I suppose at the end of the day, my advice to new mums on the breastfeeding quandary is simply to do what you can and what you are willing to do. The only expectations you need abide by are your own. Don't waste time killing yourself doing what you think you ought to be doing. Your health, both mental and physical, and that of your baby is paramount at this time, so don't dice with it. Take it slow and enjoy these precious, irreplaceable days, as they go so fast.

If you do decide to breastfeed, I have found a big comfy chair that you can safely doze in an absolute must. Make your child's bedroom as welcoming to you as it is them, as you'll find yourself spending a lot of time in there.

# CHAPTER

3

## SATURDAY 1 NOVEMBER

*10:45 a.m. Hi, The Chef here. Been sent in to capture the moment. Madeleine's got a drip in that's making it hard to write.*

*We welcomed two beautiful girls, Jelly Bean and Lolly Pop. Mum and the babies are all doing well.*

## SUNDAY 2 NOVEMBER

*9:32 p.m.* Thirty-six hours have passed, and whoa! Talk about a rollercoaster! I eventually gave up on trying to sleep not long after my last entry, quickly showered, dressed, repainted my nails, and waited . . . and waited . . . and waited.

By 10 a.m. our little angels were in our arms. Love is all around . . .

Then the anaesthetic wore off.

Holy shit balls . . . what have I done? The euphoria is wearing off too and stark reality soon hits home. Day Two begins with me barely able to drag myself from sleep for the first feed. Then I'm nodding off every five seconds. Scarily, I realise I'm talking utter gibberish. Mid-conversation with our nanny, I make some wacky comment about saving the wrapping paper from the girls' gifts for the drugs in the sticky tape. WHA—? I'm saying this with utter conviction, which is even more disquieting. The girls are terrific but I'm off on a trek through La-La Land with no orientation skills to speak of. Instead of resolving as the morning wears on, it is soon getting worse. My doctor is called and a full battery of blood tests ordered; even my oxygen levels are tested, all revealing nothing. A snappy diagnosis of extreme fatigue is made and I'm told to hit the sack as soon as the babes go down. In the back of my mind is the thought, 'How will I manage this at home?', but I shut it down. I'll deal with it when I *am* at home. In the interim I follow doctor's orders and nap.

Early afternoon I approach the nurses' station; they look me over with concern. 'Can I go downstairs and get a coffee? It might help.' The supervisor gets all supervisory and intones that my going down unaccompanied would

---

SHOPPING LIST

Trashy magazines

Bottomless pack of Tim Tams like in the ads

Vodka

Oh . . . and nursing pads

---

not be a good idea. She will escort me. As we travel toward the elevators she produces a large mug from her pocket and confides she had been dying for a coffee and I presented the perfect excuse.

Coffees purchased, we are making our way back up when she spots my doctor in the distance, headed toward the same elevator. She holds me back, hissing, 'Wait! This doesn't look good.'

So wait we do until she's confident he's gone, then she bundles me upstairs via the delivery suite and back to my room. Hilarious. The cloak and dagger world of nurses.

Post-coffee, I survive my next feed without toppling over on to a child, and the gibberish subsides.

By evening, the girls are restless. They are becoming hungry and my milk hasn't come in yet. They immediately exhaust my pitiful colostrum reserves, then just start gnawing. The gnashing of unsatisfied gums on tender breast flesh isn't anybody's idea of fun. They wake at 11:30 p.m., again at 1:30 and 4:30 a.m., then cluster feed, sometimes singularly, sometimes together, until 6:30 a.m. I feed Lolly Pop again at 7:15 a.m., then miraculously they settle. I've had two coffees, however, and am wired to the eyeballs. No nodding today!

## MONDAY 3 NOVEMBER

*9:20 a.m.* It's day three and I'm sitting on my hospital bed, holding both tiny girls in my arms, trying not to disturb their sleep with the silent sobs wracking my body. Today was weigh-in day. No, they aren't taking up boxing, but my girls' weight was taken this morning to compare to their birth weight. Anything within 10 per cent is considered acceptable. My little darlings, Jelly Bean and Lolly Pop, have lost 13 and 15 per cent respectively. The sense of failure I feel at having let them down is deep and devastating. A cheery midwife bustles into the room to take observations and spots me huddling like a shipwreck amid the pillows. Arms full of babies, I'm unable to wipe away the tears.

Her gentle reassurances just set me off, releasing a torrent of snorting, hiccuping, navel-gazing despair. I launch into a verbal self-flagellation, my voice squeaking and shaking as despair squeezes my vocal cords and I fail miserably to modulate my tone. I know I'm carrying on in

SHOPPING LIST

*My sanity*

49

the most pathetic, first-world manner possible, but my hormones are fizzing like a shaken soft drink, my emotions having all the structural resilience of a stepped-on meat pie. I'm usually so rational and impartial when it comes to the breastfeeding issue, but now something that came so easily has failed me and it seems I've bought into the dogma.

Perhaps it's just mourning the loss of how I thought things would play out over the next few months, maybe I'm just insane; I don't know but it all comes bubbling to the surface now in a nonsensical stew of feeling. Throw in a dose of fatigue, a quarter-cup of overwhelm, a dash of broken ego, two parts desperation, and the sensation of these two tiny, helpless blighters in my arms, and the whole situation is about as palatable as a dirty old tennis shoe.

## GO WITH YOUR FEELINGS

They tell you many things, doctors, parenting books and friends, but few will confess to the deep and devastating heartbreak that comes with the silliest little things following birth. I guess that with all the thrilling discoveries that come with new parenthood, it is this occasional feeling of irrational helplessness that is most readily consigned to the 'miscellaneous and useless parenting information' file: the memory that doesn't qualify as a bright and shiny Kodak moment; the days allowed to sink to the bottom of what it means to be a parent with the least ripple.

I think it's critical to acknowledge all such moments of perceived failure, however, as they inform our individual parenting style, how we handle crises small and large, and remind us that we are all fallible. Fallibility is okay, it's what we do with that knowledge that counts.

*11:10 a.m.* Minor breakdown complete, I organise to meet with the paediatrician once the girls go down. He's the 'twin whisperer', seemingly able to find solutions to twin-related problems where no answer existed before. He's in the Special Care Nursery when I come calling. Entering that glassed-in little space, I'm immediately slapped out of my 'woe is me' navel gazing, and back into reality. Incubators line the walls, each part-cocoon, part-cradle snuggling the tiniest little beings I've ever seen. There seem to be more wires and wrapping than there are babies, and the air gently vibrates with beeps and hums rather than lusty cries. It's both uplifting and devastating.

Dr Marvellous, meanwhile, is vibrant and chipper, filling the room with positivity. We discuss my concerns, then his, come to a happy medium and build a feeding plan from there. It's certainly not as dire as I had thought.

As if to drive the point home, I return to my room to be greeted by an . . . errr . . . fragrance. I'm much more familiar with this than anything by Chanel, Dior, or the latest pop sensation. Poo. Baby poo, to be specific. Not mouth-puckeringly awful but mildly unpleasant, like the aunt at Christmas who has a mythical ability to turn any small achievement you might have recently had into an anecdote about your cousin Sharon or Michael and their own stunning prowess in that particular arena.

Anyway, poo. Lolly Pop, the one whose weight has been the most unruly, has in her sleep had her own small achievement, a transitional poo: that mustardy, custardy, piccalilli-type muck that signifies your milk is coming in and finally your baby is clear of meconium. Meconium, you ask? No, it's not a rare element from a planet far far away that is deadly to superheroes and nappy-shy dads, it's baby's first poo: black, tarry and so startlingly repulsive its place is really as a special effect on a film like *Alien* rather than in your gorgeous newborn's nappy.

As bizarre as this may sound, there is something cheering about the presence of that green custard: it means she is getting some decent milk, processing it and moving it along.

I have a little chuckle to myself, part relief, part hysteria. In that moment, I must look for all the world less like a grown woman and more like my six-year-old son, Buddy, chortling over poo.

## SATURDAY 8 NOVEMBER

*12:45 p.m.* HOME! As much as I have cherished my mini-break in the luxurious surrounds of the maternity ward, with its five-channel entertainment system and exotic gastronomic wonders served on plastic trays at precisely 7 a.m., 11:30 a.m. and 5 p.m., I'm more than ready to return to my own bed and proximity to Tim Tams.

From without, all is peaceful at Chateau Catastrophe: grass neatly trimmed! Hedges clipped! Sunlight dancing over the rooftop and dappling the drive through the flowering pear trees. Birds sing, crickets chirp and Princess emerges from the front door with no pants on, screaming 'CANNONBALL!!!!!!!'

before launching herself into the gardenia bed. (Insert screeching vinyl record here.)

'Oh hi, Mum . . . I just done wee on the floor!' Yep, welcome home.

I enter with a swaddled bundle under each arm. Buddy literally walks past me, nose in his iPad. Looks up briefly, gives me a cursory greeting, then he's off upstairs. In the kitchen, Tink is using a red twirly novelty straw (one of those only available in the cheapest and nastiest of show bags, the kind I can't resist) to refresh herself from the dog's water bowl. My arms are full so I just bid her hello, step over her and move on. Thank goodness for that well-used line about anything and everything grotty being 'good for their immunity'; it certainly gets a regular work-out in this place.

Curious at the bundles Mum is cradling, Tink abandons the bowl and totters in after me, leaning over the couch to get a good view. She looks and feels so huge all of a sudden, and immediately my heart lurches, acknowledging yet another babyhood lost.

Jelly Bean starts to mewl, so Tink responds by sticking a finger in her eye. I gently remonstrate with her, explaining we have to be gentle . . . so she grabs Jelly Bean's tiny hand and thrusts THAT into her eye. Good to see healthy sibling rivalry is alive and well.

---

SHOPPING LIST

Fruit and veg: fridge is full of nothing but half-eaten take-away

House plants: ours haven't been watered and are all dead

Toilet paper: clearly we have run out as there is only a ragged pile of paper napkins from all the take-away next to each toilet

New dog – can't find M.J. Seems he's done a runner, or is just hiding . . . Fair enough.

---

## SIBLING RIVALRY! BRINGING HOME BABY TO AN ALREADY FULL HOUSE

I've said it before and I'll say it again: if I read another guide book recommending you present older siblings with a wrapped gift 'from baby' as a means of smoothing the transition of a new child into the unit, I'm going to stab myself in the eye with curling ribbon. For any child between two and six, a gift is a gift is a gift, all the better when given for no reason whatsoever. Bribery is a slippery slope, and no child should be paid off to behave appropriately around a sibling.

The safest path is via gentle introduction, reminding a child how very special they are, how lucky they are to have their very own little brother/sister/multiples(!) and how very very lucky Mummy and Daddy are to have them both. For slightly older children, it's a chance to exercise responsibility and independence. Encourage them to help more, entrust them with special jobs, and make them feel vital to the wellbeing of the entire family unit.

*3:05 p.m.* A crash course in twin feeding.
1. Make a cup of tea.
2. Purchase a twin feeding pillow (or a couple of sturdy bed pillows). Wrap said pillow around your waist à la the Michelin man.
3. Pick up twin one and arrange her under one armpit against your side along the pillow.
4. While balancing the now-lopsided ring of Saturn girdling your midsection with one hand, haul up the second twin by the scruff of their jumpsuit, laying them under the other armpit.
5. Sit, without upsetting ubiquitous cup of tea, and attempt to get comfortable. Ha ha ha ha ha . . .
6. Clamp twin one on a nipple.
7. Attempt the cat-and-mouse game of getting twin two (the more difficult and rebellious of the two already) to latch on likewise.
8. Finally all latched on: relax, let your shoulders drop. The movement shifts the whole contraption and both slip off their

breasts, dragging already-tender nipples with them. Shit.

9. Squirm about, getting them back on. Tip tea over in the process, not that it matters, it was cold by now anyway. Shitty shit!
10. Get them on, relax, doorbell rings. What the f-fruitcake???
11. Struggle up, waddle to door precariously balancing what feels like the national debt on your hips, attempt to unlatch front door with a toe. Fail. In a voice crackling with rising hysteria, yell through the door that they need to let themselves in.
12. It's the Jehovah's witnesses. $@&?!!!!!!
13. Listen, nod, manoeuvre them out the door. Resume couch position. Repeat steps 6–10.
14. Both on, relax, tense at the sound of a strained groan from twin two, swiftly followed by a squelchy, wet bottom burp and its accompanying odour.
15. Cry.
16. Open a pack of Tim Tams. Demolish.

NB: No children or besuited religious groups were harmed in the compilation of this sequence.

**3:50 p.m.** Post a very successful twin feeding session, Lolly Pop regurgitates the lot over me, the couch, the carpet, and the back seat of the car – which was still parked in the garage, that's just how comprehensive a hurl she achieved. I'm so proud; it's as if she is christening her new home.

**6 p.m.** Three hours later and the vomiting continues. Novelty value fast wearing off. I'm in my third outfit and daren't look at the laundry basket for fear of fainting at the sheer volume of material Lolly Pop has besmirched. Hmm, a lovely how-do-you-do.

**10:30 p.m.** The vomiting has continued, after feeds, during feeds and in between. Lolly Pop flops in my arms like a rag doll, barely rousing when I wake her at nappy changes. I strip her down, wipe a damp cloth over her torso, nothing. She just looks out at me, her eyes barely slits. She's so tiny, so frail in my arms. She doesn't cry – in stark contrast to her sister, who burbles away contentedly, or sweeps into frantic swells of yelping.

I don't know what to do: she's so fresh to life, so new and shiny, yet now, in this moment, I feel only that she's slipping away, and I can't control it. The Chef tries to convince me I'm overreacting but this feels so wrong. What do I do? Panic shoots through me, cold, hard and metallic. I'm so overtired and overwrought it's all I can do to breathe.

As the clock strikes 11, I make a decision. I call the hospital. When their concern matches my own I feel reassured, and welcome their recommendation that I come straight back in. Barely twelve hours out of hospital, I pack up my two tiniest babes, waking no-one, and get a cab to the hospital. One baby cries out at turns, the other remains silent. That silence is the loudest, most chilling emptiness I've ever encountered. 'Just cry, bubby,' I quietly beg. 'Please, just cry.'

## SUNDAY 9 NOVEMBER

*1:37 a.m.* Two and a half hours after arriving, Jelly Bean and I are sent home to sleep – without Lolly Pop.

Upon arrival, a number of the nurses I'd farewelled earlier in the day were back on, so naturally I flipped into 'seasoned mother/unflappable joker mode' underplaying my concerns and making cracks about laundry bills and not being able to stay away from the hospital food. Why? If I'm so *chillaxed*, so unflappable, why was I standing in a hospital corridor at the crack of midnight? These gals are veterans, however; they ushered me into the baby nursery, and as Lolly Pop was extricated from my clutches, a wad of tissues was slipped in. Sure enough, at the sight of my teensy lady being examined amid the humidicribs, the beeping, the infinitesimally fine tubing and catheters, something snapped and the tears gushed, so copious they seemed to fill the room, lapping at my ankles. Even as I talked quite calmly to the paediatric doctor in charge, the same gentle fellow who had attended my delivery, the tears streamed, initially dampening my sleeves and Jelly Bean's blanket as I tried to stem their flow, eventually just coursing over my cheeks and pooling beneath my chin unchecked.

Lolly Pop was weighed, and had naturally shed many grams. Another black mark against my name as a mother, another swift jab straight into the heart. The staff had no answers, so

SHOPPING LIST

Tissues

Antacids – either I've got horrific heartburn, or my heart is actually breaking she was admitted to be observed and bottle-fed to see how well she tolerated those precious calories.

Having hung about, skittish as a horse on speed and about as useful as a frog in a sock, I'm finally convinced by the midwife in charge to take Jelly Bean and get some sleep. I cradle Lolly Pop, shuddering with the sheer force of emotion slamming through my system. As I tenderly lay her down, I can't keep my hands off her, stroking her hair, her cheek, her tiny frame. I am all she has known since day dot. My smell, my voice, my heartbeat, more familiar to her than her own. What will she feel if I am not there? Will she feel my absence? Sense the Mummy-shaped void where I, by rights, should be hovering every moment?

As I draw myself away, it's like that old cliche about turning your back on the ocean. I pause at the nurses' station, and in a voice so small and screechy I barely recognise it, I ask if they will cuddle her. Writing the words now, I feel a right twat, but at that moment, I needed to know she would be held, treasured and not allowed to grow lonely without her other half. I am reassured of all the above, and after one more kiss I'm homeward bound with the other twin, destined for some serious tossing and turning.

It's only while I am exasperatedly pacing back and forth trying to locate my vehicle that I remember I caught a cab. Oh yeah . . .

I cry on the trip home till I'm empty and the gulping, cage-rattling sobs and hiccups subside, leaving me dry and still. I tiptoe into the sleeping house with a likewise sleeping Jelly Bean, and spot the feeding cushion where I dumped it in the hallway. Yep, here come the tears again.

*6:06 a.m.* Having held off till now, I succumb and call the hospital. Lolly Pop has continued to display her finely tuned projectile vomiting skills throughout the night, and they plan to run a battery of tests. The paediatrician wants to keep her another night to at least stabilise her. My heart, quite impressively, manages to lunge up into my throat while simultaneously plummeting deep into the pit of my stomach. I feel a wobble but keep it in check.

When Jelly Bean wakes, I feed her then can't let her go. Can she feel the absence of her little mate? Bloody kids: if they aren't driving you up the wall, they are yanking you by the noose of love you feel for them, hanging your heart out to dry.

## HOW TO CRY WITHOUT ANYONE KNOWING

Sometimes in life, you just need to have a good long weep, but the timing isn't always optimal, especially if there are young children about who will be confused and frightened by your tears. But, like a build-up of wind, or a pet with bladder-control issues, those tears are better out than in, hence you need a catalogue of feasible excuses in your back pocket, ready to whip out when the need arises.

1.  The classic: 'I've got something in my eye.'
2.  The other classic: 'I've been chopping onions.'
3.  The logical: 'My eyes are just having a quick shower.'
4.  The practical: 'My eyes are at the car wash.'
5.  The sardonic: 'My eyes wanted to have a swim.'
6.  The iconic: Wear sunglasses. Even indoors.
7.  The hypochondriac: 'I'm allergic to . . .' And if it's been a particularly rough day, 'I'm allergic to you, darling.'

# MONDAY 10 NOVEMBER

*6:45 a.m.* A new arrival puts strains on the family unit and all the relationships therein, not unlike the way a minute fissure puts a strain on a dam's holding capacity. How can something so tiny create chaos of such seismic proportions? And how on earth do you suck up the maelstrom of emotions charging through your system long enough to meet everyone's physical and emotional needs when you barely have time to have a shower? After Jelly Bean's last night feed, I don't even bother trying to go back to sleep, as the school routine must swing into action. School bags, lunchboxes, uniforms . . . I contemplate the array of lunchbox fillers I've dumped on the bench, staring as I absently stuff square after square of the kind of cheap and nasty milk chocolate into my mouth that probably came from the same showbag as Tink's curly zany straw. I'm literally immobilised. Zombified. Between night feeds with Jelly Bean and

SHOPPING LIST

*Fully functional Mummy clone. I need a break, just can't handle all this right now . . .*

fretting over Lolly Pop, I am feeling so depleted I've kind of assigned the care and attention of my other children to a single 'must do' box, where individual needs and wants have no place. I haven't organised invitations for Minnie's looming birthday party, Buddy needs to go to the dentist, Princess needs new runners, and Tink just needs some one-on-one time with Mummy, but I don't even have the patience to let her discover her new sisters properly. Naturally, she acts up and is frequently in tears. She pats Jelly Bean with the same vigour as she would MJ, and when jealousy prompts her to drag her little sister off my breast, I must admit I'm apoplectic. MJ looks forlorn.

It's so taboo, but I'm finding I just want my body to myself for five minutes. At feeding time I feel so crowded by the sea of little hands and faces that curiosity draws in and all over me, it's as if I'm drowning. I shake them off. After a quick cuddle, I put Jelly Bean down as soon as she's done rather than snuggling and cradling her as I did with all my others, and am up and fussing around over spilt Lego or the coloured pencils littering the table, rather than focusing my attention on these little urchins who really need it. I feel like I'm failing all of them, a failing that sits like a leaden weight in my gut, mingled with the shame of being so idle and fear of everything falling apart, all of which simmers away, a bubbling cesspit that's poisoning my system and leaves me stranded, leaning against the kitchen bench, stuffing my face with crappy chocolate and unable to even pack a bloody school lunch!

To cap it off, today is my gorgeous grandmother's funeral. This magnificent matriarch survived two husbands and begat seven children and more grandchildren, great-grandchildren and great-great-grandchildren than I've the time or inclination to count. At ninety-eight years of age, she finally stepped off this mortal coil the night before my girls arrived. Spooky.

My nan had been anticipating the birth of the twins with more relish than a ploughman's lunch, having been desperate to see another set of the 'Gregg twins' born within her brood. My grandfather had twin brothers, but there had not been hide nor hair of twins since, till I rocked up with my shock 'two-for-the-price-of-one-till-we-have-to-pay-for-double-the-private-education' pregnancy. Nan knew when they were due, salivating over the date, and yet in the weeks preceding her passing, had actually told the staff at her elderly care home that she would be going on Halloween, the day before their birth.

She was right.

In some deeply spiritual, cosmic manner, Mum is convinced that Nan left right then so she could return within the twins. It brings her comfort and I must say it is a lovely thought so I'm happy to ride with it . . . just have to keep an eye out for her acerbic wit in them, and the propensity for practical joking Nan called her own. Nothing quite compares to a nonagenarian greeting you with a set of false teeth balanced on her head as if they were lost sunglasses.

My mum held my nan as she softly departed this life, and commented on how tiny she felt in her arms; it was as though her soul was so immense, the essence of her being so substantial that when it departed it left little behind. The next morning, there was Mum, Nanny Gypsy to the kids, so called because of her love of long flowing garments, her wild hair and her wild heart, now clutching Jelly Bean. Through her tears she whispered how lucky she felt, how honoured to have been there holding Nan as she ended her journey, and now to be holding these tiny ladies as they began theirs.

I'm not allowed to drive, so I enlist poor Sal to don a black frock and chauffeur me to my home town. I nap on and off during the hour-and-a-half-long journey, while Jelly Bean sleeps soundly. An appropriately bleak day greets us, the pink sky blushing in sincere condolence. My entire extended family is suitably subdued, brightening only to respectfully cluck over Jelly Bean.

I'm remarkably dry-eyed through the bulk of the service, then as the family photo montage rolls out, Jelly Bean decides to vociferously request a snack. The combination of the blown-up vision of my smiling nan and a fidgeting, feeding newborn unlocks something, and the tears begin. But they are cleansing tears: a farewell, a welcome, an acknowledgement of all that has passed and all that is just beginning.

*3 p.m.* With the service complete, and feeling depleted, we head for home and little Lolly Pop. At the hospital, I learn she's been doing exceptionally well and I can take her home. Joy! And bloody terror! A final diagnosis of mild reflux has been made, the interim solution being to administer some diluted thickener at feed time, mixed in with formula or expressed breast milk, for the next few weeks. This prolonged exposure to bottle feeding may affect her ability to feed from the breast, but frankly, Scarlett, I don't give a damn! I'm so grateful she is fit and healthy, and I cannot wait to see her snuggled in her own bassinet.

With the sweet prospect of her homecoming, however, comes the realisation that this is now real. The 'no returns' policy has officially come into effect. Twins. Six kids under one roof with a very busy Chef, and a dog that knows how to open the back door but never bloody closes it . . . Crap . . .

# DEPRESSION:
# POSTNATAL AND BABY BLUES

One side-effect of childbirth and parenting which brings a note of sobriety to the celebration of new life is rarely spoken of, one which is only now starting to attract the attention it deserves: depression.

Every new parent, mothers in particular, can feel a grief often as powerful as and equal to their joy. It's a grief for many things: the life they had before, to which they can never return; the birth they had planned but which took a different direction; the elated vision they harboured during pregnancy which is difficult to maintain once the reality of new babydom, outside the safety of the maternity ward, sinks in; even grief for the loss of a full night's sleep! This feeling can seem endless and hopeless, but for most of us, as time marches on the sharp edges soften, routine emerges from chaos.

For some new mums and dads, however, the feelings of loss, apathy, anger and helplessness can set in as many as four years postpartum, and they don't just resolve. Family must be on the lookout for telltale signs that a new parent is not coping, and if we feel these emotions and cannot lift them, we need to be able to ask for help.

There are no heroes in this game, and no-one will applaud you for keeping a stiff upper lip. If enlisting the help of a counsellor feels too daunting or intrusive at first, begin by confiding in a trusted family member, a good friend, or your regular doctor. As in all things baby-wise, it's about taking baby steps.

# CHAPTER

# THURSDAY 13 NOVEMBER

**9:15 a.m.** It's immunisation time for the twins. Great. Vaccinations of all my children are something I antici- pate with the same quiet excite- ment as I would the extraction of an abscessed tooth: a necessary evil but one replete with much pain and tears – and that's just me!

I generally have the kids inocu- lated at the immunisation clinic of the Royal Children's Hospital. The

> SHOPPING LIST
>
> *Baby paracetamol. Oh, the pain, the torture, the tears – and that's just me!*

nurses are experts – this is what they do all day, and there are sights to see, things to do and naughty stuff to eat as we wait the required fifteen minutes onsite. However, I'm feeling I've seen quite enough of hospitals this year, and following an experience we had with Minnie last year, the Royal Children's now evokes some pretty painful memories.

Shall I elaborate?

Well, you have chosen to come this far with me, dear reader, so why not?

In the beginning of June last year, on an ordinary Sunday evening, Minnie somehow slipped over the balustrade of our second storey, falling close to 8 metres on to hardwood flooring. We only have security footage that captures her mid-fall (footage The Chef tortured himself with but which I will never lay eyes on). What followed was without a doubt the worst night of my life.

I heard the thump from the kitchen, a sickening sound I can recall with the same clarity I do the births of my children: a heavy, stomach-churning thud I'd rather forget but never will. Thinking the kids were throwing toys from the balcony I stormed in from the kitchen in 'Someone is gonna cop it' mode, only to find a deeply winded Minnie sprawled on the floor, gasping and contorting. At first I thought she had fallen from a height of just a few steps; the kids had taken to scaling the side of the staircase but always dropped off a few steps up. I asked her what happened, still in Robo-Mum mode. She just shook her head and said she fell. She couldn't seem to get up, though, which raised the hairs on the back of my neck. I called out to The Chef, who, in a state of fear and shock, immediately started to reprimand her for being so irresponsible and silly in front of her siblings. Minnie, somehow, managed to shoot up on to her feet, all apologies, then just crumpled back to the floor like a house of cards. It was then her eyes began to roll, not like a spoilt teen's, but far back into her head. My instincts, meanwhile, were screaming. Minnie had turned white, and grumbled of a sore arm and sore belly, between slipping into moments of near-catatonia, then asking us what had happened to her. It was when she began speaking gibberish that we decided it was time to mobilise. I called the ambulance while The Chef stretched out alongside Minnie, buoying her up with a silly story. We were still chiding ourselves for probably overreacting, even as I spelled out what had happened once the paramedics arrived, sirens screaming fit to challenge the cacophony reverberating in my own head. They blanched visibly as they looked up the stairwell to the second floor, then swung into action, loading Minnie first on to a stretcher, then into the waiting vehicle.

Climbing in beside her, I left The Chef to oversee the three other munchkins, reassuring him we would return soon, even though inside I was quaking. The Chef, always calm and level-headed in any crisis, smiled, kissed us both and soothed me, saying, 'She's fine, she's fine.' I think deep down we both knew that wasn't the case. I nearly asked him to swap duties with me.

As we drove through the quiet, end-of-the-weekend streets, Minnie began slipping in and out of consciousness. It was all I could do to keep her there with me as we approached our local emergency department.

Upon arrival, the nurse on duty ushered us directly to a cubicle. Unlike my last late-night dash to an emergency department (Buddy managed to stuff an unpopped piece of popcorn into his ear), there was no waiting.

A doctor arrived shortly after and silently examined Minnie, gently probing her clenched little body and asking us both questions in the clipped, economic tone of the professional medic, necessarily devoid of emotion. Suddenly, a battalion of white-coated and blue-smocked individuals filled our cubicle. A neck brace and body traction was swiftly fitted, Minnie weakly protesting at every turn. X-rays were ordered and results returned. Her arm, now grotesquely swollen, was shattered at the elbow. Suspected damage to her neck and legs could not be ruled out. Most frighteningly, her elbow had actually shattered coming into contact with her abdomen as she landed, perforating her bowel, injuring her spleen and various other organs tucked away in there. The X-ray showed her stomach was filling with fluid as her damaged bowel had shut up shop. The fluid would be toxic for her system if allowed to build up, so there was no other option than to intubate her. The process was harrowing: Minnie screamed, fighting against the tube being threaded through her nose and down her throat. She gagged, vomited, pleaded with me to make them stop. It was so hard to force my daughter to submit to pain, smiling through my own tears, telling her it was necessary and in her best interests. Her eyes were huge pools of tortured recrimination as she finally allowed them to fit the tube and insert drips in both arms. My baby girl, so brave; I would have done anything to take her place.

The doctor helming operation 'Put Minnie back together' finally paused for long enough to brief me, a sizeable sheaf of test results in his hand, a deep furrow in his brow.

'As I told you earlier, we can't really determine yet how much damage her neck and legs have suffered. Her arm needs to be set in a cast, and depending on how her bowel responds to the intubation, surgery may be necessary . . .' (Pause as I quietly fall apart). 'We don't have the facilities so we need to transfer her to the Royal Children's.'

Once a clear plan of action had been put in place, my Calm Mum persona took over, 100 per cent smoke and mirrors. I reassured Minnie as she was trolleyed into a waiting ambulance, taxied home to grab her some essentials, fill The Chef in, grab my own case and kiss my three sleeping babies, then onwards to the Royal Children's Hospital.

That place is a well-oiled machine. Despite the ludicrous hour, the place was humming with confidence, competence and most importantly, compassion. The medics on duty worked with an economy of motion that put me to shame, busy hands undertaking numerous tasks while they themselves exuded complete calm and a ready smile. It was close to 2 a.m. when we were ushered downstairs for some fancy X-rays, yet the technician was as bubbly and personable as a first-class flight attendant.

Finally, some good news: her hips and legs looked okay. Her neck was still a concern, however, so the brace remained in place.

By now, Minnie was beyond exhausted, and as staff worked around her, she lapsed into long periods of dozing with her eyes half open. I naturally feared concussion but a nurse assured me that in these circumstances it was quite common. When groggily awake Minnie seemed more concerned by the inconvenience she had caused, apologising profusely for my having to be here with her, and concerned that the family would be worried about her. At about 4 a.m., in a moment of lucidity, she requested that I take a photo of her so everyone would know she was just fine. I still glance at that photo on occasion, tucked away in my phone's photo album, and without fail it threatens to rip my heart straight out of my chest, for there she is, my tiny dancer, body in traction, arms laced with drips and swathed with bandages, tubing taped to her cheek, neck in a brace, straining her sleepy eyes to focus on the camera, a weary smile playing about her lips. I only pretended to send that photo to The Chef and the grandparents. If it shook me to the core seeing it in context, it would have been too much for those family members anxiously awaiting news of her condition.

Finally, Minnie slept. She began to snore which, despite the circumstances, made me smile. I held her little hand, and wisely no-one suggested I go home, take a nap, grab a coffee, or any combination of the above. It was just me and her. I wanted to gather her broken little body up in my arms and take away all the pain, but for now, just being there was the best I could do.

## PARENTAL DARK NIGHTS OF THE SOUL

Seeing your child fall and scrape a knee can send your heart surging up out of your chest and on to the floor, so an actual crisis is something we parents often dare not contemplate. However, your ability to cope will surprise you.

For me, staying functional in the aftermath of Minnie's accident was all about focusing with zeal on taking baby steps. This applies to the physical response to the crisis, which for us involved focusing on the daily medical interventions that would mend her: X-rays, blood tests, examinations, putting the cast on her arm and so on. Setting up simple routines to propel you through the day can also be enormously comforting and give you purpose when you just want to curl up into a ball.

For the two weeks I was at the hospital with Minnie, I would religiously rise while it was still dark, scrape my hair into a ponytail, slip out, grab a coffee and order a sandwich to collect later, then return to the room and complete a crossword while waiting for her to wake. I carried out this routine with military precision and it bolstered me, set me up for the day. I can't explain why but, for that period, if circumstances meant I had to deviate from my routine for whatever reason, I found it deeply distressing. It seemed that performing these simple actions kept all the fear and terror at bay. Once I had, I could deal with whatever the day threw at me.

I believe that anything such as a crossword that requires your undivided attention for even a short time gives your system a break from the emotional and physical beating that seeing your child in a crisis puts you through. Just five minutes snatched from a taxing day is not selfish; it can be the difference between calm rationality and the loony bin.

I hope you never, ever need to put these suggestions into practice, but if you do, try setting yourself an iron-clad routine and focus on those small steps to recovery. It may just save your sanity.

A week in, dear diary, and it seemed my beautiful daughter boasted regenerative powers of Lazarus-like proportions. So much so, she was sending me out in search of an ice-cream sundae for breakfast. This is probably the one time in her life when if she commanded 'Jump', I'd ask, 'How high?'.

The past few days had seen her cleared of serious neck or leg injury, and her intubation removed. I was finally given the all-clear to tenderly bathe her and wash the old vomit from her Rapunzel-like locks. Sporting a pink and purple cast on her arm, she was so busy charming every medic in sight, there wasn't time to complain about pain or discomfort. It's a lovely feeling when you not only love your child, naturally, but you see such reserves of strength and resilience in them, you also respect them.

All up, Minnie and I were guests of the Royal Children's for two weeks. We frequented the Starlight room like groupies would a back stage, and consumed McDonald's like an American socio-economic cliche. I witnessed displays of bravery from both parents and patients in those wards that would put to shame any acts of valour you might see on a battlefield. Some triumphed, some were lost. The hardest part was hearing those little people cry out in pain during the night. For some reason, those cries are so much louder, more insistent, and more heart-wrenching in the hours of darkness.

The most inspiring part, beyond the joy of seeing my daughter heal, was the attentiveness and positivity of the staff. Theirs is a job I could not do for all the Tim Tams in Woolworths. To bear witness to the pain and suffering of children is a task I cannot even begin to comprehend. Yet I am so grateful there are brave souls out there willing to undertake it. While such places exist, our children are in good hands. Now, when children's hospitals run their annual appeals, I'm the first to put my hand in my pocket.

When I do attend the hospital's immunisation department with the twins, I am recognised by a nurse who immediately asks after Minnie. I'm shocked and delighted after all this time. Despite some impressive juggling to get both babies jabbed, the whole process was reasonably painless. Being back within those walls served to remind me how priceless your child's health really is, and that we should never take it for granted.

## SATURDAY 15 NOVEMBER

*1:37 p.m.* It's Saturday. Hallelujah, I have survived a week out of hospital. How do I celebrate? By palming the four eldest off to my mother and going shopping, of course!

During the week I had made a few tentative journeys out of the house to run small errands, each time solo, each time having to summon every iota of willpower I possess not to walk out the gate and just keep going. Noosa is lovely this time of year . . . so too is Mexico . . .

As naughty as it sounds to admit it, I'm already over having little people crawling all over me 24/7; it's like I'm suffering an infestation by iPad-savvy, Barbie-toting lice. I just wanna make like Taylor Swift and shake 'em off.

It's always astounded me the patience The Chef exhibits in letting them lie all over him, the dog included, as he calmly watches TV or responds to emails. I've always been of the 'here's the boob, okay, you are done, go to sleep so I can do something useful' school of parenting, I'm ashamed to admit. At present I've a roaring case of cabin fever to go with it, so having offloaded two-thirds of the tribe I need to get out. A friend kindly agrees to drive me. The vacuum needs a service and Minnie's birthday is fast approaching. I had forgotten, however, just how long it takes to get a newborn

> ### SHOPPING LIST
>
> Golf cart. I figure I can strap a few baby seats in that little beauty, attach a sidecar, and tootle to and from the shops without having to leave my vehicle, load and reload the bloody pram, or suffer pedestrian rage when %#*-ing inconsiderate sods park their cars on the very edge of the park next to mine, so when I finally get back to the car I can't open the door to put my kids in!

out and about. Multiply it by two and you are lucky to be beginning your journey by mid-afternoon. Post-school drop-off, feeds timed and babies dozing, shared breakfast with Tink consumed (hello peanut butter on seaweed rice crackers, who knew you were so delicious?) and we are ready to go.

The trip runs smoothly once I wrangle the pram into upright and load the twins. Vacuum dropped off, I actually try on some clothes, although they all pull at boob and belly points. I even fit in a brief sojourn to the supermarket (amazingly, I manage to purchase two extra-large jars of organic peanut butter – on special, must have seen me coming – some kosher savoury snacks (hmmm, why? Did I convert one night while sleep walking?), and novelty noticeboard pins, but forget milk and toilet paper) before Lolly Pop breaks into a breathless warbling wail that clears entire aisles and sees young folk poised to dial child protective services while middle-aged women smile on in sympathy. A quick reconnoitre reveals that, yes, this shopping centre has a parents' room. I'm a seasoned user of these havens and can sniff out a good one in a single glance. Multiple change tables, check. Microwave, check. Comfy chair, check. Individual rooms with curtain? Check, check. Side table for coffee/snack/mobile phone? Check. Phew! I wheel in and immediately realise I've overlooked one crucial factor: I'm now servicing two, not one. The chair, comfy though it is, doesn't accommodate my twin pillow, so I perch awkwardly on the edge, my bottom grasping desperately at the slippery fabric. The room is too small for the pram, which hangs out, drawing up the curtain and any sense of modesty with it. Post-nappy change, I have the feed underway when Jelly Bean loads up again. I don't have any more nappies, having tried to downsize the nappy bag at the car to accommodate more shopping. I hurry them along, tickling under their chins as they threaten to doze. What was once a peaceful respite from the stresses of retail therapy ain't any more. My hitched-up curtain allows any passerby an eyeful of me tandem feeding, which invariably provokes a comment on the twins or the logistics of managing this feat, neither of which I particularly care to delve into while thus exposed. I pull them both off before they are done and hurry to the toy shop, picking up a sizeable toy horse barn for Minnie, as begged for over a number of months. A kindly assistant takes pity on me and walks it to my car, where I realise that, with the twin pram, the three baby seats, two boosters, bassinet pram inserts, over-stuffed nappy bag, twin pillow and three bags of groceries, there is nowhere for it to go. Hmm . . . guess I'll be coming back here Monday.

This time I'll bring a privacy screen.

# GETTING OUT OF THE HOUSE

If the stork has recently paid you a visit, or even if his last delivery is now old enough to manipulate an iPad, for your own sanity, strive to occasionally get out and about. Even if it is merely a leisurely stroll to the corner for a bottle of milk, the fresh air and complementary dose of vitamin D are powerful medicine: restorative and affirming.

There is something reassuring in observing that, despite the exhaustion and fogginess of new babydom, life goes on, and will continue to do so. This is just a phase, and it too shall pass. Enjoy sitting in a park with your little one(s), meeting a friend for coffee, or be extravagant and take the baby to a baby-friendly movie session.

For those struggling to get out and about with infants, feeding in public, be it via breast or bottle, can be inhibiting. The judgements of others can be enough to make you want to curl into a little ball, let alone venture out your front door. Remember, your choices are your own, and if people have issues there is squat diddly you can do about it.

If you are bottle-feeding, and feel the eyes of the 'breast is best' brigade upon you, you are obviously just not trying hard enough, too selfish or lazy to do what nature intended. Seriously? Nature intended for us to nourish our babies, by any means, and that is all that matters. Wet nurses have been all the rage since the beginning of time, so it's clear nature evolves and adapts as need be.

If breast-feeding, you are clearly just a saucy post-partum minx, using any excuse to get your bits out and wantonly arouse passers-by with your lascivious lactation. Yep, gotta say I've never felt more randy than when I'm bruised and bloated, with a healing caesarian scar, leaky breasts and a squalling infant clinging to my milk-stained shirt. 'C'mon guys, I haven't showered in a week, I'm still wearing the same tracksuit I threw on when I last showered, and the baby has hurled down my back but no-one has told me, let's GET IT ON!' Puh-lease! Again, all you are doing is nourishing your child. Other people's hang-ups are not your concern.

I had an amusing encounter recently. I toddled down to the local park with a coffee, a tray of sashimi and the twins in tow. Naturally, one became grizzly, and like dominos, one follows the other, and so I was obliged to perform the juggling act of feeding both with a haphazard assortment of rolled-up jumpers, baby blankets and wishful thinking as supports. I managed to be discreet with an artfully placed shawl but there are limits, and when a middle-aged couple wandered past, I invariably received a gawping load of evil eye from her. She turned to her husband to share the disgust, only to find he had craftily slipped on his reflective aviators to get a closer look undetected. Now, I'm not stupid, and neither was she; his intent was pretty clear. He copped a sharp elbow to the ribs for his trouble and she stormed off, leaving him to throw me a rueful smile before scuttling off in her wake.

It's important to be discreet, and to observe what is appropriate behaviour in public, but naturally your baby's needs are first and fore-most and no-one can expect you to scramble home every two hours or hide yourself away in a grotty public toilet whenever your baby rouses.

It all comes back to what you regard as appropriate. You cannot keep everyone happy all the time. There will always be someone on hand to judge when you chastise your tantrum-prone toddler in the supermarket, when you screech at your eight-year-old for mimicking Bear Grylls on the monkey bars, or reprimand your teen for refusing to drag their eyes from social media long enough to join in on a family meal at a restaurant. All you can do is what feels right for you and your family; at the end of the day that's all that matters.

Similarly, for those parents taming toddlers and too scared to leave the house for fear of being walloped with a public liability insurance claim, there are plenty of places to go and socialise, and even indulge in the long-lost art of 'adult conversation', that are both child-proof and kid-friendly.

Public play parks and gardens are the first port of call. Pack some snacks and a rug or towel, and suddenly a stroll and a play on the swings becomes a picnic and an affordable day out! If chancing expo-sure to inclement weather is not your style, there are always the indoor options. They do tend to be expensive, but what cost a few hours of sanity?

Indoor-play areas have traditionally been an orgy for viral illness and bacteria, but in recent years, stricter guidelines mean most have really picked up their game. Many are now hygienically conscientious, maintaining a strictly allergen-free environment. They frequently house small cafes with reasonably healthy food, decent coffee and newspapers to make two hours of watching your children doing their darndest to break a bone on the padded play equipment almost bearable.

Public libraries generally offer 'story time' for toddlers, followed by a craft session which allow the little ones to get their fingers in pots of craft glue and glitter at no risk to your soft furnishings.

If you are happy to pay for distractions, there are a plethora of toddler activities available in your local area: educational music classes, kinder ballet, and baby sports are programs that have had great success in my household, along with such traditional favourites as Gymbaroo. Most offer variations on a theme, designed primarily to teach the kids co-ordination, social interaction and patience – and to tire them out! Some programs require parental inclusion, but most will allow you to sit on the sidelines watching your little ones burn off some energy in a safe, controlled environment.

There are plenty of options available and this is the one time that Google may prove to be your best friend. Many local councils also offer an abundance of free children's activities, it's just a matter of looking up 'What's on?' in your area.

As your children emerge from the dependence of toddler-hood, you will be rewarded with a newfound sense of freedom, as you can get into the great outdoors with greater autonomy and possibility of adventure, plus less baggage!

Long walks, bike rides, hiking, museums, gallery tours: all become possible as their endurance, stamina and curiosity increases. Extra-curricular activities, sports and hobbies provide opportunities for both your child and you to learn new skills and socialise outside your immediate family and school communities. This is critical to your child's development, as it forces them to quickly learn social etiquette, fair play and communication skills as their boundaries are tested each time they encounter a new face. I cannot emphasise enough how important it will be to your child's development for them to develop bonds outside of their school buddies: it teaches them to be adaptable and exposes them to different cultures and different socio-economic groups, all in the name of a bit of fun, exercise and fresh air!

Just make sure you enrol them in activities close to a decent cafe because, especially through the winter months, there is an awful lot of standing around in the mud and the cold. A hot takeaway beverage in your hand can be the difference between calm, loving parental support, and sideline rage!

Parenthood is a many-splendoured thing, but even the sturdiest houseplant needs fresh air to thrive. Getting into the great outdoors with your little tackers throughout the years fosters in them a sense of adventure, togetherness and curiosity, and forges strong familial bonds that will last a lifetime.

It is all about those Kodak moments; it's all about making memories.

## MONDAY 17 NOVEMBER

**8:54 a.m.** Okay, I'm not going to say I've established a routine, but I've managed to pack the elder three ratbags off to school in reasonably presentable form, and with lunchboxes that verge on being healthy (if you count chocolate-coated muesli bars as a bona fide food group). Beds are made, hair brushed; I almost had a shower but had to abort when Princess arrived, carrying a packet of biscuits (where the hell did they come from? Had I been aware of their existence I'd have scoffed them by now) and announcing she would make breakfast. Twins were fed and back in bed before any of their older siblings had roused, and I ate a bowl of cereal SITTING DOWN! Old habits die hard, however, as I still indulged in a tablespoonful of peanut butter while standing at the sink washing dishes.

> SHOPPING LIST
>
> Just going to pop into the local grocer and have a word with the manager . . . been perusing their latest specials catalogue. It's chock-a-block full of bright and shiny ads for '2 for the price of 1' items. Someone needs to let them know '2 for the price of 1' isn't all it is cracked up to be.

Is this approaching the light at the end of the tunnel? Is the fog that accompanies newborns lifting?

Not sure I'd quite call it that but at least I didn't wake this morning in a state of urgent and irrational panic.

Feeling closer to sane than I have in some time, I make an effort to pace myself, to sit with Tink on the couch and watch cartoons with her. I found time to chat to Minnie about what her plans are for the day while doing her hair, to give Buddy a spontaneous cuddle, and to discuss the serious matter of one's sandals matching one's undies with Princess. For me, this is what matters; I don't need to bribe my children because I'm feeling guilty about the amount of time I'm NOT spending with them, knowing that this is a transitional phase and it too will pass. I regularly explain this to them and it seems to be enough that I can occasionally make it to school pick-up, I am always there at the end of the day (even if I am verging on catatonic), and I always say, 'That's wonderful, sweetie' to any comment they make . . . even when that comment revolves around having fed dog biscuits to the two-year-old.

## GETTING THE KIDS INVOLVED

Life in any family can be chaotic. Each additional sibling multiplies that chaos a little more. The sheer intensity of labour can be overwhelming, which is why the perfect way to kill several birds with one stone is to inveigle the kids into helping you.

Don't offer payment or bribes, just explain that it would mean a lot to you, and the whole family, if they could help. Even the youngest child can be of assistance in their own little way, and you would be surprised at just how much they will do just to be told you are proud of them.

### Toddlers

If you have babies, toddlers can help by bringing you nappies, wipes, cushions etc, and are often more than happy to do so. If they are buzzing about destroying the joint while you try to feed or do some work, cater to their vanity by asking them to sing a lovely lullaby to the baby, or do a dance for you. Any opportunity to perform to a captive (literally) audience will keep them occupied for at least five minutes.

### 4–6-year-olds

This age can actually take instructions; whether they fulfil them is another matter, but it's worth trying. They can be particularly handy at bath time, passing shampoo etc, laying out baby clothes, finding nappies and creams. Direct their boundless energy into doing a little legwork for you!

### 7 and over

This age group can be a triumph or a torture depending on such variables as time of day, proximity to meal times and what's on the idiot box. Remind them how critical they are to the smooth mobilisation of the whole family unit, and utilise a little mild incitement by mentioning how favourably you will look at future requests from them should they prove themselves worthy now. Their greatest strength is their ability to direct and entertain younger siblings while you feed/cook dinner/ take a bath and fall asleep, emerging like an albino prune forty-five minutes later. Children of this age can also run a baby bath, prepare snacks for siblings, themselves and you, and answer the phone/door/ screaming toddler at those awkward moments (eg when donning the twin feeding pillow which, in my case, makes me look like I'm testing out a Halloween costume featuring a giant snot-green lifesaver). Minnie takes enormous pleasure in simply comforting the twins while I arrange changes of clothes and nappies or tend to the younger ones, and acting as a firm but gentle barrier between inquisitive little hands and the babies. I'm surprised how much I rely on her running interference for me, particularly when I'm twin-feeding and Tink, having waited till my hands are otherwise engaged, drags one of the twins off me bodily. Clearly she thinks I'm under attack by a swarm of nappied pygmy terrorists and wants to save the day.

## WEDNESDAY 19 NOVEMBER

*5:47 p.m.* It's certainly cocktail hour – Molotov cocktail hour, that is! Bath time followed hot on the heels of dinner and Mummy trying to resist falling into a bottle of Riesling. Who am I kidding, right now I'd happily crawl into a cask of Fruity Lexia and then take a nap on the inflated bladder. I've hit a new low, screaming at the two-year-old for kissing the twins too enthusiastically. Then, wait for it, I screech at four-year-old Princess for asking . . . to eat fruit (!?!?!?!?). Admittedly, I had just cleared dinner and was settling down to feed the twins when she started bleating that she needed three raspberries. A tantrum ensued and I went into full meltdown mode, the combination of too much caffeine and too little sleep tipping my equilibrium overboard and my parenting instincts down the kitchen sink. It was only as I was threatening to throw her in the pool that I realised how ridiculous I was being. The child was asking for fruit! Fruit!!! And here was I doing my banana over a handful of berries!

While I'm on this confessional bout of self-flagellation, can I add that I sometimes find myself musing that one of the twins kinda resembles the love child of Yoda and a potato, while the other frequently appears to have sucked a lemon, when she isn't mimicking a chipmunk? Not that I'd tell anyone this but you, dear, candid diary.

Final confession, gotta get it off my chest: the stark contrast between my former life as actor-gal-about-town and my current situation was brought into stark relief for me this morning. The Chef and I had been discussing a few red-carpet film premieres we had been invited to (OOOOOO-errrr, aren't we fancy?) before he scurried off to work. I was busily shooting off 'Non, merci beaucoup' RSVP emails to all while feeding the twins when the morning's two long blacks began a heated discussion with my bowels and requested to make a hasty exit. Too much information, I know, but an apt demonstration of just how far I've fallen from social grace. Yep, I schlepped to the bathroom, girls still nuzzling me on the twin pillow, to do as nature intended, just in the most unnatural manner imaginable. Coffee successfully expelled, it dawned on me that I now could not, err, conclude proceedings in my current state. The girls were still feeding vigorously, and I was loath to yank them off, thereby invoking much squalling and gnashing of tiny gums and waking the rest of the still-dozing household. So I sat there, on the throne – till they were done. Pure glamour. Reckon I might change my reply to a stonking great 'Yessiree!' to a couple of those film invites. If Lady Gaga shocked the assembled media masses when she rocked a red carpet cloaked in meat, and Bjork amused them when she donned a dead swan, imagine their

SHOPPING LIST

Eggs

Bread

Milk

Detachable breasts (just wanna hand them over to someone else and let them experience the joys of twin-feeding for an hour or two, go catch a film, have a nap, and maybe grab a cocktail?)

response of my ensemble of overinflated pool ring balancing feeding twins, dirty shirt, and trackie bottoms and undies casually yet strategically draped about the ankles. Throw in a pair of Louboutins and methinks I'm *Vogue*-ready!

## THURSDAY 4 DECEMBER

*10:47 a.m.* It is the perfect storm. Minnie's ninth birthday and Buddy's school production on the same day. I'm getting shivers just contemplating being able to roll visiting relatives, fussed-over children and celebratory cake into one 24-hour chunk. Okay, maybe we don't need to limit the cake to just one day – regardless, it's joy! Buddy is just rapt that the twins will not be in attendance at his production. Don't get me wrong, he adores them, but the constant focus on them and their development can be a lot for number 1 son to take on. Whenever we pause to chat with the other school mums he immediately interjects, asking, 'So, do you wanna talk about the twins?'

> SHOPPING LIST
>
> $50 worth assorted lollies, freckles, and those tiny sugar shapes for cake decorating. I might not have time to bake a cake, but I can buy a chocolate Swiss roll, some icing mixture and some little silver balls and 'customise' it!

Must say, I'm looking forward to attending an event unencumbered, with Nanny S taking the twins and Tink for the morning. I had contemplated dragging the pair along for about five seconds, but did not relish the prospect of trying to slip in an inconspicuous feed with the entire Prep 2 community looking on.

Minnie has been in a lather all day over the contents of her remaining gifts. The longed-for horse barn was a hit. The two smaller gifts, which she does not know the contents of, are not to be opened till after school and are thus causing much speculation. Then she begins negotiating the contents of the lolly bags for her party. Can they be full of just mini chocolate bars, plus individual Lego boxes and novelty stationery? All adding up to more than the cost of the entire party? After some to-ing and fro-ing, we settle on three mini chocolate bars, good ol' fashioned lollies, and a single Lego figurine for each. Minnie nods her consent with the air of a condemned martyr. She's become terrifyingly good at negotiating in the past year and I fear what new precocity age nine will bring when she is already exhibiting the behaviour of a sixteen-year-old.

Frankly, she's lucky to be having a party at all. I managed to emerge from my addled state long enough to book the thing, then promptly forgot to send out the invitations. Nice one, Mum! The past week has seen me sending out a lot of duplicitous emails and text messages to the parents of Minnie's guest list, asking if their child can attend as the RSVP date on the 'invitations I sent had expired'.

'You didn't receive an invitation? How bizarre. I sent them out ages ago.' My deviousness disgusts even me.

The school hall is more overstuffed than an image-conscious teen's bra when we arrive to see the show. The Chef, Minnie, both sets of grandparents and I nab seats in rough proximity to each other, and I'm again thankful the mega-truck that is my double pram didn't make the door list.

My little man, when he appears amid the throng of his classmates, is gorgeous. Decked out in his Ten of Hearts card costume, knobbly knees and skinny little legs jutting out beneath, he looks so small my heart wrings, acknowledging he is just a little boy, who has kinda gotten lost and to a degree been forgotten in the maelstrom that has been the twins' arrival. His onstage gestures and the faces he pulls are so expressive, I experience a less pleasant wrench at the thought he might become an actor. Please no! Doctor? Yes! Lawyer? Yes! Garbologist? Yes! Anything with a bit more stability than my crazy career.

I applaud wildly as the curtain goes down and the kids assemble for a ragged round of bows. I vow to myself I will give my little man more attention; the question is, where do I milk another hour out of my day?

As we are filing out, Minnie pipes up again. 'Can we go and choose a cake now?'

Please believe me when I tell you I used to be one of those mums who delighted in creating gourmet gateaux for my children's birthdays. Fancy fillings, unusual shapes, the logistics of assembling a train or a swimming pool using just sponge and lashings of luridly dyed icing and tiny sugar roses really floated my boat. Now, however, my repertoire extends only about as far as making a hedgehog slice with a plastic 'happy birthday' logo wedged atop it. Even then, I'm tempted to merely stick a pile of the plain sweet biscuits together and simply smother them with icing. Job done. So my temporary, and can I again stress it IS temporary, solution is (shock, horror) bought cakes. OOOOOO, the shame!

The enormous range out there, however, brings out the arch negotiator in my beloved Minnie. This girl knows what she wants, the preferences and dietary considerations of other family members be damned. If she wants a fuchsia sponge with popping candy cream and licorice icing she will nag until she gets it. And if said cake is roundly rejected by everyone upon tasting, even herself, and just slowly decomposes in the fridge, virtually untouched, well, tough! You have to admire her spunk.

Thankfully she demands chocolate. Phew! The Chef's profession again delivers rewards as I'm able to simply order one through the bakery department, job done.

## SATURDAY 6 DECEMBER

*6 a.m.* The day of Minnie's party dawns sunny and glorious. Perfect day for being rugged up indoors, blistering your heels with ice skates.

Getting everyone to the ice rink along with lolly bags, cake and paraphernalia is a gargantuan effort and naturally I have Minnie rolling up late to her own party. Midway in, I discover the parents of most of the invitees are going to hang around (says everything about my mothering that I assumed everyone would do as I would and run for the hills at the first chance of someone minding my child for two hours) and I have failed to organise parental finger food. I rustle up a round of bad coffee, a bowl of french fries and another of lolly snakes, hoping they will buy my 'uber-retro' theme. Parental sugar hit complete, I give the twins a quick snack then, unable to quell my inner child any longer, I strap on some skates and hit the ice. That expression proves quite literal as I do just that, several times, with my butt, before finding my mojo and managing to shuffle about, execute a few turns, and make a hash of skating backwards. No serious injuries are incurred by me or the children, and we reconvene in our assigned party room, remarkable more for its insistent dampness rather than its jolly atmosphere, for deep-fried goodies and cake. Thankfully the cake is a huge hit, the parents scoffing a slice after initially refusing, then sampling their progeny's scraps before gladly accepting their own. Everyone seemed to have a genuinely great time despite the lack of fanfare, and most importantly to me, my big girl is happy.

SHOPPING LIST

*It is December, clearly I need ski gloves, woollen leggings and a freakin' hot water bottle.*

# KIDS' PARTIES

Children's birthday celebrations have become big business. But let's face it, they are more about parental ego, less about kiddy fun. The stakes keep getting higher and when attending little Ruby or little Jacob's extravaganza, you can actually smell Mum's and/or Dad's competitive ardour from a block away. It directs you to the destination more surely than satnav. Never mind the balloons on the gate, just sniff out the house reeking with adrenalised ambition.

Spending a small fortune on entertainers, catering and elaborate set-ups does not for a good time make, however, especially not for kids who, following their first giddy moments of awe, soon become fatigued by sensory overload and either retreat into their shell or your lap, whichever is most readily available, or go on a sugar-fuelled rampage, consuming or destroying everything in their path for the next five hours till they collapse in a sticky, dirty post-party coma.

I have always opted for simplicity when hosting my children's parties. Admittedly, part of that is laziness, but an equally large part is a nostalgic love of the parties of my youth, where old-fashioned, unadorned party games were the order of the day; jellies, toffees and chocolate crackles were imperfectly handmade but utterly delicious; and pass-the-parcel boasted one prize at its centre, not a mini-treat for everyone within each layer.

I have attended some parties with multiple jumping castles, coffee stations, copious alcohol at 10 a.m., a cast of costumed actors enacting scenes from films, and elaborate catering more suited to the parents' tastes than the children's, and felt embarrassed that my parties have been so lacking. However, I need only remind myself of the sheer glee I've witnessed on the attendees' faces at my soirées to feel assured that there might be some merit to my perception of what kids' parties should be all about.

One of our most successful shindigs was Buddy's sixth birthday. I ordered a batch of invites, balloons, hats etc online to match the requested theme, organised three parlour games (Pin the Tail on the Donkey, Pass the Parcel, Musical Chairs) with practical prizes such as mini stationery kits and sticker packs over plastic rubbish, and prepared the fare at my own pace, over two days (chocolate crackles, honey joys, cupcakes, sausage rolls and jellies keep fabulously well in a bit of Tupperware, so it remained only for me to whip up fairy bread and sandwiches, and to ice the cupcakes on the morning of the big day) at a tiny fraction of the cost of catering. We limited the number of invitees to six, my thinking being I wanted Buddy to actually spend time with all his special mates rather than just automatically invite the whole class. As the numbers were small, the biggest splurge was taking the crew to see a movie Buddy desperately wanted to watch (not in Gold Class). I made up snack bags for each child, along with a bottle of water bought in bulk. The highlight of the day for these little fellows was the short walk from the cinemas to our home. The thrill of independently making our way there had them inexplicably enthralled. Once home, we played games and after some initial confusion when each layer of pass-the-parcel didn't yield a prize, they had a ball. The far-from-elaborate party food was devoured in minutes, we then turned on the radio and had a dance-off (this was the other great hit of the day – amazing something so simple would prove so successful), cut the cake, and then played in the garden till the mums and dads arrived. That was my other great innovation: I was determined to have a proper children's party, not a parents' get-together dressed up as a children's party. Thus, I made it very clear that while parents were more than welcome, this was an opportunity for them to slip away for four hours (yep, I went long form, old school, none of this one-hour-forty-five-minute party malarkey) while I kept their darlings safe, fed and watered. I had requested a comprehensive list of any allergies, so there was nothing to sweat over. Clearly unaccustomed to this kind of dynamic, some parents loitered initially, but soon all took the opportunity to scamper and a great day was truly had by all.

Before you tire of the sound of me patting myself on the back, never fear, I've succumbed to party peer pressure too. I followed Buddy's party with Princess's first party, her fourth birthday, and this was an entirely different affair.

I invited the whole class, as is customary in kindergarten. Princess was desperate to dress up as a mermaid so we settled on an 'Under the sea' theme and again ordered the attendant paraphernalia online. Here is where the similarities end. As I was quite pregnant with the twins by this time, I decided to outsource and opted to hold the party at one of our restaurants, this one a newly opened space in the botanical gardens. A glassed-in area was to be ours, so I set about constructing elaborate tropical fish from paper to hang from the ceiling, thereby creating a 'fishbowl effect'. This entailed sitting up late into the night over several nights, entangled in glue, paint and paper mâché. I hired a mermaid entertainer, arranged catering specific to the parents' and the children's needs, and sourced fancy costumes for the kids, thinking all this would make my task easier, and the whole operation less stressful on the day.

What a fool.

All I did was stress! The party was just a blur of sugar and bright colours punctuated by brief, pointless conversations with near-strangers and breathless appeals for parents to eat up, lest my over-catered fare should go to waste. In the end, everyone had fun, but the whole enterprise was so overwhelming. Princess would have been happy with a candle stuck in a party pie provided she got to dress up, and frankly, I cannot even remember much of the day. Lesson learned.

My suggestion: when entertaining the idea of entertaining children, follow the KISS principle: Keep it simple, stupid. Your day might not rival the Oscars, but the kids will have a ball, and you will be relaxed enough to actually enjoy it, and those are the things that really matter.

# FRIDAY 12 DECEMBER

*7:07 a.m.* Something is wrong. I've just woken up, of my own accord, refreshed and replenished . . . something is very wrong. I hit the sack at 11 p.m., and did not rouse during the night, not even once . . . something is very very wrong . . . the twins!

I launch myself from bed, tangling a foot in the covers and tumbling to my knees. I scramble to my feet and dash from the room, skidding into a door frame and stubbing my toe on a cornice in my haste. No matter, I barrel down the hallway and up the stairs. Finally, I throw open the twins' door, propelling myself through, a panting quivering wreck . . . and there they are, cooing and giggling in their cots, Minnie is leaning over Lolly Pop, tickling her chin, Princess is perched on my feeding chair beside Jelly Bean's crib, singing her a whimsical lullaby of her own composition. All four jump at my dramatic entry: a bedraggled ogre with scarecrow hair in a faded Rolling Stones T-shirt.

'Oh, hi Mum,' sing the two big sisters in unison, while the little ones treat me to syrupy grins and start pumping their arms and legs in joyful anticipation of breakfast.

The twins slept through the night! And rather than being slapped out of my slumber by a squalling chorus, here I find two contented babies being serenaded by their sisters.

Life is never perfect, but this moment comes pretty darn close – and after a full night of slumber, I feel almost human, or at least, less like Daffy Duck, continually falling off cliffs and having my beak re-arranged by baseball bats. Maybe, just maybe, I can do this after all, but as my reaction to the gift of unbroken sleep suggests, perhaps the sheer enormity of the task before me – dragging up half a cricket team in the age of the nuclear family – will break me before I'm even in sight of the finish line. Is such a Herculean feat possible to undertake with sanity intact? Can the peg that is such a large family ever fit into the 2.4 children hole allotted to families by modern social standards? Will the car survive? Will the house survive? Will the nanny survive? Only one way to tell, and that is to jump in feet first. There is no going back now: look out world, here I come with my DIY entourage.

For now, it's all about enjoying and living in the moment, and as I sit, smothered by love on all sides, that is precisely what I am doing.

# CHAPTER

5

# THURSDAY 18 DECEMBER

**6 a.m.** The littlest girls are well into their second month. Minnie is nine! Princess and Tink are striding through their fourth and second years respectively, and come April, Buddy will be a little man of seven, thus legally able to sit alongside me in the front seat, as he keeps solemnly reminding me.

> SHOPPING LIST
>
> Crack-filler. It never ceases to amaze me that with all the home improvement going on, I'm surrounded by cracks! Bent-over builders, that is: utility belts at half mast, butt cracks brazenly saluting the sun. I'm practically blinded by the reflected glare bouncing off all those lily-white glutes. I suppose if I wanna see change, I'm gonna need a sea change!

Despite limping along like a three-legged junkyard dog, the family is still a functional unit: fed (kinda), dressed (more often than not) and loved (always).

The same cannot be said for our front yard, where the building works have begun with gusto. Here's a scenario guaranteed to strike fear into the heart:

**7 a.m.** Ding dong . . .

Kids half-dressed, toast going cold, no fresh bread for school lunches, babies screaming, boobs aching, T-shirt sagging at the neck from being stretched to give the babies chest access too often, and there's a construction crew on my doorstop. Within fifteen minutes the jackhammers will start pounding and thus it will remain for the rest of the day. The yard is now a churned-up, boggy quagmire we can longer access vehicularly, instead being forced to park on the street. Chances of nabbing a car park anywhere in the vicinity of our front gate? Just give me a moment while I choke on the hilarity. I'm left schlepping six children several blocks to my car just to buy a loaf of bread. Yes, I could walk them all to the shops, but, having done the maths and considered the logic of such a journey, there's a decent chance I'll lose one along the way.

There are only two options left to us now: get outta here OR sit cross-legged in a corner, rocking, while tunelessly humming Taylor Swift's 'Shake It Off' for the next three months . . .

Hmmm . . . 'Kids! Go pack your bags!'

# SATURDAY 20 DECEMBER

*6:55 a.m.* Ahhhhh, the beach at summertime: sun, sand, surf, tiger snakes. Then there are the summer tourists, swarming over every available inch of sand, clogging up the queues at the bakery, snaffling up the last neenish tart. Rude. I get a bit proprietary about the stretch of sand and surf we call our turf. I just figure if you pay property tax on a place you deserve an automatic exemption from queuing at local stores and amenities, automatic claim to the choicest baked goods at the local bakery (offload the spinach and cheese sausage rolls on the tourists, the beef ones are for us locals) and automatic access to the one toilet in the public beachside block that still has toilet paper left. Too much to ask? I think not.

> SHOPPING LIST
>
> Christmas wrapping paper
>
> Toilet paper
>
> Fly paper (or was that only actually available in the Thirties and my gorgeous Nan, ever resourceful, just kept trotting out the same strip, every summer, for seventy-odd years?)
>
> Frozen sausage rolls (taste like paper, but have no other choice)

Just getting to the house requires a military-style operation, naturally. Knowing our little hideaway, itself in the last painful throes of completion, would be besmirched by the ongoing presence of builders (oodles of dust, handprints on walls, grotty boot prints on floors, lunch refuse scattered helter skelter, and the odd toilet left unflushed) I had organised for a cleaner to come. I'd also arranged to take delivery of a Christmas tree from the local nursery, and for an electrician to come and help me string Christmas lights. Unfortunately, maths ain't my strong suit (umm, hello? Actor! Clearly not paid to think!) and I had booked everyone for 10 a.m., forgetting it takes two hours to drive there, dang! Hence, the kids went to bed fully dressed in their clothes for the next day, breakfast is pre-made sandwiches, and I have coordinated the babies' feeds from 2 a.m. to ensure we are on the road by 7:30 a.m. Then of course a builder for the renovation in Melbourne rocks up late, some plants arrive as I'm trying to feed, and Jelly Bean then presents me with a massive hurl, all over her, all over the floor, all over the carpet in the next room. That's some powerful projection. Fan-bloody-tastic.

*7:42 a.m.* We are finally making tracks. The car heaves with pantry staples, clothes, prams, kiddy paraphernalia, fragile Christmas decorations (I've packed extra, tipping at least 30 per cent will arrive pulverised), some mysterious boxes I'm 'helping Santa's elves with' (take up half the bloody car, that lot) and the children. With the amount of cargo I'm shipping, I could easily be forgiven for securely buckling in a lavishly wrapped vase and leaving a child standing, bewildered, on the doorstep.

*9:47 a.m.* We are quarter of an hour on the wrong side of our destination, but just have to stop at a service station and release the hordes from the car. Out they tumble, ankle-deep in dumped cling wrap, drink bottles and dirty nappies. Gotta love a road trip.

For the last twenty minutes Buddy and Princess have been busy in the boot clawing each other's eyes out because he was singing along to Katy Perry too loudly. Lolly Pop is screaming, Tink is cooing 'go to sweep' to Jelly Bean while sticking her finger in her eye, and Minnie is screeching that she is trying to listen to the radio. In the midst of the cacophony my agent chooses to call. Am I interested in being on *I'm a Celebrity Get Me Out of Here*? Apparently the producers are really keen. I instruct her to take a listen; the kids obligingly ramp up the bickering. Being dumped in a remote, fetid swamp amid feral animals is just an average afternoon at my place, and given said animals wouldn't require me to spoon feed them, bathe them, or change their nappies, it would be a bloody holiday! Message received loud and clear. Before she rings off, my eternally patient agent asks when I would be ready to step back on to a set, there being a few new projects floating around for which I would be well suited. Considering my most significant achievement of late (outside of feeding/cleaning/clothing my half a football side) has been managing to apply fake tan to my legs, I'm tipping I'm not quite ready to dip my toe back in the pool of professional engagement just yet.

*10:05 a.m.* Finally pulling in to the house, we see a large, jovial-looking man wrestling with a large, jovial-looking conifer in the driveway. The resemblance to St Nick is undeniable. I contemplate telling the kids he might be Santa in disguise but it looks like he has his hands full already without a tribe of tiny warriors climbing all over him requesting Lego and ice-skating Elsa dolls. Sadly, his merriment doesn't extend beyond appearance. Despite dragging the tree up an impressive number of stairs, when I ask for his assistance in getting the wilted conifer upright and into its stand, he baulks. Not part of his job description, apparently. Changes his tune pretty quick smart when I slide him twenty bucks, however. Yeah, merry freakin' Christmas to you too.

The electrician arrives shortly thereafter and we spend the rest of the afternoon tangled in eco-friendly solar LED fairy lights and attempting a bit of arty-farty placement of the illuminated reindeers I found online. By evening, the yard presents a restrained Christmas wonderland amid the dense bush surrounding us on three sides. Indoors, the tree is twinkling, alive with sparkling baubles. It only took two hours and three smashed pieces before Tink finally ceased fiddling with the ornaments on the lower branches and the job was done. Christmas for eight, here we come!

## TUESDAY 23 DECEMBER

*4:43 p.m.*: Beyond gin and Valium, online shopping is a mother's best friend. Without it, this year Santa would be delivering a jar of peanut butter, post-it notes, some loose change and a handful of rubber bands all artfully stuffed into an empty tissue box.

With the exception of a few large-scale items (soda stream anyone?) I've managed to complete my shopping duties, in my pyjamas, online.

SHOPPING LIST

*Shop? Why shop when you can eBay? Apparently it's the new black.*

I'm obliged, however, to make one pre-Chrissy run to the city to collect the makings of Christmas lunch and copious amounts of alcohol, and to drag Buddy in for a long-overdue dental appointment. Melbourne is abuzz with festive merry-making. I've brought along Tink and the twins to ease the load on The Chef (who am I kidding, I wanna play Mother Martyr and luxuriate in a bit of admiring pity!) and they are already getting giddy on the commercial Yuletide hype.

Buddy behaves beautifully throughout the appointment, Tink insists on fiddling with every piece of instrumentation in sight (but haven't we all wanted to do just that?) and the twins break out in a squalling chorus. As we wrap up, the hygienist takes pity on me and offers one of the cubicles for me to feed in. Thank goodness I brought along my trusty twin feeding cushion – subtle as a sledgehammer. We slip in, and the older two are given pencils and paper to keep them occupied. Mid-feed, Tink, who has been loitering around the periphery of the room, darts to the door, manages to wrangle the lock into submission, and slips out. Bloody hell. There's nothing to do but to hoist myself up, twins riding sidesaddle, and chase her. Down the hall, round the bend, and into the waiting room, heaving with patients. I pause on the threshold, arms clutching cushion, twins noisily nuzzling, boobs baby bound, and a partridge in a pear tree. Merry bloody Christmas.

I extract Tink from the toy corner, collect Buddy and offload the twins into the pram, while manhandling the mammaries back into their maternity cups in an attempt to exit with some shred of dignity. As we pass the reception desk Buddy drops a clanger by ever so politely rounding on the receptionist with, 'Um, my mum said I'd get a lollipop if I was good!' (Oh, Buddy, don't mention sugary bribes at the *dentist*!!!)

'No darling,' I hiss with a smile, 'that's when you go to the doctor.'

## CHRISTMAS DAY

*12:43 a.m.* The children . . . are still . . . awake . . .

I cannot even count how many times I've threatened them with a no-show by Santa, it hasn't made a single dent in their apparent determination to see the sun rise. I glance forlornly at the tree, its base still bereft of gifts. Strung out and overtired, Princess stomps around the kitchen in nightgown and

> SHOPPING LIST
>
> *Whatever it is, I hope 7/11 stocks it. Cos nothing else is bloody well open!*

gumboots, heaving with huge, hiccuping sobs but unable to tell me why. Tink just flings herself on the floor in a straight-out tantrum. Buddy darts from room to room, mocking my attempts to brush his teeth, while Minnie follows me about asking deep, philosophical questions about the meaning of Christmas, intercut with sly quizzes on what she can expect under the tree.

'How would I know? It's up to Santa.' She gives me the kind of look exclusive to tween girls and deadly vipers.

Desperate times call for desperate measures. Once all are herded into one bedroom, I put on a DVD, set them up with a snack and slip out. Tink, my two-year-old, still very much a baby, is the first to nod, and the rest, thankfully, soon follow, visions of sugar plums dancing in their heads.

I'm tipping the box of gifts down from the laundry shelf when, right on cue, the twins wake. The Chef, who had been prepping Christmas lunch all night with his brother Top Gun, is enjoying a quiet drink, and so is passed the mantle of Santa's helper-cum-gift-arranger, while I toddle upstairs for a last feed and long nap (if I get that it *will* be a Christmas miracle). Merry Christmas to all and to all a good night . . . till 2 a.m. and then again at 4:30 a.m. . . . and when the rest of the tribe rouse at 6. Yeah . . . merry bloody Christmas.

## PLAYING HOST

Playing Santa to numerous children and host to too many guests this holiday season? Here's a handy survival tip: disappear. Excuse yourself on the pretext of tending to the endless piles of washing, then lock yourself in the laundry with a bottle of riesling and a pack of mince pies and don't emerge till New Year's Eve. Eventually your guests will start taking care of themselves and with so much food going around, there should be ample scraps on the benches, tables and floor to sustain your children.

Bonus: the melodious hum of a washer-dryer can be surprisingly soothing for frayed, Yule-weary nerves.

## SUNDAY 28 DECEMBER

*6:47 p.m.* Having hosted numerous guests over the festive period, our cupboard is totally 'Old Mother Hubbard'. I attempted a quick supermarket shop in the morning but was greeted by bumper to bumper traffic clogging the coastal road at the end of our driveway, so swiftly retreated, only emerging again at 5 p.m. for a second attempt with Tink and the twins in tow. The traffic congestion had eased everywhere but inside the little local grocery, which was teeming with every type of holidaymaker imaginable. From your garden-variety cara-

SHOPPING LIST

*Anything! I'll take it!*

*Tinned mackerel in tomato sauce and a bag of matzo ball mixture? Gimme!*

vaners and grey nomads to aspirational hotel-dwellers who'd booked two years in advance, to the surfer dudes shacking up in their vans and the dreadlocked music festival ticket-holders roughing it in tents pitched in the most improbable and possibly illegal destinations.

Everyone was there, haggling over everything from quinoa to footy franks. Like Moses parting the Red Sea, I surged through the throngs, my bulk-pack nappy/Salada/peanut butter/Tim Tam-laden trolley helmed by Tink in the toddler seat, Lolly Pop in the capsule and Jelly Bean dangling precariously from the Baby Bjorn. It was harrowing, the only balm being when a brace of young dudes referred to me as a 'milf' in the household cleaning aisle as I reached for the spray 'n' wipe.

The queue for the checkout was several shades of hell, however: twenty deep with only a handful of uninterested cashiers ploddingly swiping items through. As I finally reached the head of the queue, a now-screaming Lolly Pop bouncing on my hip beside her Baby Bjorn-bound sister, a nasally teen announced that trolleys couldn't go through that aisle and I'd have to detour to register number three. I pointed out that register number three also boasted a twenty-deep queue, to which she replied I should have read the sign. I glanced about me, bewildered, finally spotting said sign, indeed advising 'no large trolleys allowed', but totally obscured by a cardboard stand spruiking festive novelties and assorted crap. Speechless, I dutifully wheeled my over-stuffed trolley and wailing children to aisle three. When a gentle dear ahead of me smiled and commented how brave I was, I actually burst into tears! Lest she feared she was trapped in the queue with a loony while trying to purchase 500 g of Desiree potatoes, I explained the situation, gaining great satisfaction and validation from the disgusted expression it evoked. My new friend took it one step further, however, telling everyone else in the queue, and, like Chinese whispers, it passed on till it somehow reached the manager! Before you could say 'price check on aisle 3' my trolley-load was being scanned through and bagged, then personally escorted to and packed into my car! Tink was mollified with a fistful of chocolate Santas, and the twins were being cooed over and generally occupied while the manager apologised emphatically. I felt terribly embarrassed. Had my tears unwittingly put an end to the nasal young lady's holiday employment? Had I over-reacted? She was probably only following the rules; was all this necessary? The manager grinned at my concern then pointed to my car boot, every available crevice stuffed to bursting with environmentally friendly shopping bags, as it is every shopping trip, several times a week.

'Miss, I seen you in here with all the kids, and we don't wanna lose customers like you.'

Ahh, now I see: it's all good business, and frankly something a lot of retailers and cafes would do well to remember: mums equal money. Playing temporary creche rakes in the cashola. Yes, children are messy, screamy, whiny and all the other dwarves, but if made to feel cared for and valued, be it at the market, the fruit shop or a local cafe, a mother will be your most loyal customer. She will tell her friends and essentially guarantee you years and years of trade. That's years and years of spending, at least 40 per cent of it on wine alone! It cannot hurt to diplomatically remind your local store-owner/cafe proprietor of this next time the aisles are so clogged with poorly placed product you can't manoeuvre your trolley through or the barista snorts derisively at your next latte-with-three-babyccinos order. Over the course of, say, twelve years, that's a lot of exorbitantly overpriced nappies and $2.50 frothed milks purchased without complaint. With a little consideration and show of respect, the booming mummy market can be a savvy retailer's Mecca.

## MONDAY 29 DECEMBER

*6:59 p.m.* The Chef has returned to Melbourne for a work engagement and has just pulled into the driveway back home. It would appear that in my befuddled, pre-Christmas, stressed-out, sleep-deprived state, I'd watered the garden on my last visit home then left the hose running . . . for days . . . thereby flooding the garden, the deck, and the basement.

I have experience in these matters. At seventeen, I flooded my first apartment, a concrete box in a dodgy suburb, by falling asleep while running a bath. Admittedly I had been knocked sideways by a shocking flu and passed out for four hours. This did not change the fact that I awoke to find things floating past my bed. The carpet had lifted, so I couldn't open the door and release the foot-high deluge, and my only option was to take what tools I had (a saucepan and a teacup) and ladle water down the sink, down the toilet, and out the window. I worked valiantly through tears and snot for some seven hours, then tugged up the sodden carpet,

SHOPPING LIST

6-man tent

Glitter glue

Fluoro pink shoelaces

A bird cage

Cheese . . . zzzzzzzzz

Huh? Sorry . . . what?

wrangled it out the door and downstairs to dry in the concreted car park. I mopped, wiped, dabbed, checked the efficacy of the electricals (impressively sound) then emptied an entire can of deodorant in an attempt to sweeten the damp floorboards. The fug of synthetic watermelon fragrance mingled with a perfume akin to wet dog lingered for months. Two days later I dragged the carpets, dry but now rigor-mortis stiff, back up and attempted to re-lay them with ordinary stationery staples. Epic failure there, but a year on I still got my bond back!

Funny how the stupidity of our youth frequently fails to teach us a bloody thing beyond how to open a beer bottle with our bare teeth and that peanut butter is delicious smeared on anything. Here I was, despite all the wisdom gleaned from some twenty intervening years, flooding stuff again. Merry . . . bloody . . . Christmas.

## GETTING ENOUGH SLEEP

When you become a mum, there is something in the old adage that 'You can kiss sleep goodbye for the next twenty years (perhaps forever).' Yes, the broken sleep of new babydom is par for the course, along with the stops and starts that come with children wetting beds, having nightmares, and just refusing to sleep in general.

For me, the frustration is that, even when my children fall into a regular pattern of sleeping through the night, I still wake up. It's as though my ears are so sensitively attuned to any sounds of wakefulness among my brood, I wake up before they do. Part of this, I'm sure, is that I've always zealously guarded the sleep of the rest of the family (read: if someone wakes it's enough to have to coerce them back to slumber without any others joining in!).

The reality is that the human brain, and these infernal contraptions we call our bodies, need satisfactory rest in order to function. Lack of sleep has a negative impact on every aspect of our lives, from decision-making processes, spatial awareness and perception to fitness, mood and appetite. On too little sleep, you can be a danger to yourself and others. After a string of rough nights, I find myself drifting through the days in an impenetrable fog, making silly little mistakes like forgetting where I put things, losing the thread in conversation or leaving the hose running. Fatigue even has its insidious way with my vocabulary, and I'll find myself grasping even for embarrassingly simple words like 'that' or 'stable', suggesting I'm anything but. This scatty focus and broken concentration suggests my judgement is impaired and thus I feel nervous about driving and making important decisions, sometimes avoiding both until I get some decent rest (which may never happen). I become stressed, which in turn makes sleep even more elusive, and thus the vicious cycle continues like a dog chasing its tail.

Getting babies to sleep through the night as quickly as possible helps immensely. With each of my babies, I employed a feeding regime that seemed to work and has had most of them sleeping through the night, most nights, from around six weeks. Now before you feel compelled to tear me a second . . . um . . . Number Two hole, let me preface this by saying we have to be realistic about what 'sleeping through the night' constitutes. I'm not talking 7 p.m.–7 a.m. No way! Anyone claiming that their young baby is sleeping twelve hours is talking Number Twos. Small babies simply cannot obtain enough calories from a single feed to sustain their metabolism for such a stretch, so we can call BS on that notion. I'm talking more in the realm of 11 p.m.–5 a.m.

My method has been to 'cluster feed' my babies from around 8 p.m. This means I keep them semi-awake – allowing for short dozes – but keep offering them a breast or bottle for a period of around two hours. Sounds onerous but use this time with them in your arms to read, watch a film, or answer emails. I like to write, read scripts, or make lists (yes, I'm a devoted 'lister' of just about anything: shopping, to-do, interesting positions to assume while watching paint dry). After two hours of playing and feeding, the baby is generally so tired and so full, they are out like a light and will sleep till 4–5 a.m. Just ensure that once you put them down, you jump straight into bed yourself, or, as in my case, shuffle until your legs hit the mattress, then just topple forward, face-first, on to the bed fully clothed.

Take advantage of any opportunity to rest. Many espouse taking naps when babies sleep during the day. This is all very well when you've just the baby to contend with, but add older children to the equation and it's simply not possible or practical. Also, if you are anything like me, I simply cannot sleep during daylight hours unless I'm on a sun lounge by a pool and the thermometer is tipping 30°C, but moving to Barbados probably isn't a practical solution at this time.

Toddlers tend to present a problem at the other end of the day. Getting them to sleep can be a challenge, and getting them to stay in bed once there can verge on impossible, particularly when you have just made the transition from cot to bed and they discover they can escape at will. Woo hoo!

I used to be of the school of thought that if they burned off as much energy as possible right before bed they would fall immediately into sweet slumber . . . WRONG! They just become overwrought, hooning through the house like whirling dervishes until the wee small hours. Now I encourage physical play in the morning and afternoon, but post-dinner and bath it is all about low-impact activities. Reading a storybook, yes, if my arms aren't already full of smaller children, or some quiet drawing/colouring-in, or a simple game. Repetitive actions like colouring or laying out and picking up cards seems to induce sleepiness and is very calming, thus conducive to good sleep.

Bedtime can present just as many challenges for older children too in this age of constant streaming media and the boundless stimulation that goes with it. Like most parents, I've been so desperate for rest (or just a break from the kids, let's be honest here) I've let my children stay up too late, watch too much television, even (shock, horror) take the iPad to bed with them, all in the misguided hope they will sleep soundly. However, the best sleep medicine is to implement a few hard and fast rules around bedtime, and a rock-solid, unwavering routine.

I've had the most success when I've made them aware of what time they must be in bed by and refuse to deviate from that under pretty much any circumstances. Apart from the odd special occasion during the holidays, Minnie must hit the sack by 8:30 p.m., Buddy by 8 p.m., Princess – try as she might to defer it – is under the covers, story read, by 7:30 p.m., Tink by 7 p.m. As much as I'd like to shoo them all off to Dreamland as a collective, the staggered approach means they all get a bit of Mummy or Daddy time, which seems to settle them more effectively. Princess and Tink share a room, which can be tricky, particularly when Princess pulls Tink from the cot so they can come and petition us as a united front, or worse, when Princess decides to climb in too for a play when Tink has already nodded off, but overall, they enjoy each other's company and sleep better when the other is present. How that dynamic will play out when the twins are booted out of my office into the girls room with Princess and Tink remains to be seen.

Set bedtimes and stick to them, and that includes for yourself. Don't complain if you do manage to have the house to yourself by 8 p.m., then watch an entire season of *Game of Thrones*,* only to hit the hay just in time to hear the cock crow.

Get sleep when and where you can: parents who sacrifice their rest for the sake of parenthood find it pretty hard to be good parents after all.

*Binge sessions of *Game of Thrones* are only marginally less important than sleep, so to enjoy the best of both worlds, offload the kids on a grandparent or friend one weekend, stockpile wine, chocolate and a take-away delivery menu, warm up the DVD player by 9 a.m., and binge away. A good twelve-hour session means you'll be in bed by 9 p.m., and will wake the next morning fresh as a daisy. The perfect crime.

# WEDNESDAY 31 DECEMBER

*9:37 p.m.* New Year's Eve. After a day of backyard cricket in the driveway and dips in the pool with only a few lost balls and mild sunburn, The Chef's brother (affectionately known as Wings because, beyond being an accomplished pilot, he is truly remarkable at everything and manages to rise above any challenge, regardless of how great) whips up a Middle Eastern lamb shoulder (champion) and I a plum pudding parfait (yep, mashed-up pudding leftovers stirred through softened chocolate ice-cream then refrozen – *Masterchef*, eat your heart out!). The kids toast marshmallows, the adults toast the new year with amaretto sours, and as the clock strikes nine I'm in bed watching a doco on air crash investigations. Happy new year!

SHOPPING LIST

World peace

An end to global hunger

Universal harmony

One of those things on the infomercials that make vegetable spaghetti

# THURSDAY 1 JANUARY

*10:15 a.m.* Happy new year!

Time to practise that time-honoured tradition of making resolutions and breaking them roughly four days later. I've done them all, from planned fitness regimes that aim to keep you Lycra-bound until Christmas, and diet plans so aggressive even using a heavy-bottomed saucepan to cook with seems counter-intuitive. I've ruthlessly feng shui-ed to the point of virtual renovation and attempted sobriety so extreme even I found myself pompous and irritating. Eau de party-pooper, anyone?

Resolutions and I don't have a great track record. However, it is a new year, and this time, my resolution looks, feels and smells quite simple: To give each of the children more one-on-one time (insert incredulous laughter here). My method is to institute a divide-and-conquer policy, whereby I offload the others through:

a. Distraction: drawing, games or *gulp* iPad/TV allowance.
b. Palming them off on someone else: we have had so many people through the house over the festive period, their board can be child-minding, thank you very much.
c. Inclusion. Let one child select the activity and invite the others to participate, on the leading child's terms, thus making them the centre of attention.

> SHOPPING LIST
>
> Resolution solution. Just dissolve 1 tsp concrete in a glass of water to immediately stiffen your upper lip, gird your loins and cement your willpower, making sure THIS year's resolutions get a fighting chance. Put a bit of concrete in it and harden up!

Despite successfully hitting the sack early last night, little Tink awoke at precisely 11:45 p.m., seeming determined to herald in the new year. I settled her, she got up again. I settled her, she got up again. The routine continued until close to 2 a.m., at which point I decided to use this as an opportunity to practise my new policy: here we had the perfect conditions for a little one-on-one time, bugger the hour. And so, in the quiet pre-dawn hours we played a little game with her dolls, I read her a few of her favourite books, and finally, I sang her to sleep in my arms. Singing a child to sleep is the stuff of fairy tales, and was something I had only done with Minnie when I still had the luxury of time and energy. But to feel the warm weight of their little body in your arms, big eyes gazing at you, watching as their lids slowly droop, lashes fluttering over cheeks as sleep overwhelms them, is one of the most precious, memorable moments a parent can experience. It is one we might indulge in with our babies, but is often swiftly put aside as they grow and other demands overtake us. But when you actually take the time, you immediately wonder why you don't more often – and the bonus is they never complain about your singing.

## DIVIDE AND CONQUER: SPENDING ONE-ON-ONE TIME WITH CHILDREN

One-on-one time with your children is a wonderful thing, but as life becomes busier, schedules tighter, and, in my case, families larger, it can be one of the first sacrifices made just to get by. I strive to give my kids a little 'Mummy time' each, but I also think it's very important that they learn early on that Mummy or Daddy time is possible even when Mummy or Daddy are doing other things and also when other siblings are in attendance.

As I mentioned earlier, one method I use to make a child feel important and the focus of my attention is to play a game where the nominated child is the leader and calls the shots without being challenged. Also, asking one child to accompany and assist me with a household chore (folding laundry, prepping dinner, whatever is age-appropriate) is an opportunity to have private chats about things that interest them while getting a few jobs done!

Another favourite is to allow one child a sleepover with a grandparent or special friend, where they'll be spoiled rotten in the process. All the children understand their turn will come and so accept the situation with good grace. Naturally, it puts a substantial dent in your babysitting allowance with Grandma should you actually want a proper night out yourself, but sometimes we need to make sacrifices for a higher purpose. That, and it is the greatest instrument of bribery you will ever exercise over your progeny.

One final suggestion we always have fun with: select a bunch of assorted veg, slice up two proteins (e.g. beef and chicken), and assemble some basic stir-fry sauces (oyster, soy, teriyaki).

Now set the kids up at the table or bench with a kid-safe knife and chopping board and let them select and chop their own veg. I tell mine they have to choose a minimum of three. This keeps them joyously occupied for at least fifteen minutes. Now let them choose a protein and a sauce, and have them 'assist' you to quickly stir-fry their individual meal. Having had the freedom of choice (ha ha, the fools!) you will be amazed at how quickly they scoff their handiwork. They have been fed something nutritious, clean-up is minimal, and most importantly, they feel both clever and special: an esteem-boosting combo for any child. Follow this up with a make-your-own-sundae session and you will be the best parent in the world (and who knew sliced fruit dressed up with a scoop of ice-cream could taste so deceptively good?). Even better if you get in early and just blend banana with assorted fruits and freeze to create 100 per cent fruit ice-cream. Whoa! Where's that Parent of the Year award? Pin it here!

## SATURDAY 3 JANUARY

*6:54 a.m.* My very favourite time of the day. Most of the house is still silent in slumber. Soft fingers of dawn light thread slowly through the dark sky, caressing the horizon with a tender touch. It's just the twins and me. Lolly Pop has now decided she will only take the breast when she feels like it so there's a complicated dance of setting them both up, only to have Lolly Pop frequently snub my offering while Jelly Bean just lies back, watching proceedings with a mouthful of boob. I set myself up in bed with the girls, an assortment of pillows for support, a coffee, a peanut butter-flavoured protein ball (mmm, just like peanut butter but virtually indigestible and with a hint of cardboard) and my iPad, and write until the muse departs, the twins fuss, or I remember an item I haven't added to my online shopping list. Now it's time to make the switch to the online supermarket for some real fun. I have not got a gambling bone in my body, and extreme sports and thrill-seeking tend to involve sweat and difficult-to-remove stains (no thanks; I've been changing nappies for nine years without a pause – that's about as much muck, sweat and tears as I can handle), but as I've mentioned, I love a good list, and while I source all our meats, veg and bakery requirements from farmers' markets, there is something verging on erotic about compiling a list for a fortnight's worth of all those other household necessities (ahem . . . Tim Tams), then trawling virtual supermarket aisles, nabbing said grocery items at bargain prices. It feels like a substantial achievement,

SHOPPING LIST

*Don't feel the need to make a list, just gonna perv at what is on special online.*

and all from the comfort of my bed, nightgown-clad, at quarter to seven in the morning.

Online shopping presents the ultimate chance to multi-task. Do it while you are cooking, folding laundry, nursing, or any number of mundane domestic chores that bore the pants off you but, sadly, must be done. Then there is the delight of that shopping list, having been sent out into the electronic ether, being delivered to your door at a time nominated by you. You might still be in that nightgown, but who cares, because the fridge is stocked, the pantry heaves with goodies, there are nappies in abundance (if only someone retailed an extra set of self-cleaning hands designed specifically for nappy changing while you read the paper and scoff Tim Tams. While we are on it, how about retailing an extra set of lactating breasts someone else can strap on while you catch a few extra Zs? They would sell out in seconds and the server would go into meltdown almost immediately!). Job done; now you can move on to more important things like eating cheese straight from the packet, water divining, or a session of heavy-duty stain removal.

No, there's no accumulated grime in my laundry basket from abseiling down a cliff face or flinging myself from a plane at 30 000 feet, but there are the results of some epic nappy failures which, for most people, are infinitely more terrifying.

## SIMPLIFY, SIMPLIFY, SIMPLIFY

Surviving parenthood with your sanity intact week in week out really depends on your ability to make things a little easier, a little simpler, thereby creating room in your schedule for the things that make you happy, the things that keep you sane.

One perfect example is the supermarket shop. An arduous task at best but one that must be done.

With a gaggle of children in tow, this chore tends to go one of two ways: you take the whole tribe and spend an hour saying 'No, you can't have . . . (insert noxious junk food or crappy plastic trinket here)', returning rubbish they have secreted into the trolley back to the shelf, enduring judgemental stares from passers-by as a toddler chucks a massive wobbly in Aisle 6, trying to distract their attention from the range of chocolate and lollies strategically placed at child's-eye level at the checkout, and finally wrangling them into the car only to realise one of them has shoplifted a round of brie (true story; can't fault my children's palates) or you have forgotten to buy half of what you needed thanks to the distracting powers of your rug rats. Either way, you need to load 'em up and head back in for sixty more minutes of hell. The other option is you dart in by yourself and end up rushing around the aisles in an adrenalised state, equivalent to an aerobics class (hopefully minus head-to-toe Lycra, but that depends on the suburb you live in), again to discover that in your haste all you have managed to grab is milk, bread, dry pasta, a packet of Tim Tams and possibly a round of Brie, and now the babies will have to go to bed tonight with their nether regions wrapped in cling wrap because you forgot nappies, and as much as you would love to go back in, the neighbour who kindly offered to mind the kids while you slipped out is probably now bald from hair-pulling, your fifteen-minute car park has expired, and you are crying with frustration, so should you return to the aisles you would probably grab the wrong thing in your current state of blindness (like those novelty-flavoured Tim Tams, eww!), so what's the point?

Solution? Get online. Set up an account and save your time, your sanity and your neighbour's hairline. I recommend taking it one step further and set up pen and paper stations all around the house at those hotspots where you run out of things and are likely to forget to list them: kitchen, lounge, dining area, bedrooms, bathrooms, and at any nappy-changing stations. This way your final list, when all the other anally compiled ones are tallied up, is comprehensive and no additional quick trips to the shops will be required. Online supermarket services also feature a list function so you can note down items throughout the week before placing a final order.

Now . . . if only you could find an autobot on eBay that would neatly label and put away all those groceries while you kick back with a cold glass of vino. I'm trying to train those miscreant children in the fine art of butlering but sadly it hasn't stuck; once the delivery arrives they are always too busy chucking wobblies over my failure to purchase Coco Pops, or having withdrawals from the lack of stolen Brie. The system still ain't perfect.

# CHAPTER

# SUNDAY 4 JANUARY

*6:15 a.m.* AAAAARRRGH! Just rolled gingerly on to my side and AAAaaRrgh! Red-hot searing pain, a smouldering ember scorching through my chest wall and down my right arm. Nooooooo! The inevitable has happened. Lolly Pop's breast fussiness has had dire consequences. Little Jelly Bean just can't keep up with emptying both barrels and now it would seem I have MASTITIS.

For the uninitiated, mastitis is not the name of a band, a cocktail or a type of tennis elbow incurred from too much masturbation. Mastitis is when a breastfeeding mother develops an infection in her milk ducts and the world falls apart.

Mastitis is cracked nipples so dry they put the Sahara to shame.

Mastitis is expressing molten lava through some of the most delicate epidermis on the human body (quick shout out to all those people passing kidney stones out there!).

Mastitis is a Brazilian wax multiplied by infinity.

Right now, if one of my children were to ask that old existential chestnut 'Where is Hell?' I'd say: 'It's in my chest!'

That is mastitis.

> SHOPPING LIST
>
> Ice
>
> Heat pack
>
> Cabbage leaves
>
> Does Woolworths stock pethidine?

Breasts are, in many ways, a cross women are born to bear. We hit puberty and are crucified on the cross – the 'cross your heart' bra that will be our constant companion for many years to come. We are sacrificed on the altar that is the lingerie department checkout. Breasts are, in a sense, the cups of life; they give life and they can take life away, as writ large by the devastation of breast cancer. Breasts can stock milk, but that doesn't make us milk bars, and as much as we appreciate our partner's efforts, they are not udders and do not need to be wrenched likewise!

Funny, isn't it? Breasts are so fascinating, except when they are performing the function for which they are designed. Bazza down the end of the bar can scream 'Show us yer tits!', but when you do, on the tram, to quell a screaming infant, there is an uproar! There is a time and place, of course, and men may well argue that they don't make a habit of down-trousering to flash their tackle in public (well at least not all of them) and that argument might just have a leg to stand on if so many of them didn't behave like they have said genitals sprouting from the top of their heads. But I shouldn't generalise; that is a condition to which both sexes are sadly susceptible.

Sorry to get so snitchy but my boobs . . . really . . . HURT!

Why do men have breasts, anyway? Is it to taunt us? Having gone through nine months of figure-destroying pregnancy, we are expected to breastfeed and embrace all the joys that go with it . . . such as MASTITIS! Sure, men have the equipment, but they'll be buggered if they will use it to feed their progeny. The ultimate slap in the face is that some men have bigger breasts than their female counterparts!

Like the Bermuda Triangle, the construction of the pyramids, and how the heck they get those model ships inside those tiny bottles, those mounds of feminine flesh have bewitched mankind from the beginning of time. But right now, I'm crying into my breast pump, desperately trying to clear house, the promise of a fever moistening my brow, wilting cabbage leaves stuffing my maternity bra. What is the deal with breasts? Whoever invented them had a very sick sense of humour.


*5:10 p.m.* The Chef has had to return to Melbourne for work tomorrow. Of the two local doctors, one is booked out, the other is on holiday. This fever ain't abating and I'm going through cabbage leaves at a rate of knots. At this rate, we will be making sauerkraut with the leftovers for the next week.

I'm biting the kids' heads off over the smallest infractions. Little Tink, confused by Mum's unwarranted grumpiness, flings herself at me for a comforting cuddle but when a small arm grazes one throbbing mammary I go through the roof. Tears, tantrums and general hysteria follows . . . and Tink gets a bit upset too.

I serve up dinner. The kids know something isn't right, and you could cut the tension in the air with a blunt Play-doh tool. When the phone jingles we all jump. Assuming, at this hour, that it is The Chef, having forgotten something, I snap into the phone, 'What?'

'Oh!' a startled little voice answers. 'Ms West, just wanted to let you know the doctor will stay back to see you tonight. Can you be here in thirty minutes?' Hallelujah! A glorious ray of sunshine parts the grey clouds of my misery.

'I will be there with bells on! And so sorry for biting your head off there – thought you were my husband. See you soon!'

I turn to the dinner table, already strewn with bits of rice, meat and vegetable matter, along with a suspicious-looking puddle where Princess has clearly spilt a portion of her juice.

'Right, kids, eat up – now!'

With visions of the almost palpable relief promised by those antibiotics dancing tantalisingly before me, I rush the kids through dinner, alternating between cajoling and screeching. Empty dishes collected, I push little arms into coat sleeves and sock-less feet into runners, and begin ushering the team towards the garage for the great buckle-up. Buddy sidles up behind me as I perform the juggling act that is snapping the twins into their rear-facing baby seats.

'Mu-um,' he whines, twisting the bottom of his jacket between his fingers, 'when's dessert?'

'Not right now, Buddy, gotta move.'

Something snaps behind those big brown eyes and their inconceivably long lashes.

'WHAT?' he roars, and is gone. Back into the hall, out the front entry and down the hill.

Not now! I don't have time for a juvenile wobbly, not when I'm on the verge of throwing one myself. For a millisecond, I contemplate driving off, then think better of it . . . just.

Leaving the rest of the team strapped in, listening to the warbling of a highly strung, over-pampered, spoilt boy band, I go in search of my own, and find him halfway down the hill, muttering to himself. I pause long enough to hear he is *practising* the argument he is going to present to me.

'All you do is yell at me . . . then you say you are sorry? How can you say you are sorry when you always yell at me? You don't love me . . . you never hug me. You don't love me . . . I don't even do anything wrong and you still yell at me!'

The pain in my chest suddenly wasn't a shade on the pain in my heart.

I gently coaxed him back up to the house and we perched together, side by side, on the stairs. It was time to admit I was in the wrong.

'I'm really, really, truly sorry, Buddy.'

I watched his face change as those beautiful eyes registered first shock, then disbelief.

'I've been very yelly lately and it's not right. You kids have not done anything wrong, you are all just being kids and I should not have been so angry. I'm sorry.'

I could have gone on, expanded on how the pain in my chest fouled my mood, justified my snappiness by pointing out how loud and rambunctious they were being, qualified my reactions in relation to his reaction when told dessert was a no-go. But I didn't, I simply had to acknowledge my little fella was hurting, and own responsibility for my part in that.

Buddy appraised me solemnly.

'It's okay, Mum. I'm sorry too.'

For the second time this evening the heavens opened, raining glorious light upon us both. Breakthrough!

Time was ticking by but we shared a long cuddle. It was so lovely to press his warm little body, now developing the knobbly angularity of boyhood, the plump curves of his toddler days gone too soon, against mine, avoiding the red-hot rage of my right boob.

I explained to him how special he was, and as my only boy, he was extra special to me.

'But what if you have more?' he asked with genuine concern. I had to suppress a guffaw.

'No way, Buddy! Six is enough!'

'But some families have eight kids . . .'

'And those families probably have to live in the zoo.'

'Are you sure you won't have more?'

'Absolutely.'

'So the doctor said you can't have more?'

Given that is precisely what the doctor said last time I was written a script for uber-strong contraceptives, only for them to deliver me a double whammy, such an assurance isn't terribly reassuring, but if Buddy had faith so be it.

'That's right, sweetheart.'

War over, we returned to the car hand in hand. The twins were screaming, Tink was belting Princess over the head with her My Little Pony, and Minnie glared at us in recrimination for taking so long, but I couldn't wipe the smile off my face.

Kids – can't live with them, can try to live without them but leaving them on a stranger's doorstep is illegal in all states and territories.

## TREAT 'EM MEAN, KEEP 'EM KEEN

The perfect parent—child relationship, to my mind, is one where the child knows and is secure in that knowledge that you are their greatest champion, love them unconditionally, and will go to the ends of the earth for them, BUT they are also keenly aware of who wears the pants – and we are not talking the pull-up variety.

This ideal scenario does not come about through your screaming at them like a wounded banshee, nor from threats or aggression, no way! My children are so accustomed to my fishwife-like screeching they barely raise an eyebrow. However, a modulated, quiet, steady voice, and a request made at their eye level in terms they understand, e.g. 'Continue with this behaviour and you will never see your iPad again,' really deliver.

I know many parents will quake at my suggesting you occasionally have your child walking on eggshells, but let's face it, it isn't really *fear*, it's respect – for you, your role as their leader and guide, and for what is appropriate behaviour within society and the family unit. Helicoptering, cotton-wooling, reasoning and cajoling ain't gonna work because young minds are not built for logic. They are primitive, serving the wants and needs of the ego. By appealing to their instinctive fight-or-flight response, they learn, like all wild animals. But don't think they'll feel in any way less loved, or that they'll love you any less.

Lead by example and your children will have something to emulate; they'll have boundaries for behaviour which make them feel secure. It is very much a case of 'do as I say AND as I do'. The result is kids who are well adjusted, who will challenge you but know when they have crossed the line. Save your tonsils and keep them on their toes; in time they will thank you for it.

# TUESDAY 6 JANUARY

*8.50 a.m.* The children are enjoying their usual holiday sleep-in. With the twins back in their cot and several coffees ingested, I'm enjoying cutting fruit salad with intent to tackle that most pleasurable of tasks: cleaning out the dishwasher filter. Who would have thought a dose of strong painkillers and the combination of hot towels and a breast pump could prove so motivating?

Suddenly, the still morning is torn asunder by a series of yelping screeches from Buddy.

As any parent will tell you, kids are noisy buggers, but there is a distinct difference between the usual screams and roars of rowdy rug rats, and the cry of a child in pain. Hearing the latter variety pierce the air, I scuttle to the bedroom Minnie and Buddy share, to be met by a similarly alerted Chef and my little man, twisted and contorted, his head leaning heavily on one shoulder, the opposite arm curled awkwardly against his side.

'He can't move his head,' Minnie intones, and sure enough, the slightest attempt to move sets him off, yelps and whines ricocheting off the walls. My blood immediately drains from every extremity, seemingly replaced by icy water, coursing through my system. Is it? Could it be? I can barely even think the word, so terrifying is the thought. Meningitis?

Okay, I pull on my Calm Mummy boots and assemble a mental checklist: Temperature? No. Sore throat? No. Headache? Yes . . . damn. Stiffness at back of neck? No, just to one side. Rash? No. Right. I tenderly sit Buddy up and begin the process of gently massaging his neck and shoulder. His yelps subside somewhat, and with gentle manipulation, he is able to lift both arms above his head. Good sign. He is still decidedly lopsided but manages to down a little kids' Nurofen, and follow me gingerly to the kitchen for breakfast. The act of spooning Weetbix from bowl to mouth is all too daunting, provoking fresh tears, but, amazingly, a choc chip muesli bar is snapped up and manipulated with ease when offered. I'm suspecting a crick neck, as my dear old Nan would have diagnosed it, but I keep a hawk's eye on him regardless.

'Mum . . .' Minnie approaches me as I clear away breakfast, her voice wavering with a hint of concern. Hmmm, I smell a confession coming.

'Um . . . last night . . . um . . . me and Buddy sneaked out our iPads and . . . um . . . watched them in bed. Um . . . he was still watching his when I fell asleep and he was kinda lying funny. Maybe that hurt his neck?'

Of course: awkwardly-positioned-iPad-induced crick neck, the little bugger. I kiss Minnie appreciatively atop her head.

'Thank you for telling the truth, sweetheart. Now you are banned from the iPad for the day, Buddy for two days. Run along.'

Phew.

## SERIOUS ILLNESS IN CHILDREN

Realistically, the chances of your child contracting a serious illness are minimal. However, should the unthinkable happen, the consequences can be devastating. Catastrophising and predicting the worst-case scenario is a common ailment among parents, but if a little embarrassment is what you must suffer nine times out of ten to ensure that tenth diagnosis of something serious is caught in time, then it is well worth it. I speak from personal experience here, as we had a serious health scare with Minnie when she was three. As you are still following on the journey, I am confident you will forgive yet another detour. Besides, you are a diary, and by your very nature you are obliged to bear witness to any number of rambling dissertations and heartfelt yearnings.

So here goes . . .

August 2008: Work has again dragged The Chef overseas, this time to Europe, but the payoff is a family holiday at the tail end of the trip in glorious Tuscany.

I was to fly into Rome. Sounds glamorous but I was packing a tiny Minnie and a four-month-old Buddy so chances were I would be landing at Rome International looking like a pannier-laden packhorse, up to my neck in disposable nappies, wipes and inappropriately large baby movers. Whatever; it was more than worth it for a few weeks of sunshine, vino and some serious carbs.

Perched in the Qantas lounge at Tullamarine, the hour fast approaching midnight, I slipped Minnie a small dose of Phenergan. For the uninitiated, Phenergan is a children's antihistamine, with the delicious side-effect of inducing sleepiness. Yep, I was drugging my child in the hope of enjoying my Emirates business-class meal and a new-release film, molested only by the needs of a breastfeeding infant. This being my first attempt to cross oceans with a toddler and baby on board, I did not know, and no seasoned parent had warned me as I now warn you, dear diary, that it is best to give Phenergan a trial run prior to actual travel, lest it have the reverse effect on your child. That's right: rather than sending your beloved child peacefully off to La La land, Phenergan can magically transform them into a psychotic whirling dervish, careening into surrounding objects like a Pumpkin-Patch-clad pinball set on wrecking havoc with every rebound.

Can you guess which of the two paths Phenergan led my little angel? Yep, turned her into a demon and sent my hopes of a peaceful leg between Melbourne and Dubai to hell in a handbasket. She collapsed into a restless sleep only as we touched down, presenting me with the joy of lugging two small children, one unable to walk, one refusing to, through the terminal. Finally ensconced in the lounge, Minnie refused any food bar a miniature tub of chocolate ice-cream, which eventually melted in its container, untouched. She complained of a sore throat and that her head 'had a toothache', and she was very warm to the touch. The temperature rise might have been due to her onboard exertions, I hedged, but still, I was packing children's Panadol and I wasn't afraid to use it.

Back on board, Minnie curled into my side and was soon fast asleep. An hour into our journey, absorbed in *The Notebook* (my little air-travel indulgence) I noticed Minnie felt increasingly like a hot little ember burrowing in beside me, and sitting her upright, I found her fevered and clammy to the touch. Now roused, she broke into hiccupy sobs, whimpering that her throat hurt. I turned the overhead light on and she recoiled, shielding her eyes from the glare, then yelped again, crying she had a sore neck. Sure enough, she was holding it stiffly, and when I asked her to look up at the ceiling, she could not; she just burst into a fresh shower of tears. Crap . . .

Mind shifting into overdrive, I immediately recalled the symptom checklists for the numerous communicable and non-communicable diseases I'd been taught at immunisation sessions I had attended with the kids. The terrifying shadow of meningococcal disease loomed large and, petrified, I buzzed the attendant.

The natty young man's 'Some roasted nuts, Madam? Perhaps an aperitif before dinner?' smile fled, and he visibly blanched when he spotted Minnie huddled on my lap. I explained I feared she was seriously ill, and without missing a beat he contacted Medivac, the 'hospital of the skies'. Once I had listed Minnie's symptoms, the medic at the end of the line confirmed my fears in theory, and recommended the flight head for Rome International ASAP. I called The Chef on the inflight phone. No answer. Meanwhile, my dapper attendant had moved our little trio to the pointy end of the plane and our own petite suite, before putting out a call for any doctors on board to please come forward, like something from a B-grade straight-to-DVD film.

Three passengers hit their buzzers in response and miraculously, one was a paediatrician from New Zealand. I called The Chef again, and again it went straight through to the keeper. What the heck was he doing?

Tense, exhausted and terrified, Minnie lay stretched out atop my prone form (bless the seats that unfold into beds in first class!) as this lovely woman tenderly examined her. After I'd managed to quickly feed a neglected Buddy in the moments between, the sweet attendant solicitously held him, giving him a gentle jiggle, which ultimately proved unwise as Buddy presented him with the contents of his snack, all down one lapel of his beautiful silk Emirates suit.

'Not to worry!' he assured me as he shifted Buddy to the other hip, where my darling child swiftly unloaded the rest down the second lapel, and a small portion down our Florence Nightingale's back. The guy goes above and beyond to help us out and this is how Buddy rewards him, clearly jealous of all the attention Minnie was receiving. To his credit, the young man merely grinned tightly in response to my agitated flapping, and disappeared momentarily, Buddy in tow, only to return with Buddy cleaned up and said jacket disposed of.

Having thoroughly examined Minnie, the paediatrician delivered some good news. While she had a raging temperature and tenderness in the neck area, this could be simply due to a sore throat, and the fact her body remained flaccid rather than rigid was a good sign, as was the absence of any significant rash. However, she recommended a full battery of tests once we were in Rome, just to be certain. I hazarded a small, relieved, outward breath and practically inhaled the glass of bubbly pressed upon me. Both my babies had nodded off in my arms and I held them fiercely to me for the remainder of the flight, fending off any threat to their little beings, be it physical, viral or bacterial, just by sheer force of motherly willpower. I dialled The Chef again. Nothing. Bloody hell!

Rome International airport suddenly stretched out below us. Our welcoming runway was distinguished by the presence of an ambulance, from which emerged a clutch of blue-clad figures in Hazmat suits as we touched down. Notified of our plight, air traffic control had given our flight airspace priority, meaning the four hours to Rome had been shaved down to less than three, and we were now being greeted by this brace of blue medics fitted out for biological warfare, face masks and all. Confronted by these alien-like creatures, Minnie went into meltdown, climbing up and huddling into my lap as they attempted to stretcher her out. Eventually it was me prone upon the stretcher, my children smothering me like icing on a cake. As we were swung aboard the ambulance, The Chef finally called. He'd been rightfully enjoying a long Tuscan lunch, and as my calls from the plane had been unlisted he'd assumed they were telemarketers and so ignored them. The joy in his voice at knowing we were finally in Rome disappeared faster than an open pack of Tim Tams when I filled him in and announced we were all, at that moment, aboard an ambulance. His voice a little shaky with poorly concealed concern, he announced he was getting in the car that moment. My initial irritation quelled by our mutual fear, I instructed him to hold tight until we at least had a diagnosis. He acquiesced reluctantly and begged to speak to Minnie, who was by now too exhausted to do more than mumble.

I would later learn that our fellow passengers had to wait aboard the plane, idling on the tarmac, until Minnie had been diagnosed, lest they all proved to be carrying some infectious horror and unwittingly passed it on to numerous innocent Italians. Whoops. Sorry folks!

The journey to Rome base hospital was memorable only for its speed and the reckless swerving along the autostrada. The blue aliens did their best to minister to Minnie, but their appearance and the comforting words uttered in a foreign tongue only sent her into a tizz so they all backed off, merely smiling at me reassuringly from time to time. Her energetic response must have reassured them also as they all deigned to remove their headwear, which mollified Minnie somewhat, and certainly alleviated some of my panic as it surely signalled she wasn't toxic.

Deposited at the entry to the Emergency Department, all three of us were heaped into a wheelchair and ferried to a consulting room which looked, frankly, more suburban accountant's office than sophisticated treatment area. Regardless, we were soon joined by an English-speaking doctor, who could have examined Minnie up a bloody tree for all I cared, so great was my gratitude at finally having her before a doctor in a hospital. Clearly I've watched too much *ER*, as I was quietly anticipating a George Clooney-type figure in a beautifully cut suit, perhaps straddling a Vespa, to be attending us. Our doctor was a squat, hirsute little man boasting a substantial monobrow. However, he had the joyous, mischievous brown eyes of a naughty little boy, the kind of smile so filled with compassion it would move you to tears, and most importantly, he understood what I was saying.

A swift, efficient examination followed, along with a battery of tests, before he disappeared down one of the rabbit holes comprising the consulting suites of the hospital.

When our merry little physician bustled in again shortly after, I was mid-breastfeed, yet he didn't even blink. I liked the guy.

'Tonsillitis!' he announced with such relish that, combined with his glorious accent, made the condition sound like some irresistible dessert. I crumpled, then shot up to give him a spontaneous hug, relief surging through my system with such force I nearly swooned. Again, that naked boob entered the equation, jiggling about like a cherry-topped vanilla blancmange, but our saviour didn't flinch. He explained that he would administer a mild antibiotic and wanted us to stick around for an hour or two so Minnie could be observed in case of a reaction, but then we were free to go.

The wait flew by; I was so buoyed up by relief and spent adrenaline I barely noticed. Two meal trays arrived. Amazingly, it would seem bad hospital food is a universal constant, even in countries renowned for their gastronomy. A cut salami and cheese sandwich, tub of wilted salad, juice box and mini dessert bowl filled with a congealed yellow substance of dubious provenance. Some things never change, and this little piece of home was so reassuring I almost ate it; it was just the promise of a mammoth bowl of pasta and jug of chianti once we were reunited with The Chef that stilled my fork.

The combination of painkillers and antibiotics boosted Minnie immeasurably, and she was soon sitting up, fiddling with her tray of food.

Enormous credit to Emirates. Having sped up our flight, organised our hospital detour and smiled on as my baby vomited upon them, when we emerged blinking from Emergency into the golden blaze of a Roman summer day, we found our pre-booked driver had come to collect us from the hospital with all our luggage safely stowed inside the car! Emirates had collected our cases, cleared Customs and packed them before collecting us. Tuscan carbs, here we come!

## WEDNESDAY 7 JANUARY

*11 a.m.* Just read a bit of marketing gossip online, suggesting Cadbury was releasing a chocolate block with Vegemite! What crazy, umami-seeking food scientist thought to put that combination together? What drugs was she or he on? Where can I get some?

> SHOPPING LIST
>
> *Vegemite chocolate!!!!*

## THURSDAY 8 JANUARY

*11 a.m.* Inspired by that Vegemite chocolate rumour, I toasted shredded coconut, mixed it with melted 80 per cent couverture chocolate, spread it out on waxed paper, sprinkled it with salt and allowed it to set. Whoa! The BEST coconut rough ever! Ashamed to admit, over the course of the next three hours, I consumed the lot, lurking in the pantry trying to look busy.

Need more supplies . . .

> SHOPPING LIST
>
> *Shredded coconut*
>
> *Dark chocolate*
>
> *River salt flakes*

## FRIDAY 9 JANUARY

*8.20 p.m.* Three days in and the antibiotics have wrestled this mastitis to the ground and given it a stern talking-to. I've had both Jelly Bean and Lolly Pop working overtime to clear the ducts (sounds like I'm having my heating system serviced – charming!) and the fever has retreated. The only downside is my system feels toxic.

The joys of a groaning Christmas table, a very full-on new year, summer barbecues and my penchant for hoovering leftovers from the kids' plates (sometimes before they have even finished), coupled with a decent whack of flora-decimating penicillin, has left me with a sensation of sludge coursing through my veins (well, my digestive tract at the very least). I've been slamming down so much probiotic yoghurt I've practically curdled myself, though all that culture has left me with an urge to don a cravat and smoking jacket and tune in to the opera channel. Still, I suspect clearing out my system will require more than mere good bacteria, I'm thinking of hiring in a team of men in Hazmat suits and a disposal unit suited to handling radioactive waste.

SHOPPING LIST

Probiotics

Prunes

Panadol (does common paracetamol work for chocolate hangovers? Uuuurggh . . .)

I have to do something; like a leaky engine, I'm not operating at my optimum level, and frankly, our kids need us to be at our best 24/7. I owe it to them to be fit and healthy – a paragon of good nutrition, smiling through the deprivation; glowing despite a growling gut.

So what to do? There is really only one logical solution when your lifestyle requires a well-thought-out and balanced health and exercise overhaul: go on a wacky fad diet, of course!

It's always easy to pick the poor sucker 'on a diet' – just don't go too close if you've ingested fast food in the past forty-eight hours in case they smell you coming and try to gnaw your face off.

I've tried a few different diets in my time. The Zone, Atkins, Pritikin . . . one involved licking the photos in cookery books. I was really seeing results until I developed a taste for paper. The local library suspended my membership – they had a 'no taste testing' policy, apparently. The poor newsagent reached the point of having to lock up shop, and his supply of *Gourmet Traveller*, whenever he saw me coming.

Another stand out was the 'Orange Diet', which involved eating only foods that are orange in colour. That was the only rule. Not terribly helpful when that means your 'allowed meals' could therefore embrace a breakfast of Cheezels covered in orange juice. I know these things are about modifying your diet but, really, some guidelines would have been helpful. It's all too easy to feel completely justified in simply adding Fanta to your meal deal, knowing that by the time it's ingested the whole meal with be orange anyway.

There is such a range of diets to choose from too, and each week women's magazines add a few more to further the confusion. A personal favourite you will frequently see advertised is the 'No-diet Diet'. You would have to worry if you found yourself on that one. The No-diet Diet? It's a bit like buying some 'No-clothing clothing'.

'Look, I'm wearing "No-clothing clothes".'

No wonder we are confused.

This obsession with diet is too frequently categorised as an XX chromosome thing, though if men were bombarded with half the media pressure to conform to bodily perfection that women cop, then it would become obvious this particular peccadillo has a lot more to do with culture than biology!

Still, few are the men who will admit to being on a diet. No! They just decide to get fit! Just as men are never overweight – they just need to get fitter! 'Me? Fat? Nah, this is just potential muscle!'

The Chef epitomises this mentality. He works out every day, watches what he eats, and allows himself the odd indulgence without fretting about the consequences.

I, on the other hand, have a piece of chocolate, then, because it is 70 per cent dark couverture, feel justified in having twelve more. My solution is then to run back and forth to the laundry with single items of dirty clothing, making one trip into many, and to charge up and down the stairs, putting away one item at a time. Heaven forbid I should go to a gym. I might get tinia!

I'm willing to concede that the fellas do seem to have a better grip on the whole dieting paradigm.

Guys seem to be able to take the approach: 'If I want to lose weight, I need to cut back on a few things and exercise more.' Then the blighters go and do just that without losing their minds! Whereas my rationale, and that of many of my friends, runs more along the lines of:

'I've eaten nothing all day, so surely it's acceptable if I now down three glasses of wine and a bag of Caramello koalas, right?'

Or we resolve to eat nothing but lettuce and green tea for a month, then by Day Two would hijack a busy convenience store for a quick hit of instant noodles.

The Female 'Diet' tends to have a recurring pattern, which runs something like this:

Breakfast: 'I'm gonna be so good today. Just fruit and low-fat yoghurt.'

Lunch: 'Nah, thanks. I'm not up for the dim sum banquet. Back at the office I've got tuna and some wheat crackers *whimper*.'

Late afternoon: 'Yes, thanks, I will have fries with that!'

Considering that the true definition of 'diet' is: 'the foodstuffs we consume regularly to support the healthy functioning of our body', we are all on a diet, essentially, every day of our lives, regardless of what we consume. The exception would be those skeletal celebrities who, in interview after interview, gloat that they never diet. As sceptical as we might be, they are actually telling the truth. They never diet – because they never EAT. ANYTHING. EVER!!!

Oxygen and cigarettes do not a diet make.

And there is no way I will be reverting to the extremes I practised in my youth when wanting to 'tone up' or shift a few kilos. Besides, pouring myself into skinny jeans is no longer my end goal. I'm more concerned with keeping my organs (rearranged so comprehensively by so many pregnancies) all in the right place, boosting my stamina, nurturing my bowel health (sorry if you are snacking as you read), and hopefully halting, or at least slowing the rapid slippage of my bottom down the back of my thighs.

Also, the journey of every morsel I consume from the plate into my mouth now has an audience of six impressionable little monkeys, keen to find any excuse to inhale junk themselves.

So, as their gourmet guiding light, and in desperate need of a health and fitness overhaul, I owe it to myself and my family to adopt some sensible, long-term practices when it comes to diet . . .

Just need to pop to the chemist first. I saw they have this amazing powdered drink that turns to jelly in your stomach so you feel full, vitamins that suppress appetite, and these incredible tablets that literally absorb fat and flush it straight out so you can eat anything! Amazing!

## SATURDAY 10 JANUARY

*10:15 a.m.* A new day and, despite the presence of much Yuletide pâté in the pantry and foie gras in the fridge, my healthy eating resolution is holding firm. Though it would be unfair to say we do not eat healthily, per se. One definite benefit of being entangled with a Very Good Chef has been the education I have received on the benefits of eating seasonally, organically and close to the source. Likewise, I'm sure The Chef has benefited from my insights on how to achieve best results with a straightening iron and sip coffee without smearing your lipstick. Sadly, he has never taken on my brow-plucking tips. My beloved boasts some seriously splendid eyebrows; hence, manicuring them is the one tip from me he could genuinely make use of. (He once received a terribly tongue-in-cheek letter at the restaurant, threatening to report him to the RSPCA on charges of cruelty to animals – for gluing these enormous furry caterpillars to his forehead!)

When it comes to the family diet, however, we try to be uber-conscientious about what we put into our mouths and the mouths of our children. I'm no purist

SHOPPING LIST

*A medal. I'm such a martyr, a paragon of discipline and virtue! (Just don't point a Twistie in my direction, please.)*

('O Tim Tam, Tim Tam, wherefore art thou Tim Tam?') but I only shop organic when it comes to comestibles, and am lucky enough to be able to order our meat and vegetables through the restaurant, which has access to the very best producers on the market.

My problem is, I will buy the 70 per cent couverture chocolate with goji berries and chia, or the spelt loaf with whole grains, and while still patting myself on the back for making such wise purchases, eat the lot. Too much of a good thing is still too much.

So with a steely will and having consumed much black coffee and porridge to quell the demon appetite, I have dragged the troops out to a fantastic nursery and organics store on the coast to stock up on the good stuff.

In an attempt to get them enthusiastic about produce, we tour the nursery, admiring the tomatoes, smelling the herbs and learning their names, before a little treat of morning tea at the marvellous certified organic cafe. There is a near-miss when Princess attempts to push Tink in the pond in search of tadpoles, and a minor meltdown over who got the 'fattest' gingerbread man from Buddy, but we finally make it to the store section, all six still intact. I'm just about to select some heavily perfumed stone fruit when I hear it. Whoosh-SPLAT, splat, splat, SPLAT! That's Jelly Bean . . . and then put put put SPLAT! Putputputput . . . SPLAT! This time from Lolly Pop. Suddenly my downsized handbag resolution comes back to haunt me. I've just one nappy between two besmirched little bottoms. I'd taken the cumbersome nappy bag out of the car earlier to make room for the groceries (when you are seating six, something's gotta give) and now here we are, in the middle of this gorgeous store, but one sadly bereft of nappies in this, our hour of need. Suffice to say my dash around the aisles grabbing random organics probably set a new land speed record, and the twenty-minute drive home with two baby bums clad in abundant paper towelling sealed in by plastic bags with two holes for legs (the lovely shop assistant had a few sneaky ones behind the counter for emergencies, and this certainly qualified) was only soothed by the inhalation of two organic, biodynamic dark chocolate bars, and the bags of lentil chips I bribed the kids with. One resolution hadn't served me so well today, the others can wait till tomorrow.

## TUESDAY 13 JANUARY

*3:36 a.m.* Have you ever lost time? Literally let a deluge of small details, like following stepping stones set in endless circles, overwhelm the clock until you find yourself looking back, wondering, what happened?

That has been the past forty-eight hours.

Setting out on what was to be a lightning trip home so The Chef can complete a day of filming *Masterchef* before thirty-six hours in London cooking for Australia Day, the day closes on a mildly vomitty Jelly Bean, adding more than her fair share of soiled clothes to the washing basket. Twelve hours later, she has not kept down a single feed, projectiling neatly past her own couture and all over me. Cheers . . .

Naturally, it is not until 8:30 p.m., when all the doctors' offices are closed, that I notice her neck seems a little stiff and tender. Is this Groundhog Day? Am I stuck on an endless loop I cannot escape? With a calmness bred of familiarity, I clear up the dinner refuse, put Tink to bed, kiss the eldest three (most of whom are naked, savouring the warm night with a bit of hose horse-play in the back yard with Dad) and drive the twins directly to the nearest emergency department. Don't get me wrong, I'd eliminated the obvious causes and tried introducing some formula with thickener, all to no avail. Without gilding the lily, the doctor who sees us, post haste, is as bewildered as I am, given Jelly Bean isn't febrile (that's 'has no fever' to you or me, and those select medics who speak the common tongue).

SHOPPING LIST

Huh? What happened?

Where am I?

Who are you?

Who am I?

But at least he has some suggestions. His (admittedly aggressive) suggested course of action, however – putting in catheters, drips etc – leaves me cold. We have been able to rule out serious infectious disease, so my instincts scream that battering her tiny body so early on is probably unwarranted. Thankfully, the doctor and his team are quite supportive of my plea to wait and see till morning, given most of the important tests such as ultrasounds and blood work could not be carried out until then, anyway.

I feed Jelly Bean, while Lolly Pop, already a seasoned smiler and eyelash-flutterer at eleven weeks, flirts gooily with the nurses, and we head home, with instructions to return in the morning.

The feed stays down until 4 a.m., at which point the cycle begins again. I've gone through twelve baby suits and five baths in the past twenty-four hours, with no signs of it abating.

As dawn strips back the shadows on what promises to be a scorcher, my resolve is set. I'm not taking any chances on the Russian roulette of emergency department doctors today. Instead I leave a heartfelt plea on the voicemail of the paediatrician who delivered the girls and cross my fingers.

By lunchtime I'm cleaning puke from the sofa in said paediatrician's reception room. Thankfully it is minimal simply because Jelly Bean let loose within the confines of the Baby Bjorn, and thus my summer frock has absorbed the bulk. I brought along two changes of baby clothes . . . alas, none for myself. I force a bashful smile when the pretty receptionist swoops in with a clutch of wet towelettes, trying to keep the deluge in check, my breathing a ragged overture to tears, the frustration of the last two days threatening to spill over.

Doc checks Jelly Bean over thoroughly; her vitals are all good, but she's clearly not her usual chirpy self. Her wan complexion and listless gaze contrast sharply with the tubby little Buddha that is Lolly Pop, cooing at the doctor whenever he meets her syrupy gaze.

A flurry of tests are ordered, and we return to the neonatal nursery where the girls were first washed and weighed, where Lolly Pop spent those critical early days, to have blood drawn and a special urine-collection bag fitted. Downstairs, an ultrasound of her stomach and duodenum is attempted and aborted due to gas obscuring the image. I'm to return three hours post her next feed which, when given, resurfaces immediately anyway. By late afternoon we are all at the end of our tether. When gas again blurs the second attempted ultrasound, I request that we persevere, moving Jelly Bean around, massaging her belly, giving her another feed, after which the radiographer finally succeeds and the question of growths, obstructions and muscle deformities can finally be put to rest. It is reassuring but we still have no answers, and I'm about to take out shares in Omo and Cuddly.

With all the tests run thus far coming back clear, our doctor considers allergies. I'm about as useful as a fifth wheel on this score, having never been intolerant of anything (beyond sightseers driving at half the speed limit on coastal roads then refusing to let you pass) and none of the kids have ever been allergic to anything. Rather than fiddle with formulas, he recommends I cut out all dairy. Looks like the healthy diet regime I've been battling since New Year's will be enforced after all and my secret stash of Tim Tams will remain just that. Thankfully he's not suggesting anaphylaxis. Diet schmiet: anyone who dares try to interfere in my sordid affair with peanut butter might just lose an eye for their troubles.

## FRIDAY 16 JANUARY

*6:54 p.m.* Three vomit-free days and I feel courageous enough to return to the beach for one final week of bliss. In addition to Jelly Bean's dramas, the few days in Melbourne were further made uncomfortable as the front yard has been chewed up and spat out, while the days are punctuated by the meanderings of tradespersons around the property, into the house, and even into the kitchen to microwave last night's lasagna while I was in a precarious state of semi-undress mopping up one of the many couture-clinging hurls. Must say they were quite ingenious, though, hooking up a complicated network of extension leads to provide themselves with a toasted sanga station and tea and coffee facilities (read: jaffle iron and an electric kettle).

I'm up at 3:30 a.m. with the twins, so once they are fed, I load the car and wake the kids for a dawn take-off (it's been a long week; I think I can be forgiven for the occasional brain blip).

Wrestling still-zombified children into the car with the promise of a hot chocolate en route proves well worth the trouble, just to see the morning light bouncing off the waves when we hit the coast an hour later.

Unloading the troops and a hyper MJ (I suspect someone, probably the kinder-aged cannonball, has fed him her muesli bar), all finally feels right with the world. That is until I unload Jelly Bean and her head flops suddenly forward with enough force to bring on tears. I had noticed she seemed a little floppy but had put it down to lingering weakness from a few days of dehydration. Now, however, I feel convinced she is struggling to support her head. There's only one logical solution: get on Google.

Several searches later, I've convinced myself she has somehow suffered a head or neck injury, probably delivered by 'I love you so much I'm gonna suffocate you with kisses' Tink, so the vomiting was probably due to concussion and Jelly Bean could possibly now have brain damage.

I'm not even going to give my psychosis the credit of a detailed description; suffice to say I called NurseOnline in a state of mounting hysteria, was directed to the nearest emergency department, and was soon zooming back the way we had just come with a carload of disgruntled children.

Two hours later, after yet another thorough physical examination, Jelly Bean's diagnosis was: weakness caused by dehydration.

Bloody hell.

Despite all the pleasures of bored fiddling with medical equipment, possibly contracting golden staph in the process, and having their heads bitten off by me, my brood are unaccountably sullen, even when bribed with a dinner of fruit smoothies, completely undercut by a hot-chip chaser.

Back at the house, I release the team into the warm twilit evening for a run around with MJ while I settle the twins. Minnie loiters in the lounge, about to settle into an iPad session. 'Mu-um?' The slight ululation tells me she wants something. My reserves are depleted, my nerves frayed, but that is no excuse for the snapped response I deliver.

'What now?'

Huge, wounded puppy dog eyes immediately brim with tears, bottom lip trembles, cheeks flush fit to rival the setting sun. Come to think of it, Minnie has been quick to cry quite a lot lately – how have I not noticed? Something is going on here . . . hmm, might need to Google it.

SHOPPING LIST

Tim Tams, please come back.
I'm sorry. I cannot live without
you! Please come back,
all is forgiven.

# DON'T GOOGLE!

Why even bother with seeing a doctor? Why waste your precious time when there is a plethora of anecdotal medical knowledge at your fingertips? Why? When there's a carefully collated virtual knowledge bank fit to rival a Harvard medical degree just one keyboard click away?

Why? I'll tell you why: for all of us plebs out there self-diagnosing, self-medicating and self-destructing with the aid of the myriad search engines administering medical advice for free, only a minute minority actually has sufficient knowledge to properly interpret what they read and glean the relevant information in a useful and meaningful way. The rest of us are just like bad soap actors: blindly bumping into props and hoping for the best. I should know!

Sadly, what's at risk is not a mere Logie nomination, it's your health, and that of those you love. Your GP, paediatrician, chiropractor, psychologist, whatever, didn't slog out all those years studying just for the honour of swaggering about in a white coat – any bad soap actor can do that (again, I should know). They actually know a thing or two about their chosen field and shock! horror! actually want to help you. Startling, I know!

When it comes to children, only a fool relies on guesswork, especially in the case of young children. Babies and toddlers cannot tell you what ails them, their symptoms can be hard to decipher, rapidly changing and some disguising others. A small child's wellbeing can deteriorate in the blink of an eye. Why would you even hesitate? Of course it is uncomfortable, feeling like you are jumping the gun in rushing your little one to the emergency ward, but what cost is a little embarrassment?

When it comes to your family's health, get off Doctor Google and get thee to a GP. Gauging your health or that of a loved one based on internet results is like skipping a trip to the hairdresser just because you have a mirror and a pair of secateurs in the shed: both are quick and easy, but done at your own peril. Lest you end up bald or bed-ridden, let the professionals do the job for which they are trained, and let the internet serve the purpose for which it was designed: online shopping and watching cute cat clips on YouTube.

Follow your instincts: no-one knows your child better than you. If you feel something isn't right, there's a very good chance you are correct, but don't trust your iPad to diagnose the cause.

## SATURDAY 17 JANUARY

*6:15 a.m.* Feeding the twins, watching the day dawn, reading back copies of the digital edition of the newspaper on my iPad. A couple of tradespeople I didn't know were coming walk past my un-curtained bedroom window. Can't be bothered getting up, don't care. I took all six out for a day of smudged zinc, soggy sandwiches, windburn and shivering at a water fun park yesterday and have woken bone tired and a little brain dead. Then I happen across an article, the content of which sits me bolt upright with such force Jelly Bean loses her starfish-like sucker grip on my milk bar and starts to squawk.

Small child reattached, I peruse the story in depth and am amazed and a little terrified to see it describes Minnie's recent ills perfectly, and actually gives a cause . . . all before my fingers have even had a chance to itch with the temptation of seeking another Google-driven diagnosis.

The article concerns *adrenarche*, or adrenal puberty, and the hormonal changes heralded by maturation of the adrenal glands in children aged between seven and nine. It is the precursor to the physical puberty to come a few years later, but a sure sign that the inevitable is on its way.

Bloody hell.

While adrenarche has no physical symptoms, it plays havoc with a child's emotional stability, and has lately become the subject of numerous studies on the implications of hormonal fluxes on a child's behaviour. Adrenarche can cause distress, withdrawal, aggression, you name it; if it's an emotion-based malady, adrenarche may be the cause of it.

I think back on Minnie's recent irritability, her propensity for tears, her unbidden flashes of anger, and it becomes all too clear. My little fairy princess, my tiny dancer, is growing up, and I, so busy drowning

SHOPPING LIST

Training bra?

Make-up?

Sanitary napkin starter kit?

Or do I just get a maxi-freezer and start cryogenically freezing my children as they approach age twelve? If I defrost them at seventeen, can we avoid puberty altogether?

125

in children, have not noticed. Her moods scream 'Hey! I'm on the cusp of womanhood here' and I, still lost amid the nappies, tantrums and puréed food, did not hear. In many ways, by constantly reinforcing how much more cognitively and physically capable she is than her younger siblings (read: able to do stuff for *me*) I've forced her to take on more responsibility than her young shoulders can carry, and made her grow up before her time. She is just a little girl, and suddenly it seems that precious time is slipping away. All those cliches about kids growing up too quickly have materialised. Suddenly she is on the verge of being a hormonal teen, and there is nothing I can do to change it.

But maybe I can help her in other ways.

Time to implement 'Project: Support Minnie'.

In the brief period between when the twins doze and the rest of the horde rouses, I read as much as I can on adrenarche, and how best to support tween-agers who are experiencing it. The rest will depend on instinct and simply listening. With the constant screeching which in recent years has become the soundtrack to my life, I've become very good at blocking out extraneous noise, but sometimes I forget to hear what is really important. My firstborn needs her mum, and now Mummy needs to listen.

*2:15 p.m.* My, my, my . . . I have a lot of children. What has finally prompted this realisation? Is it the fact I've been changing nappies for nine years without pause? That I've been either breastfeeding or pregnant for the same term? Is it the stares in the supermarket car park as I unload one after another, like clowns unfolding from a Mini Minor? Is it knowing that soon I will need to roast two whole chickens for dinner, potentially three? No, it's none of these obvious markers: it is the quiet comprehension that as I study the enigma that is a child reaching maturity, I'm still nursing two tiny babies. I'm covering both ends of the parenting spectrum: one child finding her wings, taking the first clumsy steps towards leaving the nest, which two new chicks have only just entered. Okay, I'm exaggerating, but it is still an odd sensation, an awakening to facts I simply cannot fathom.

I'm ill-prepared. I'm not ready.

How can my baby be reaching maturity when I'm still such an immature twat? How do I answer her questions? How do I keep her on an even keel? How do I steer her in the right direction when I get lost using satellite navigation, and what degree of control do I have when bribes of a trip to the toy department no longer cut it?

# ROLE MODELS

I've never been much of a subscriber to the notion of 'role models' being key motivators in the journey of life. I certainly admire talent and ability, willpower and ambition, but have never felt compelled to measure my own achievements by those of others. I tend to believe this can get you in a world of trouble. What if you fall short of the mark? What if you don't measure up? Perceived failure based solely on what another person has achieved in different circumstances at a different time creates a slippery slope toward self-doubt, depression and giving up.

I'm a big believer in achieving one's personal best, and my personal motto is 'don't make excuses, make it happen'. The only thing making excuses guarantees is a front row seat to watching the world pass you by.

Accordingly, I want my kids to be self-motivators, to have healthy egos and to believe in themselves. I like to think this approach will also prove pivotal in helping Minnie through this weird and wonderful new phase in her life.

I begin by really listening to her observations, and rather than greeting them with the usual 'uh-huh', I encourage her to elaborate and explain why she came to that conclusion and what it means. I attempt to give her thoughts and feelings weight and importance, thus making her feel important.

Next is, naturally, spending more time with her. As I've said before, 'one-on-one time' is most effective, and in my case is only possible, when it is integrated into everyday activities. Hence, I ask her to help me fold laundry/water the garden/unload the dishwasher/come to the shops, and while we complete the domestic chore, we talk. For me, making a child the focus of 98 per cent of my attention while multi-tasking with a few necessary chores is the most effective way to emphasise how important they are, and that I hold them and their opinions in high regard.

Feeling loved and feeling respected are two very different beasts, but they are equally important in ensuring your child cultivates a healthy sense of self-esteem.

*8:15 p.m.* Is it wrong to encourage your kid to help out folding the laundry, then ask them for a glass of water, and while they are gone quickly re-fold their lot, stuffing it at the bottom of the pile, only to lavish praise on their efforts upon their return? If so, cuff me, officer.

Minnie and I have spent a glorious afternoon chatting, folding, drying dishes, sweeping, looking at random age-appropriate stuff on the internet and cooking. She's become so grown-up, so lovely in a young-lady kind of way, past the cuteness of childhood. My girl is clever, witty, and those negotiation skills are only becoming magnified with age. How have I not noticed till now? Regardless, I'm not wasting time on self-flagellation, I've recognised the problem and now am determined to implement the solution. Parents make mistakes: that's being human. When you learn from your mistakes, that is being clever.

The family winds up the evening watching a movie together, with the spectacle of homemade choc-tops thrown in (it's not a successful evening if you don't finish it needing to bathe the kids again and having to scrape melted chocolate off the couch).

Once all are in bed, I retire to the laundry (naturally) to soak a couple of stains, when a little voice pipes up from the doorway.

'Mu-um . . . can I sleep with you?'

There she is, my not-so-big girl, in her kitten nightie, golden tresses tumbling about her face and shoulders, looking much younger than her nine years. She will be my baby forever, and with The Chef still away, why not?

'Yes, go on, I'll be there in a minute.'

For her, I'll be there forever.

## SUNDAY 18 JANUARY

*9:05 a.m.* I'm redoubling my efforts to be attentive to Minnie, and while the younger girls seem oblivious, too busy drawing on the walls and themselves with a craftily swiped lipstick, Buddy senses something is going on. As if there has been some seismic shift in the force, his juvenile 'someone is getting attention' antennae have pricked up, alerting him to the fact that that someone isn't him. From the moment he wakes he is mopey. Maybe the approach I'm taking with the nine-year-old Miss will deliver similar results if applied to the six-year-old Mister?

'Buddy?! I need your help at the shops . . .'

# HANDLING THE SIX-YEAR-OLD TANTRUM 101

*9:43 a.m.* Arrive at the chemist. Just dash in for baby Panadol. Buddy wants a plastic pistol. No. Generic or brand name? Buddy wants some tubs of modelling clay. No. Hmm, do we need band aids? Buddy wants a bag of black jelly beans. No. 'Will that be on a card?' Buddy wants a chocolate. No. 'Need a bag?' Buddy wants a toy car. No. 'Yep, see you next time.' Buddy runs from the shop, tantrum in full steam, and flings himself on the concrete, screeching like a banshee, drawing gaping disapproval from all within a 100-metre radius.

I size up to him, swoop in and wrap my arms around him tight.

I feel the flinch, as if he expected a slap, then the tense confusion as the instinctive fight-or-flight response kicks in. I nestle my face into his still baby-soft neck and his blond bowl-cut tickles my cheek. I breathe in the sweet smell of salty sunshine that is a sweaty little boy.

'Buddy, please don't act that way. We don't need treats today. When you behave like this, screaming and running off, it makes me sad. I love you so much, please don't make me sad.'

SHOPPING LIST

Can that cryogenic freezer I've put on order have a cloning option? I really need a few more of me to go around . . .

It's all delivered as a tender whisper, just for him and me, no spectacle for the gawping crowd, no public humiliation, no derision . . . just a mum and her boy.

He stiffens, and as the anger and adrenaline subside, so too does the frustration. His breathing quickens, catches, a deep sob relieves the tension and suddenly those little arms reach up and wrap about my waist.

'Sorry, Mum.'

'I love you, Buddy.'

'I love you, too.'

Now a warm little hand, pudgy with the last pads of baby fat, slips compliantly into mine as we head amicably toward the post office.

Bloody hell . . . it worked!

# TUESDAY 3 FEBRUARY

**7:09 a.m.** Having well and truly wrung the last dregs from the holidays, it's time to return to the merriment and mania of school. Despite arriving at the house late last night, by 7 a.m. The Chef had headed to the gym for a workout before facing another long day, and I had bags packed, uniforms laid out, breakfast prepped, fruit cut. My frenzied flitting about the kitchen, hovering between one task and the next, was not unlike the sensation when one too many lattes have been inhaled: your heart starts rattling around your chest like a toddler on red jelly beans let loose in a shopping centre, and you just know you should have switched to decaf two lattes ago. Finally, I sit to feed the twins and quite frankly don't think I can get back up. Bloody school . . .

Five minutes into the feed, Tink starts screeching from her cot that she wants to be a princess. Okay; put the twins down to extricate and nappy-change her. Twins starts squawking. Now Princess wakes. Finish Tink, start to dress Princess. She yanks her dress down awkwardly and a button catches in her hair. Crisis! I note Jelly Bean's cries increase in volume and pitch. Quick check reveals, yes, Tink has crawled into the bassinet with her and is 'helpfully' trying to wrench her out by the head. I pull Tink out instead and create a barrier to the study-cum-nursery door with a chair, a still-unwrapped but large birth present to the twins (the 'shake test' suggests it's a plastic-based toy of many small parts, hence my reluctance to open it), a pair of Buddy's runners and a toy tambourine. If that thing goes off I know Tink has breached security.

I drag up Buddy and Minnie. There's a bit of argy-bargy about new school shoes and potential blisters. Blah blah blah. Put some concrete in it and harden up, kids! Still, I do apply a slathering of preventative band-aids and slap copious 50+ on them before herding them downstairs as Sal arrives. Finally I can dress myself. No time for a shower today, just a liberal spray of deodorant. Whatever.

Downstairs, I start on the breakfast dishes, just because it's an excuse to eat the kids' leftovers and thereby dodge having to make anything myself. Aaah, the simple rewards of motherhood. Right, brush teeth and load everyone into

> SHOPPING LIST
>
> A diary – too much to do, too much to remember.
>
> Hang on, what are YOU then?
>
> Get your act together, diary!!!

the car. As they pile in, I notice Princess has left behind her backpack and her new school hat is sitting oddly on her head, lumpily tumescent. When I enquire, she whips said hat off to reveal the contents of her lunchbox crammed inside. Why? I ask as she repositions sandwich-, muesli slice-, apple- and grape-stuffed headgear. 'I don't need a lunchbox, I've got a new hat.' Guess you can't argue with that logic, can you?

## THE JOY OF THE PACKED LUNCH

Organisation. Whoa! How can one word have so many implications and interpretations? And yet I cannot stress its importance enough. It is one thing to know which days the rugrats have library, and to be able to get them to after-school activities on time, but true organisation lies in those little bits and pieces that make the entire household move forward harmoniously.

Lunchboxes are one such onerous, unrelenting daily task that can make or break the average week. My advice? Make them a day ahead and refrigerate. I've tried out the ol' 'make a week's worth of sandwiches and freeze them', but found I wasn't happy to sacrifice an entire Sunday in the process, and was very limited in fillings that didn't prompt the mush factor.

Just whip up said lunchboxes while making something similar (such as lunch for yourself and any toddlers).

### Assembling a lunchbox your children will actually want to eat

For as long as I can remember, I've experienced a secret thrill from packing a varied, nutritious, attractive lunchbox. Sad, isn't it? What a cheap date I must be. But if my child's lunchbox doesn't look like something you might see in those 'back-to-school' advertisements in women's magazines, then I'm just not satisfied. However, a pretty lunchbox isn't worth losing your mind over. I'm mildly insane, there is no need to pussyfoot around it. But the same doesn't need to be the case for you! Follow a few basic rules and Operation: Lunchbox can be with accomplished with minimal blood (slipped cutting up an orange) sweat (running out of cling film at a crucial moment and having to dash out for more?) and tears (realising I could potentially be doing this most mornings for the next eighteen years, which with time served, brings the total to twenty-three years of lunchboxes!).

Anyway, here are my favourite lunchbox tips as honed over years of trial and error:

- Stick to sandwich basics, like cheese, ham and cheese, chicken and so on, then pop in a sealed tub of add-ons which might sog the sandwich if added before packing. Grated carrot, sliced tomato, lettuce, some mayo, corn kernels and even mashed egg. My kids get such a kick out of having a mini salad bar in their lunchbox they will happily stuff their sandwich with vegies and not even be aware it's healthy.
- On the red-button topic of sandwich fillings:
Beetroot and tinned tuna between
Should never be seen.
Need I say more?
- Carrot sticks are good, but whole baby carrots (preferably organic Dutch, but let's not quibble, no need for racial tension over produce) go down a whole lot better. Most good organic shops will offer a variety of carrots. My lot love purple ones just because they are purple.
- Those carefully choreographed, glossy shots of lunchbox fillers always feature kid-friendly dips and crudités. I'm bang up for a vegie stick but dips? Really? Pre-mashed avocado goes brown, and squeeze on too much lemon juice and the kids will rebel. Cottage cheese separates, yoghurts go warm, cheese spreads get smelly, and hummus? Puh-lease. My answer to a dip has always been a small tub of nut butter (if the school allows it) or pack a small ripe avocado and a plastic spoon. Instruct your child to cut the avo in half using the handle of the spoon (thereby averting the kind of crisis that would arise should a knife be brandished in the classroom) and then mash up the flesh. Instant guacamole! Add some crackers and crudités and away you go! Vegemite as a dip for celery and cheese sticks is also a hit in these parts.
- Bake your own muesli bars or cookies. Go nuts and cram them with everything healthy you can lay your hands on: oats, grains, seeds, dried fruit, quinoa flakes, goji berries and so on, then decorate with

a thin drizzle of CHOCOLATE. Hey presto! They are suddenly a treat and the kids will suck 'em down.

- Wraps: don't waste your time. They are guaranteed to sog, warp and fall apart, and no matter how carefully you construct them, they will never look like those pristine little kitchen-paper-and-twine-bound bundles in the food mags. (As a general rule, food magazines are just porn, copping more photo-shopping than your average Hollywood a-lister and requiring as much diva-pampering too.)
- Once a month, or if you are keen, once a week, do a 'themed' lunchbox. Use broad categories such as cuisine styles (Japanese: sushi rolls, cold noodle salad, pickled veggies, anything slathered in kewpie mayonnaise. Italian: cold meatballs, pasta salad, breadsticks and tomato salad. Chinese: fried rice, stir-fried veg – or fabulous take-away leftovers!) or specific events. Last Halloween I had a ball jazzing up their lunchboxes. Cold spaghetti in a pesto dressing was wriggly worms, a boiled egg was dressed as an eyeball, a marshmallow in kitchen paper with a face penned on was a ghost and so on. Plan ahead with the kids and let them get involved. Guaranteed THAT lunchbox will come home empty.
- Tinned tuna with some chopped vegies.
- Frozen tubs or squeeze packs of yoghurt are a must, with a frozen orange doubling as chiller and a nutrient-packed summer thirst quencher.
- As a treat, I love to write them a little note on kitchen paper, wishing them a good day or just to say I love them (I draw a little picture for the littlies who can't yet read) and wrap it around a sweet biscuit or a single piece of chocolate like a tiny gift. Very well received. An occasional treat is good for the soul.
- Whole fruit. Unless you are again happy to squeeze on lemon juice and risk a puckered-up rejection, pre-sliced fruit will generally go brown or mushy and give them an excuse to chuck it. It's also important for kids to appreciate that food does not come in perfectly compartmentalised little pieces, and learn to enjoy it in its natural form.
- Leftovers: most evening meals can be reimagined as lunchbox fillers. Even if it's just a small slice of cold quiche or tub of pasta. If it's a dish favoured by your child, they are guaranteed to eat it, for the novelty factor if nothing else. This approach also saves a lot of time and resources.

- Allergies. When packing lunchboxes, be hyper-aware of the presence of allergens. Not just for your child but also their classmates. Ask your child's teachers what specific foods should be avoided to ensure a happy, healthy classroom.
- The flipside of that is, don't dress up your child's intolerance or dislike of a food as an allergy. This puts everyone at a disadvantage, and the risk is that, like the boy who cried wolf, if everything is constantly off limits, other parents may well develop 'allergy exhaustion' and risk placing potential allergens in their child's lunchbox out of frustration. Describing a dislike or mild intolerance as a genuine allergy is not a behaviour unique to children. Adults are particularly inclined to do it, and it's just plain ridiculous. Working in hospitality, The Chef is regularly sent extensive lists of 'allergies' from diners prior to their visit. His wonderful chefs always adhere to these limitations on their creativity but it must be deeply frustrating when diners claim to be allergic to an ingredient then, seeing a dish delivered to another diner they like the look of, they will order it, and when told it contains said allergen will reply 'oh, a little bit won't hurt'. In the case of genuine allergies (rather than intolerances), a little bit will hurt a lot. Being led to believe 'a little bit won't hurt' engenders a lackadaisical approach to food preparation and hygiene that can risk lives. If you don't like something, or it gives you a bit of gas, own it! And to those who insist on having their salad dressing on the side, won't have their fish come in contact with olive oil, must have skim milk because they are allergic to fat/oil/cream/whole milk, that's not an allergy, that's an eating disorder. And that's one habit we most certainly don't want to pass on to our children via their lunchboxes.

## THURSDAY 5 FEBRUARY

*6:01 a.m.* Today, I have an audition. First in a long time. Yes, I'm nervous, excited, anxious, slightly nauseous, but above all, the concern that keeps spinning through my mind, strumming my nerves like taut guitar strings is: how the heck will I manage if I get the job?

Ludicrous, I know, but utterly relevant. The role is in an American film shooting interstate. How would I do it? I cannot clone Sal, so I would need more help. The whole family could come along sporadically but with school and The Chef's endless commitments, only Tink and the twins could come full time – and we aren't the Pitt-Jolies; we don't pack an entourage every move we make. We can't afford it and nor do we want it.

Having completed the morning ritual, I slip into my mini-office to go through the script while waiting for the twins to wake. Sitting between their cradles, I'm treated to that symphony of sounds unique to rousing babies. Grunts, squeaks, sighs and some serious bottom action. Lolly Pop gets in first with a tootle on her trouser trumpet, then Jelly Bean harmonises with a bottom burp of her own. There's Lolly Pop, cutting the cheese with alacrity, before Jelly Bean drops her guts again, a little too forcefully as announced by the definite splat splat ker-BLAT notes of a mighty shart. Next comes the frenzied suckling of tiny hands, heralding they are awake and hungry, before the first whimpers commence, rising to the lusty crescendo equally loved and despaired over by parents everywhere. And there it is, the most perfectly composed concerto known to motherkind. Let the feeding commence.

*9:04 a.m.* Oh, the many and varied joys of home improvement just keep on coming. Kids safely deposited at school, I settle the twins and kiss Tink, then make to head out for my audition. Opening the front door reveals my car is locked in by a concreting truck, which, of course, cannot be moved until the job is done.

Bloody home improvement!

In a tizz, I contemplate booking a taxi, but know at this rate I will be horribly late. Taking my frenzied call, my agent suggests I simply record my audition on the iPhone and send it in. Brilliant! Let me just turn on the stage lights in my home studio and dust off the hair and make-up team down in the cellar.

> SHOPPING LIST
>
> *Nerve repellent*
>
> *Anxiety remover*
>
> *Confidence super-booster*

I find what I hope will be a flattering sunny spot in the sitting room to set up as my 'set' and peel a sweat-soaked Chef away from his beloved gym equipment to act as director, cameraman and prompter. The Chef's devotion to fitness is truly impressive. Every day, rain, hail or hangover, he's either pumping iron or pounding the pavement. Me? The only bicep curls my arms undergo are those required to apply mascara, though I must say nine years of daily lifting, carrying and settling small children does give you some serious definition. Still, when this final term in my breastfeeding career ends, and my mammaries join my ovaries in retirement, I fear for the state of my thighs.

Anyway, with my sweaty director in place, delivering his half of the lines with all the conviction of an MP confessing to Cabcharge rorting, I suddenly found myself stagestruck! Beset by nerves, frozen by the kind of performance anxiety I've only ever experienced when I returned to work after being hit by a bus. Yep, a bus. Is it time to skew off on a tangent? I think so! Let me set the scene:

*June 2002, 9 p.m.* It's an unseasonably warm evening in Sydney. Far too warm for the favourite olive-green roll neck jumper I've borrowed yet again from my mother. After a full day on set at *Neighbours*, I had jumped on a plane, still with a face full of stage make-up, to arrive in Sydney in time for hosting duties at a Kids Helpline function the next day. Arriving at my hotel with a howling stomach (this was when I was deeply entrenched in veganism and inflight fare was not yet the vego-friendly, gluten-free, paleo-wonderland it is today) to discover the hotel's restaurant was closed. Being on Oxford Street, I was confident of finding something decent, so set out to hunt down a meal. A twenty-minute mini-mart shop later, I recall standing ON THE PAVEMENT, beside a bus stop, looking for the traffic lights which would guide me back to my hotel.

That's all I remember.

What actually occurred was that a bus, travelling at considerable speed, pulled in to the bus stop, mounted the pavement and collected me with it. I bore the brunt of the impact on the left side of my face, was thrown some 10 feet, and skidded another two along the asphalt on my face – leaving a considerable amount of epidermis in my wake. Possibly could have gone back to collect it, but being grated by sidewalk grime, old chewing gum and cigarette stubs is not my favoured form of microdermabrasion.

Now for the kicker: as I lay there, unconscious in the gutter, some clever end, some twisted cretin, stole my wallet! Hence, when the police and ambulance crew arrived, there was no way to identify me. I was officially Jane Doe, and given that I suffered amnesia for a few days when I finally roused, the situation was pretty messy. Thankfully, I did have that Kids Helpline function to host, so when I didn't show, the organisers contacted my agent, who did the dramatic ring-around to hospitals and police stations before finding me at St Vincent's Hospital.

Oh, the duality of human nature. In a suitably Dickensian twist, after said cretin had stolen my wallet, two ladies of the night, into whose turf the bus had smashed me, held me, mopped up my bleeding head and called the ambulance, waiting with me until it arrived before disappearing into the night. I have since made requests for them to come forward, hoping to thank them personally, without luck.

Injury-wise, I suffered three skull fractures, the worst running underneath my brain shelf, which gaped, releasing cerebral fluid (which, to my palate, tastes not unlike chewing on aluminium foil) and filling my cerebellum with bubbles of air. Thankfully it closed after a few days and didn't require serious surgery. There was a cerebral hematoma and haemorrhaging where my brain ricocheted around inside my skull upon impact, broken teeth, and all the blood vessels burst in my eyes. The point of impact suffered a crush injury, meaning the skin died and had to be cut away and sewn over, taking my eyebrow in the process, while one whole side of my face was a giant flesh wound. Again, I'm so lucky my agent found me before I was operated on, as I was locked in to just have a run-of-the-mill stitch-up job, but my agent insisted that, as I was an actor, any patch-up needed to be performed by a proper facial surgeon. It was the closest I've ever come to having plastic surgery, and believe me, it was close enough. Had I had the foresight (or had I been conscious) I might have requested a little nose refinement and some delicate lifting on the eye area – who would have known?! However, I was still in my early twenties, back when two-minute noodles were a food group, drinking til 2 a.m. was a respectable hobby and I boasted the epidermal elasticity of a rubber band.

In a shout-out to the wonders of stage make-up, mine, having survived the rigours of a fourteen-hour day on set, played an important role in confirming the vehicle that did the damage. It adhered to the windscreen. Yep, at the point of impact, there was a perfect imprint: foundation, rouge, lipstick, even a hint of mascara, all intact. A policeman I spoke to days later, clearly dissatisfied with walking the beat and keen to branch out into comedy, told me, 'Well, we have located the vehicle in question, Miss West, cos you left your face on it.' Oh, I laughed and laughed, until I saw my face in a mirror.

It was about a week later when I was finally able to hobble to the bathroom, against my doctor's advice, to check out the damage. I didn't recognise myself.

My face was swollen to twice its normal size, mottled black and purple in an alarmingly accurate homage to a stepped-on meat pie. Both eyes were blood red à la *Robocop*, teeth decimated, and a mess of bandages concealed the fresh rows of stitches and raw, oozing wounds that was once the left side of my face.

In that moment, I wanted to die. Having so narrowly avoided that very fate only days before, I was ready to step off this mortal coil and bid the life *dramatique* a fond *adieu*.

Why? Because I was young, I was making my way in a profession I loved, and I made the superficial but common mistake of believing my appearance was the most important thing about me. To my understanding, the way I looked was all I had to offer. I thought that all my hopes and dreams, my wit, my personality, my talents and disposition were summed up by and only equal to my visage . . . and once that was fundamentally flawed, well, the rest went to hell in a handbasket too.

What a fool.

Admittedly, much of my concern stemmed from the fact that I worked within a deeply appearance-oriented industry. Acting was my great love, one I'd pursued since childhood, sacrificed a potential legal career to follow, and simply could not escape. It's like an addiction, a drug for which there is no substitute, a malady from which there is no recovery or cure. I was young and stupid and didn't really comprehend that where there is a will there is a way. I was so blinkered by my ambition I couldn't see there is more to life than one's job title.

In the weeks and months that followed, as I slowly healed, and through therapy refined my motor skills, I really had to question why I had become an actor in the first place. Was it for the sheer love of performance, telling amazing stories and entertaining people? Or was it to be on the cover of *TV Week* in a bikini?

For me, it was always the former, and once I'd finally grasped that, I understood that if I was truly passionate about entertainment, there were plenty of avenues I could take. Stage, my first home, is generally less obsessed with physical perfection, and film and TV are slowly evolving to embrace the reality that different shapes and sizes lend interest and character. There is also production: producing, directing, writing! And who hasn't heard that old standard, 'You've got a great head for radio'?

Once I had embraced these possibilities, I began to feel excited about the future again and where it would take me. Regardless of what the magazines feed us, regardless of what the celebrities endorse, regardless of what the majority of us think when we look in the mirror, the way we look makes up the tiniest portion of who we are. If we limit all we have to offer to that minute fraction, how much do we lose? How much does the world miss out on? I guess you could say, what I learnt, and now tell my children every day, is that sheer force of willpower will take you further than fancy clothes or Botox, and truly the most attractive thing you can do is believe in yourself. Don't make excuses, make it happen! If I was prepared to throw away a hard-won career over a few dents and busted teeth, I didn't deserve that career in the first place.

Miraculously, I was back on set at *Neighbours* eight weeks later. Yes, it was exceptionally difficult. The make-up team had to do a job verging on prosthesis to disguise my various lumps and bumps. I seemed to be held together by hardcore painkillers, industrial-strength foundation and pity for those first few months, and my short-term memory was kaput, so even learning the simplest of lines proved a gargantuan task. My confidence and self-esteem were the greatest casualties initially, but I now came at my career with passion, drive and an unassailable determination to succeed, whatever the odds. I also had a newfound respect for the privileged position I enjoyed in being paid to do something I loved, and was more prepared to take risks and more appreciative of the opportunities that came my way. Finally, I knew what it meant to be brave. Bravery is more than war zones, medals or getting starkers on TV before a national audience. Bravery is having the audacity to say 'This is what I want, and I'm gonna get it.'

When you become a parent, you really understand what it is to be brave; what it means to stand by your choices when everyone has an opinion. Society is quick to judge and no matter what path you take, those little critters are along for the ride, experiencing every bump you encounter. It's a brave choice to return to work, an equally brave one to stay at home, with a vociferous chorus to boo and hiss both sides. Only you know what is right for you and those you love. I knew I was doing what was right for me then, returning to work when doctors, family and even my producers suggested otherwise, just as I know I'm ready to dabble a toe back in the workforce now, though a cast of thousands would say I shouldn't. My line of work does not call for a 9–5, five-day-a-week commitment, but it does require travel, extraordinarily long hours, and serious commitment for those weeks or months of filming. With six littlies, there is very little I get to do purely for myself. No laborious beauty treatments, catching a film, or time-consuming hobbies. But when I work, it is for me. My being a mother informs how I work. It makes me more dedicated and frankly better at doing my job, because if it means I have to be away from my babies to do it, I'd better do it well.

So as I stood before The Chef, who grinned encouragingly at me from behind my phone, I shook off my self-doubt for a moment, and let that old determination and belief I had discovered all those years ago settle in. I stumbled a little, and fluffed a few lines, but I was playing make-believe, not tinkering with nuclear weaponry, so if it wasn't perfect the world was not going to end. I actually had a bit of fun and quite enjoyed myself!

I suppose that if there is one truth my career has taught me, and motherhood reaffirms every day: if you want something and you are prepared to work hard for it, and you believe in yourself, then nothing can stop you, not even an out-of-control bus!

Author's note: Didn't get the job; probably just as well, but I got my groove back!

## MONDAY 9 FEBRUARY

*11:56 a.m.* I'm absolutely, utterly, to-the-marrow exhausted. Simply put, this morning I attempted a challenge of mammoth proportions. Epic in its complications, this task was emotionally draining, technically improbable, a true mission impossible: yes, I had to get Princess and the twins to pose for passable passport photos. Might as well have tried to cure cancer and climb Everest while I was at it.

The prescribed pose is so ludicrous as to be almost criminal: head straight, looking straight at the camera, eyes open wide, mouth closed, no smiling. Wha—? No smiling? Who in their right mind points a camera at a child and tells them not to smile? It's just cruel. It's a sin up there with the cashier packing your bread under the tinned goods. Mangled compressed sandwich

> SHOPPING LIST
>
> *Are there deportment classes for babies and toddlers? My lot see a camera and turn into flippin' gremlins!*

140

might sound like molecular gastronomy but it ain't. I know a smile can be transformative, but I'm pretty certain a grinning assassin doesn't look significantly different to a moping one, especially when they are four years old.

Little Princess could not help herself: that gorgeous smile kept sneaking out, much as we tried to suppress it. What are you supposed to do?

'Think sad thoughts, darling.' Or 'Okay, look at the camera and say "Santa isn't coming this year!"'

We finally got a shot of Princess looking suitably depressed, then it was Jelly Bean's turn. The extremely patient assistant at our local pharmacy laid out a white sheet (the passport office demands photos must have an unpatterned white background – obviously wallpaper screams terrorist, and don't get me started on flocking) and I put Jelly Bean down on it. With her wobbly head, she couldn't stay still. When she finally did, her eyes started roaming the room, refusing to focus on the red Old Spice box I was rattling above her. Jelly Bean finally barrelled the camera, and the assistant snapped her just before she broke into a beauteous smile. Perfect.

Lolly Pop, woken from a deep nanna nap, wasn't having a bar of it, crying plaintively, real tears streaming down her cheeks. Offering cuddles, a dummy, singing to her and making loud noises had no impact. We were reduced to sitting, poised to snap her during one of her momentary gasps for breath. After ten torturous minutes I take her for a stroll. Thank goodness Sal was with me; she takes Tink and Princess home so I can make another attempt at capturing a non-smiling, non-crying, dummy-free, camera-focusing Lolly Pop.

After a brief shop for bananas and a-hem, peanut butter (it's on special! Sure, I need toilet paper, cheese, bread and milk, but some things have to take priority) we return, to discover the assistant has set up a makeshift studio in the beauty treatment room. 'I thought Lolly Pop might prefer it in here,' she said.

Prefer it she did. Lounging on the pristine white treatment bed, the soothing strains of a rainforest symphony filtering through a discreet sound system, the heady scents of sandalwood incense and some delicious face cream concoction redolent of jasmine, Lolly Pop turned it on for the camera. She was actually cooing, fluttering those impossibly long lashes straight down the lens. Snap snap snap. We managed not just a passable passport shot but a veritable portfolio! Mission: accomplished. I know my kids are terrors but here's hoping these mugshots suggest otherwise.

When we return home, I'm knackered, face aching from trying to settle the twins by pulling faces, back shattered by hovering, tensed up, above them as we attempted to capture the shot, I pull the photos out to start the application process, and can't help but spend a moment admiring how sweet the girls are. I wincingly glance at my own renewal photo: what a difference ten years makes! Then I notice there is a little blob on my shoulder in the shot. What is that? I go and look at myself in the mirror. Yep, there it is – baby puke. It's been there all this time and no-one told me. Charming. Now it will be captured, as if for posterity, on my passport for the next ten years. Bloody passport photos.

*5:21 p.m.* I suspect Jelly Bean, my little McNugget, is weaning herself. There seems to be a definite lack of interest when I drag out the sad sacks at certain times of day, particularly in the afternoons when my supply is at its lowest ebb, like my patience. I can almost sense her frustration. Why make all that effort, waste all that time and energy, when there are perfectly good bottles on the market?

On one hand I'm relieved; on the other, I'm just so sad. What is it about breastfeeding that is so addictive, beyond the pervasive ideology that it's the most natural thing in the world and the best possible start for your baby? For me, it is the warm weight of your little one, cradled just so in your arms, that perfect rosebud mouth seeking insistently, their little face flitting from dozy rapture to gooey smiles around a milky mouthful. It's their fluffy-duck little head nestled in the crook of your arm, tiny eyelashes fluttering against your skin. It's being snuggled together deep in the night, when silence reigns and all the world sleeps.

But it's also cracked nipples, constant fatigue and inopportune leakages when you finally make it out for dinner. It is sitting attached to bipping, thunking, sucking pumps like dairy cattle. It's ending the night with boobs of rock should you hazard a big night out, your friend holding your hair back so you can literally milk a little of the backlog into a sink. It's an appetite almost embarrassing in its boundlessness. What's on the menu? Umm . . . a steak, double serve of potatoes, bearnaise sauce, the tiramisu, and can you throw in a pack of Wagon Wheels?

It is bonding at its most elemental, and when your little one decides of their own accord that they are done, it can feel like rejection: a cold, hard slap, a cord severed, a tender tearing of the ties that bind. I tuck a snubbed nipple back in its increasingly loose maternity bra, Jelly Bean having reared and bucked away when offered it recently. They have done their duty.

Stiff upper lip and all that. Sure enough, however, at the next feed she wouldn't have a bar of the proffered bottle, and gaped at my shirt like a landed carp till she found her target, and happily dined, eyes closed in slurping bliss.

That is the greatest challenge of parenting, of rearing these little people: gracefully accepting that we work to their clock, we run on time borrowed from them, and they are truly ours for only the briefest moment before the wide world claims them for itself. That is my fundamental truth; there is no point fighting it. So while Minnie still wants to sleep in my bed, Buddy still wants to kiss me at school drop-off, Princess still wants to hear my made-up fairy tales, Tink still cries out for me in the middle of the night, Lolly Pop still fits perfectly dozing upon my chest, and Jelly Bean still seeks me for her dinner, I will be mindful of treasuring every moment, and once these things end, I will try to smile at their memory while looking forward to what fresh wonders each new phase will bring.

## TUESDAY 10 FEBRUARY

*3:05 p.m.* Fresh wonders? This one is about as fresh as a batch of prawns left in the sun. Buddy has another dental appointment, this time involving the use of happy gas available in mango, berry, peach, vanilla, cotton candy, cola, Fanta grape or classic Fanta orange flavours . . . seriously. I decide we will make a proper day of it, mum and son, with the twins along as optional extras. We park in the heart of the CBD and catch a tram to the dentist. All goes smoothly and Buddy is a delight, relishing being the subject of my undivided attention, entertaining me with vivid stories and elaborate explanations of why things are as they are, as well as throwing in some curly questions I truly have no answers for.

'Why are the babies' clothes called "jumpsuits"?'

'Good question, Buddy, I've no idea!'

Back on the tram we head to a sparkly new shopping metropolis for some concentrated toy-browsing and a naughty lunch – may involve ice-cream; will definitely involve gratuitous and unnecessary use of calories. A small toy is selected without fuss, some items are put on layby for his coming birthday, lunch is devoured with the appropriate degree of appreciation. The drive home revolves around pleasant chatter on a range of topics; we pull in, put the twins to bed, greet Sal, Princess and Tink, I ask him to have a quick shower so he will be ready for karate, and it happens: the meltdown.

'No.'

'Buddy, shower time.'

'No!'

'Buddy!'

'Nononononono! No way, NOOOOOO!'

He then proceeds to run around the lounge in a frenzy, before flinging himself on the floor, screeching and ululating like a demented banshee – that or a Collingwood fan post-defeat. A mildly stunned expression flits across his face as he realises that flinging himself on to polished concrete surfaces actually hurts quite a bit, before nudging up the decibels a bit just to ensure the neighbours a few streets down are also party to his distress.

I'm standing in the kitchen, gobsmacked: where did that come from? After a long day of fussing over him, I'm biting my lip trying to keep my 'You ungrateful little $&@*! Back in my day . . .' demon under control. Two more minutes and I could be spewing forth a tirade of vitriol, if not green slime. Confession time: I have never been slap-happy, but in that moment the palm of my hand was itching.

> SHOPPING LIST
>
> *Unicorns and flying pigs: will wonders never cease?*

Then a remarkable thing happened. Little Tink, clutching her lay-lay, her beloved blanket, approached the roaring wreck that is her older brother, and asked, 'Buh-dee . . . you okay?' She then proceeded to pat his back ever so tenderly.

'Issss aw-right, Buh-dee . . . isssss aw-right. You okay . . .'

And the maelstrom ceased. Buddy pressed pause on the meltdown and let himself be stroked.

Princess, who had been devotedly tearing images from her colouring book and scattering them on the floor to make a Disney princess-themed carpet, now joined in too.

'What's wong, Buddy? Why are you cwying?'

'Because I'm tired . . . I don't wanna have a shower yet.'

'Oh . . . well, have one anuvver day.'

'I have to have it now cos I've got karate soon.'

'Oh . . . have it now, then.'

'Yeah . . .'

And that was that. Buddy got up and with shoulders slumped, lurched off to the bathroom while the little girls resumed their ripping and cartoon watching. How did such a simple exchange yield such immediate results? They actually had a discussion! Granted, Buddy's tone was still ripe with petulance but he spoke with more respect and in more measured tones to his little sisters than he had to me in some time. Those girls seem to have the power of persuasion in buckets. Either they will both secure positions in the UN, or they will make kick-arse telemarketers.

## INDEPENDENT INFANTILE DISPUTE RESOLUTION, OR LET THE KIDS SORT IT OUT AMONGST THEMSELVES

Though I have absolutely no scientific proof, I am absolutely convinced children have an inborn, deeply complicated language unto themselves which only they understand. Why? Try listening in. At the height of a screaming frenzy, while we can only stand back, a little dazed and very confused, they seem to carry on an intense dialogue amid the cacophony. Similarly, when deep in play, speaking toddler gobbledygook, they actually converse, exchanging ideas, listening and responding in kind.

It is wise, therefore, to let them sort out their angst among themselves. They are better equipped to find a fair and equitable solution than we will ever be, and being utterly egocentric, they approach their biffos without the baggage of emotion and guilt we burden ourselves and all our interactions with.

I was always very quick to step in when ructions broke out between members of my tribe, trampling all over the delicate interconnections of sibling relations, generally inflaming the problem and making everything worse. Now I just step back, and as they alternate coming to me, sobbing, to dob on the other, I push repeat on a favourite mantra: 'Sort it out amongst yourselves.'

Miraculously, eventually, they do! Remove yourself from the equation and soon enough those red faces and guttural cries will be replaced by smiles and laughter as they move on to the next phase of whatever complex game they are playing.

I'm not suggesting total abandonment here; all kids have a limited capacity for diplomacy, but as a general rule, they are more than capable of resolving their own spats. Honing these skills within the safety of the home sets them up for life. In the real world no-one will be there to hold their hand through dispute resolution (not without a hefty fee, anyway) and sadly your future self won't be rocking up to your child's workplace, walking stick in hand, to seperate warring colleagues and send them to the naughty corner on your child's behalf. Conflict is healthy, finding an equitable solution a critical life skill, and self-regulation must be learnt and exercised by the self, it can't be done for them. Just don't encourage too much physical resolution – no-one needs a trip to the emergency department. I should know!

## THURSDAY 12 FEBRUARY

*12:45 p.m.* Speaking of epic tantrum-chuckers, Princess, my four-year-old pink pudding rolled in sequins and tied in a bow, isn't throwing so many at the moment. With Sal stationed at home with the younger trio all snug in their cradles and cots, I collect Princess from kinder to find her in a delicious mood, full of mischievous giggles and busting to tell me about her day. She sings a few made-up ditties as we stroll to the greengrocers for beans, impersonating a raucous seagull when I throw her one to sample. With a little time on my hands, the day's finger painting and glitter clinging to hers, we pause for a coffee and a sushi roll. With great gravity she informs me we need to create a cover page together for her kindy portfolio. We can use collage, photos or poetry, but it has to be about her. Whipping out a pen and stealing a cafe napkin, I prompt Princess to tell me things about herself and what she likes, before a swift detour to the newsagent for a few craft supplies. Back home, opting for a little mixed media, Princess does a bit of collage and a few throat-clenchingly cute family portraits, while I attempt to string a few of her thoughts about herself together. I write out the result in paint pen between her exuberant bursts of collage and illustrations of mermaids on a large sheet of coloured cardboard. Princess wriggles around next to me like a puppy in proximity to a barbecue, excited I am actually making something with her. I need to do this more often . . . and there it is. Once again, a lovely mummy–daughter moment is sabotaged as the ugly spectre of Mother Guilt appears. Princess and I work harmoniously together, she humming one of her made-up ditties, me rediscovering the simple pleasures of wielding glue stick and glitter. It's a perfect moment, yet all I can think is that I should be doing this more often, or at least photographing it for posterity. How utterly ridiculous. Why do we focus so exclusively on what we don't do while disregarding what we do manage? We are so busy projecting images of perfect parenting on our lives, all we can see is where we are lacking, blinkering out so many wonderful moments in the process.

On the Sunday just gone, I spent the morning whizzing about the house tidying, clearing the week's laundry backlog, prepping lunch and whipping up a cake for lunchboxes. This slightly crazed blur of activity was so I could clear my schedule and spend some quality time with the kids and The Chef before the week wrapped me in its tentacles again. So I sweated, stressed and barked at my little people for getting underfoot, but once it was done I was so knackered I was in no mood to play anyway! Shoulda, coulda, woulda. I should have dropped the ironing and joined in the hide-and-seek game they were relishing. I could have asked them to help me bake the cake rather than shoving the batter-dripping beaters into their sweaty little hands then directing them to disappear. I would have enjoyed my day more if I'd been a little more inclusive rather than exclusive, made a game of the chores that really needed doing and left the others for some other time.

This preoccupation with 'quality time', seen as being so essential to good parenting, is a bit of a farce anyway. Moments snatched with your kids are more about time and not so much about quality; just being with you means more than carefully curated schedules and calibrated outings. An impromptu walk around the block to check out the neighbours' roses yields more rewards than a textbook trip to a theme park, and once the obligation to have a great, enriching family experience because it costs so bloody much to go to such places is removed, genuine enjoyment of each other's company fills the void.

> **SHOPPING LIST**
>
> Glue stick
>
> Blu-tak
>
> Glitter
>
> Cardboard in assorted colours
>
> Whiteboard markers (have no actual use for them, but do find if you sniff them, the world suddenly becomes a much nicer place)

Whenever The Chef is away, and I'm pulling my hair out playing solo, my only source of distraction keeping the kids from destroying the soft furnishings, the pantry, and each other, I make a point of resurrecting the classic evening stroll. I must look a sight with one twin strapped in the carrier, another beside Tink in the twin stroller, and my three little ducks, Minnie, Buddy and Princess, trooping along behind me, but we have a ball precisely because we are doing nothing. The point is we are doing it together. No expectations, no plans: just strolling, conversing and laughing. That is a moment worth treasuring.

# FRIDAY 13 FEBRUARY

*5:10 p.m.* It's been a long few months, and so I must admit that it's with a fair bit of excitement that I greet The Chef's suggestion of dinner at the restaurant – until, that is, he lets me know I will be 'hosting' some guests, or in other words, total strangers. In other words, I have to be on best behaviour and can only watch on with a Mona Lisa smile as they imbibe some of the world's finest wines.

Still, a night out is a night out; can't look a gift horse in the mouth and all that.

I bound upstairs to select a frock that will camouflage my still-wobbly knick-knacks, only to be confronted with the terrifying prospect of transferring whatever things I need for the evening from my day-to-day carry-all into a sleek little clutch that better matches my outfit. Any such procedure requires effort and planning. To begin, a thorough examination of the contents currently occupying said handbag. Within its once streamlined leather confines I discover:
- Wallet
- Phone
- Keys
- Chewing gum
- Tube of lip gloss and a pink lipstick
- Purse pack of tissues
- . . . all good and reasonable so far . . .
- Three disposable nappies (one of which was no longer in the intended child's size)
- Two mini-packs hygienic wipes, one of which has dried out completely

and is encrusted with dust, crumbs and a now-desiccated sultana
- One bib
- One sock
- Two dummies
- . . . okay, not too unreasonable for a busy mum about town . . .
- A soiled romper suit I'd forgotten to take out and wash
- A packet of birthday candles
- A tube of zinc and castor oil cream
- An empty box the desiccated sultana belonged to
- A teaspoon and numerous broken pieces of plastic cutlery
- . . . then things got a little weird . . .
- Several sachets of sugar, salt and pepper (clearly preparing for the next world war)
- A finger puppet
- A folded newspaper crossword splattered with what looks like dried tomato sauce
- An information pamphlet on a local stamp collectors' group
- Take-away menus for Vietnamese, Italian and Lebanese cuisine
- Portion of the wrapper from a pack of Iced VoVos
- A stiletto heel, without the shoe
- Two muesli bars (Uncle Toby's white choc chip, and a Brooksfarm gluten-free, for those sticklers for details out there) both partially eaten and put back in their wrappers
- A mouldy cheese stick
- Some coins from Thailand
- Rubber bands
- Hair bands
- A few broken rice crackers
- Red nail polish
- Shoe polish
- Floor polish (I swear . . . it was a sample given to me on a shopping-centre expedition)
- Something that could once have been a dried apricot . . . or an oyster, not sure which.

Disgust and curiosity aptly described my reaction. When had I become, quite literally, a bag lady? This had to end; drastic measures were required, and so I undertook the greatest act of rebellion I could think of: I removed the wallet, keys and phone, then upended the rest straight into the big green wheely bin amidst the pooey nappies and other unidentifiable nasties. No coming back from there. I then selected the most petite clutch in my little collection and filled it with only my phone, a lipstick, credit card, and a single stick of gum.

Ohhhh! I felt so light! So free! So liberated!

I went out that night with a decided spring in my step, a rebel's swagger, an air of anarchy.

The next morning my newfound euphoria still hadn't abated. I was a new woman, the bag lady banished, a tiny tote-bearer now in residence. I threw caution to the wind and used that clutch all day – after I'd stuffed in a nappy, of course, just in case . . . and a tiny bottle of hand sanitiser . . . and a muesli bar, a really small one.

## WE'VE ALL GOT ONE, AND IF YOU HAVEN'T, YOU HAVEN'T LIVED!

I've got one – I have! Every woman's best friend. Actually, I've amassed a grand total of twelve – so far. But we all have at least one, don't we? C'mon ladies, admit it! You're probably using it right now!

I love mine, I do. We share a very special bond. It's an enormous part of my life and if I'm honest, I couldn't function without it. If I were to lose mine, I couldn't go on – yet if I were then to find it again, I could never use it again. It wouldn't be the same, not after someone else had . . . well . . . used it. Ew! Grubby fingers all over it. Yuck!

Men have quite an issue with them, don't they? They are very curious about them and why we insist on using them so much. 'Why do you need to bring that? You seem more attached to it than you are me!'

I think men are secretly jealous of them! Though to their credit some men have come around and are actually using them. How and for what purpose, however, doesn't bear thinking about. Because there is something a little . . . um, odd . . . about a man with a . . . a handbag.

What? Did you think I was talking about something else? Dirty-minded beasts!

There is something deeply special about one's relationship with one's handbag. Women are quite attached to them; men at times seem terrified by them. Is it the bag or the hidden contents that are sooooo daunting? What unseen horror lurking within could evoke such fear? Make-up? A tampon? An ex-girlfriend who alerts you to when your man is lying? Perhaps it's just a fear of the unknown. A man's only real comeback is the bumbag. That fashion aberration of the eighties still has some traction with the male market, if only because by its very placement it ostensibly draws the eye to that region of the masculine anatomy so many fellas go to great lengths to get noticed. Apparently there is a misguided belief out there that the combination of their crown jewels AND a handbag in the same vicinity will prove absolutely IRRESISTIBLE! Sadly, for most women, the mere sight of a bumbag provokes quite the opposite reaction.

Whatever, the handbag is a woman's secret weapon and one she should not take lightly. It is the one domain truly ruled by women and the one dominion we should never allow to be usurped or parted from us.

Thus, it is truly a sad day when the worlds of HANDbag and NAPPYbag collide.

Usually, these carriers, crucial in their own unique ways, are mutually exclusive. Both are designed with a specific purpose in mind, and used to carry stuff from A to B. That is where the similarities end. But with motherhood comes baby stuff and so what was once solely the handbag's domain must be shared with the nappybag. Worn in unison, the handbag and the nappybag combo, along with the pram/sling/baby Bjorn, leave us looking more packhorse than clothes horse.

Then, one day, out and about on a quick trip to the shops, you realise it is easier to just slip a nappy in your handbag for emergencies rather than lug along the nappybag, and thus, the dreaded handbag/nappybag hybrid is born. The transition is insidious. Suddenly, that lone nappy sitting discreetly amid the compact confines of your favourite clutch becomes two, then five, to be joined by a travel pack of wipes, then hand sanitiser, tissues, then you are suddenly looking for something a little larger, more of a 'carry-all', so you can squeeze in an extra wrap, bibs, a change mat, snacks, the kitchen sink and half the laundry.

Attempts to escape this mega-clutch's clutches can prove futile as you wrestle with a need to overpack just in case . . . just in case of what? You become trapped in the eveningwear section of a department store and need to set up camp with a three-person tent, barbecue and Nespresso coffee machine?

Yes, babies will mess themselves and toddlers will too, so a spare nappy, a minimal change of clothes and so on are definitely warranted additions to one's packing, but a whole co-ordinated ensemble? With shoes? And accessories? Not so much.

As a concession, I have collated what I now refer to as a Car Bag for when I am out and about. This is basically a nappy bag with the whole catastrophe, which resides in the boot of my car for if and when I should need it. If I'm in the middle of a kids' department spending spree and someone commits a number three (explosive expulsion of contents of either tummy, bowel, or both) I consider it easier to hoof it back to the car for reinforcements and on to the parents' room to do battle with the bombed-out romper than it is to lug the equivalent of the Dead Sea scrolls around in a glorified carry-all.

Should we be making the day trip by pram alone, I put a couple of extra bucks in my wallet. If there are no childrenswear shops in the vicinity of my destination to replace said decimated onesie, there will at least be a supermarket or convenience store. Because if all else fails, a box of tissues, some cling film and strategically placed face washers can be transformed, MacGyver-style, into a perfectly service-able temporary outfit – and it's waterproof too!

## SATURDAY 14 FEBRUARY

*1:10 a.m.* Great night, great food, great wine . . . and bubbly . . . and cocktails . . . and nightcaps . . . not that I got within a maraschino cherry-length of even one of them.

Naturally, the minute we set foot in the door and usher out the babysitter, the twins decide to rally and punish me for daring to have a night out.

Gee, I miss the days of going out, actually going out, drinking copiously and laughing raucously before falling into bed, not to rouse till midday. Having had a semblance of adult conversation, it has only served to emphasise what a huge void the absence of a once-vibrant social life has left, a void I've filled with chores, obligations and mundanity. Gotta get out more, but how?

I'm half-out of my frock, still stumbling in my heels (yep, blisters galore, woo hoo!) when Jelly Bean starts, soon to be joined by Lolly Pop in a raucous chorus. By the time I've wobbled down to their bedroom, changed two wet bottoms, and returned with my cooing armload of cuddliness, The Chef is deep asleep and snoring.

SHOPPING LIST

*A few more sets of arms, please, like Durga*

## HOW TO BOTTLE-FEED AND BREASTFEED TWINS SIMULTANEOUSLY

Sit on a comfortable surface that provides back support, preferably a bed boasting overstuffed pillows, legs out in front, with one bended at the knee.

Prop one little poppet within the cradle formed by the crook of your knee. This formation also acts as a fabulous makeshift bouncer, keeping the bouncee amused and giving the bouncer a butt workout with serious burn.

Cradle Poppet Two in the opposite arm, and either attach to the boob or put a bottle in their mouth, balancing its base in your armpit.

With your free arm, put a second bottle in the first one's mouth.

Halfway through, change positions, lest one butt cheek becomes over-perky while the other continues its gravity-induced slide down your leg.

Now try to relax. Just don't move . . . or breathe . . .

## MARCH 2 MONDAY

*11:12 a.m.* Weigh-in day with the maternal health nurse. Gee, I'd love to be having a coffee and a chat right now, rather than contemplating the load of washing that awaits me at home. The lunchboxes to be made, the dinner to be prepared, the bums to be changed.

On a lighter note, both Jelly Bean and Lolly Pop are well within the healthy weight range for their ages. They are responsive (I'm quietly telling myself they are advanced) and reaching all milestones, despite a bumpy start. Loading up the pram I allow myself a small victory dance, then somehow jam the pram's brakes on. Not going anywhere soon. Bloody fandangled brakes. Ah well, the road to health, wealth and prosperity is never smooth.

*1:19 p.m.* Finally extricate myself from the little people long enough to dash to the supermarket. Arrive, laden with groceries, at the checkout, to discover I've left my purse somewhere at home, or at the doctor's. Keep calm . . . breathe . . .

*3:22 p.m.* School pick-up. All going well, then get pulled aside by a mum in need of a gossip fix, and all three, Minnie, Princess and Buddy, disappear. Poof! Gone. Tearing my hair out, I spend the next thirty minutes reassembling them. Finally coax them all back to the car . . . and find I've received a parking fine. Try to visualise myself as Switzerland: impartial, detached, cool and collected . . . but inside, I'm bloody Chernobyl!

*5:13 p.m.* 'F#%K . . . F!!! . . . SH!!! . . .'
I'm in the bathroom, shower pounding, radio blaring, extraction fan humming, letting off some steam. I'm angry, fuming, ropeable, for no good reason, and desperately need to expend a little of this unaccountable rage lest I short-circuit and set the kitchen alight.

That is the worst part. I don't know why I feel so mad. I just am. There has been no one incident, no discernible trigger, just a slow accumulation of irritants, quietly building to a malignant head, like an awkwardly positioned pimple, now ripely ready to squeeze, the mildest provocation or pressure precipitating an eruption of mammoth proportions.

So I'm screaming obscenities. In the bathroom. With the shower on.

Five minutes in, I've unleashed sufficient rage to again focus on my image in the mirror without wanting to punch said reflection square in the nose. Instead, I burst into deep, racking sobs, bone-rattling hiccups that bring a sunset blush to my cheeks and swell after swell of tears to my eyes.

SHOPPING LIST

Gin

Valium

Smelling salts

Crikey! What the heck is wrong with me?

Back downstairs, I resume the dinner assembly, offering no explanation to Sal's probing and clearly concerned gaze, just focusing very intently on chopping tomatoes lest the wild banshee reappear and I am unable to rein her in.

Tink tumbles in looking for 'foo foo' and my voice crackles, squeaking like a plastic-covered couch when I snap that dinner will be ready soon. The rage simmers just below my skin, ready to rumble into a rolling boil at the slightest provocation. I'm immediately remorseful, down tools and wrap her in my arms. Her busy little body against mine dissolves the fury, leaving a deep sense of unease, hopelessness and failure. Roller coaster!

Tink squirms away and I feel rejected, unwanted, un-needed. Tears. Bloody hell!

Dinner time. As Sal departs, she lays a hand on my shoulder, no words needed, and it is all I can do to suppress a wail and avoid melting to the floor. The kids eat with gusto, despite my threats to put Buddy out with the rubbish when he spills a few peas. It's bit of a worry that they accept my raging with such equanimity, but then I have made the rookie mistake of leaving the TV on during dinner, so really, the spectacle that is my meltdown is just the less interesting of two diversions.

Plates cleared, it's time for my moody version of dessert: I hand out biscuits and the kids skittle outside to escape the black cloud I've conjured. I absently move around piles of notes, bills and other paraphernalia while gnawing on the kids' leftovers. One pile is the bits and pieces related to the twins' passport applications and my own renewal. My stomach clenches with white-hot disappointment. The Chef and I had been booked on a week-long cruise through some amazing European ports, him cooking, me MCing, with the twins along for the ride. Inhouse nannies had been organised, wardrobes purchased, diaries cleared; everything was tied up with a bow except for the flights, which were well on their way. The Chef needed to arrive a week before me for other work, I couldn't get out of a few commitments at home and wasn't comfortable leaving the kids for any longer than a week anyway.

The plan was for me to fly in later, twins in tow, and meet him in Rome to commence the cruise. T's were being crossed and i's dotted when a little-known fact came to light: airlines will not allow a solo parent to travel with twins. I was initially outraged, ready to rock up to the Qantas head office and give them a piece of my mind; then I thought about it and realised that as babies require the bolt-in bassinets at the pointy end of the plane, the second one in my case would impede on someone else's leg room. Perhaps a little unfair. As cute as they are, I'm also sure no-one wants to be forced to share airspace at close proximity to two screeching infants while I juggle nappies, wipes and the warming of bottles unless they are their own flesh and blood, and even then the temptation to turn up the volume in the earphones and pull on a sleep mask is pretty strong.

In any case, me flying solo with twins is not going to work. The Chef could not leave later nor I earlier to allow us to travel together. Thus, the only options are: for us to hire a second set of hands purely to travel with the twins and me, as nannies were already booked for the cruise, or leave the twins at home in the care of the grandparents.

I consider it. If I fly out just in time to meet the boat on the day it sets out, and return the day it docks, I will still be away eleven days. I can hear the fear in the voices of both grandmothers when I broach the possibility with them. Both say 'of course', but you could drive a bus into the pause between my asking and their agreeing. I then juggle the notion of carving up the family further: Princess and Tink go to my mum's for a week, Minnie, Buddy and the twins with Sal, then swap: Minnie and Buddy OR the twins to The Chef's mum, the others to my mum or Sal, OR the twins with Sal the whole time, the older four juggled between grandparents like hot potatoes – but that would require missing school for close to two weeks, which would stick in my throat no matter how smoothly those deckside cocktails would slide down.

Eleven days: can I even contemplate being away from my babies for such a stretch, my bigger ones included? In fact, breastfeeding aside, I'm certain that at the moment, my bigger babies need me more.

I'm torn: the need for an adventure and time away with The Chef tugs me in one direction, the needs of my little ones and all the emotions tied up with that wrenches me in the other.

Hence my anger, hence my frustration, hence my afternoon meltdown. Ah, yes, it all makes sense now. Subconsciously brooding on the amazing trip I am going to have to sacrifice on the altar of domestic reality, I am rebelling!

Fatigue, unbalanced emotions and pent-up frustrations are all firing, exploding like kamikaze warfare, ricocheting off the walls and around each room I enter. I'm trapped by iron bars of my own making. It's a cage gilded by love but it's a cage all the same. I feel deeply ashamed to be thinking this way but it's true. In this moment, I resent my children.

It is not personal, it's just the whole package. The promise of two weeks of sun, vino, and mental stimulation (hallelujah!) is being snatched away, to be replaced by two weeks crowded out by school runs, lunchboxes, nappy changes, tantrums at dinner time and revolts over going to bed (aka business as usual). It all just feels too cruel, too much to bear. I feel deeply ashamed, but suddenly the degree to which my world, and the opportunities I can pursue, have been curtailed by having so many children, is all too clear. How selfish, I know, but I cannot help how I feel and this is an honest account, warts and all.

How many job offers have I had to turn down because I couldn't reconcile my parenting commitments with the hours required? The jobs I have taken have been no bundle of laughs either, dashing to and from set in a frenzy to relieve babysitters, freaking out whenever overtime is called, feeling guilty that I can finish my coffee while it's hot, without spills, and have a quiet lunch alone, or with other adults, no little hands grasping at my plate, wanting the very same items they rejected from their own plates purely because they are on mine.

I can count on two fingers the times I've been out for drinks in recent years, or to dinner later than the 5 p.m. family-friendly sitting with at least half of the tribe in tow. The house is only ever in order around the midnight hours, despite my best efforts, and no matter where I look there is always some domestic chore that needs doing.

I feel a similar resentment radiating off The Chef at times when he just wants to watch the news without being screamed at or crawled over, and Minnie when she just wants a breather in her own room without being crowded out by her little sisters, so I know I'm not alone, but that isn't terribly reassuring.

I frequently feel suffocated, and while I'm having this little pity party for one, I can confess that I crave adult conversation, so sick am I of trying to interpret baby babble, and having every word I speak, every instruction I impart being summarily ignored. I'm convinced my children have the ability to completely tune out the specific frequency of my voice. It never ceases to amaze me that I can harp on for a good fifteen minutes appealing to them to brush their teeth, begging them to don their school blazers, demanding they get out the door and get in the car, raising barely an eyebrow in response. Then The Chef needs only to intone, 'Kids, c'mon,' and they are up. 'Yes, Dad? What is it?'

Then, after attempting to assemble a meal that caters to all their finicky little individual likes and dislikes, there is a 70/30 chance they will hate it anyway, each for their individual reasons. Gotta stand out from the crowd, I guess. After my many futile threats of 'No dessert', all proclaim to be full (only the dinner stomach, mind you, dessert stomach has plenty of room). Once the table is cleared, dishes done, and I've thrown a few scraps at a plate in the name of the 'adult meal', they will saunter up, one by one, proclaiming those dreaded words, 'I'm hungry'. AARRGGHH!!

I'm headed back upstairs to scream into a pillow when the phone rings. The Chef, clearly calling on the run, speaks to me in small bursts between greeting people, dispersing instructions and bantering with someone about gutting a fish. He finally pauses long enough to let me know we are going out to dine at Heston Blumenthal's The Fat Duck (at Crown Casino, Melbourne, not Bray, England, but who's complaining?).

Hallelujah! The thundering clouds of my grey-sky mood suddenly part, a thin, fragile ray of light pierces my misery, not entirely banishing it but sweeping it under the rug for another time – as all mothers do.

There's a spring to my step as I scamper downstairs. Tink has stolen a roll of toilet paper from the powder room and is sitting atop the dining table, using the dregs of her apple juice to make paper mâché. Whatever. I hand her a Freddo Frog and pat her on the head. All that matters right now is that this weekend, Mummy is going out for dinner.

## TUESDAY 3 MARCH

*11:15 a.m.* I volunteer to go along as the parent helper for Buddy's class swimming lesson. After three hours of cramped bus rides, politely asking other people's children not to run around the edge of the pool, ushering shivering little bodies into the shower and cramming small, damp feet into small, sweaty socks, I return to my car, resembling a steamed fish with frizzy hair, to find I've copped a parking ticket for being 3 minutes late. Who cares? This weekend, Mummy is going out for dinner.

## WEDNESDAY 4 MARCH

*10:21 a.m.* Morning chores complete, twins fed, I sneak into the city for a moment of dress shopping. I wrestle my way into the car park and have just ordered a pre-retail-fix caffeine hit when the school rings. Princess has a tummy ache.

Plans abandoned, I collect a surprisingly smug-looking four-year-old. Once home, she reveals she wasn't sick, she just didn't like the play lunch I had packed her. 'And I'm hungry.'

No big deal. This weekend, Mummy is going out for dinner.

SHOPPING LIST

*A whistle, because I cannot, and I'd like to, while I work!*

## THURSDAY 5 MARCH

*12:15 p.m.* Tink is having a meltdown of seismic proportions. She's been fed and watered and now desperately needs a nap before school pick-up or the afternoon will be a write-off. I've read to her, snuggled her up with all her toys and tried building with blocks; nothing will settle her.

'I want Dora.' With the twins asleep I've been luxuriating in the silence; the last thing I want is the inane soundtrack of Dora and her red-booted chimp chiming through my lounge room. All up, I've been listening to that Mexican minx screeching 'Aloha!' for nine years. As each child has recovered from their Nickelodeon addiction there has been another waiting in the wings, ready to savour their first D-D-D-Dora fix. Nine years! I'm shocked I'm not fluent in Spanish.

SHOPPING LIST

*A smile so the world smiles with me.*

Tink attempts to hug the wide-screen TV, clutching lay-lay before her as in prayer, pleading with me for just one shot, just a little taste of Dora action. Ahhh, well. What's one more quiet afternoon blown to smithereens? This weekend, Mummy's going out for dinner.

# FRIDAY 6 MARCH

**3:35 p.m.** At the school gate, Minnie proudly hands me a colourful creation she's concocted in art class.

'And I couldn't find my smock.' Huh? She opens her blazer to reveal that the front of her school dress is splattered with drips of oil paint. Breathe. It's okay.

TONIGHT, MUMMY IS GOING OUT FOR DINNER!!!

**5:30 p.m.** Having given Sal the day off, I've prepped a very, very simple pasta for dinner, and the moment she walked in the door I basically offered a brisk wave by way of greeting, handballed the whole fiasco that is Friday afternoon at the ranch in her general direction and disappeared upstairs.

Oh my! Make-up! Hair straighteners! A bra that isn't of the maternity persuasion! I contemplate actually wearing my hair out, but just looking at the hairdryer, round brush, and smoothing serum is enough to make me want to curl into the foetal position so think better of it, lest tempting fate will mean I end up cancelling the whole thing.

I try to jazz up the existing half-tucked ponytail number, my standard hairdo of late, with a bit of teasing and hairspray. It'll just have to do. I'm so out of form when it comes to dressing up, the prospect of attempting a serviceable style for an adult evening out brings on heart palpitations. Now a slap of foundation, some eyeliner, poke myself in the eye with the mascara wand, end up with a nasty black blob tangled in my eyelashes, try to remove it with a cotton bud and merely smear it down one cheek. Shit. Wash face, start again.

Okay. War paint in place, I actually paint my toenails! The paint is so old it's gone stiff and clumps unappealingly in my cuticles; whatever. As I slip my strappy heels on, the strap trails one unset clump up my foot. Thankfully it's disguised by the strap itself, so it can stay there. Smoke and mirrors, my friends!

Frock time. I discover the summery number I had pinned my hopes on, which worked so well at Christmas down at the beach house, does not work with a conventional bra; only a bikini top really works. Hm, I've left all my swimwear at the beach house. Can I customise a bra to fit, using pins, threads

160

and a pulley system, MacGyver-style? Who am I kidding? I attempt a pair of those 'invisible' bra straps, which to their credit do manage to deceive the eye, except that where my armpit fat used to be there now look to be miniature bottoms, two cheeks apiece.

With time ticking, I whip on an old favourite, sucking in one deep breath to haul in all those still-displaced organs while zipping up. Success.

Downstairs, I am ready to have one more pre-dinner empty-out courtesy of Jelly Bean, when I discover my dress, my old faithful, was not designed with breastfeeding in mind. Should I change? Cover up? Bugger it, I haul the entire frock up and over my shoulder on first the right side, then the left, giving my children, The Chef and Sal an eyeful of my squishy belly, lily-white thighs, and my 'going out' fancy undies (lest I get hit by a bus again) Sadly, this is clearly nothing new to any in attendance and no-one bats an eye.

Right, boobs clear? Check. Dress wrestled back into place? Check. Children farewelled, even though they ignore me cause the TV is on? Check and check.

Okay. Mummy is going out for dinner.

*11:29 p.m.* What . . . a . . . night! The food! The wine! The company! The wine! The riveting conversation! The wine! The slipping in and out of hailed taxis without concern over baby seats and whether the pram will fit in the boot! The wine! I might have had a teensy weensy bit TOO much to drink. I might have a teensy-weensy headache in the morning. I might have had a teensy-weensy trip over as I tottered up the front steps and smashed a heel off my shoe and ripped a teensy-weensy tear up one side of my dress. Ahh well, it was worth it. I feel so relaxed, so free, so empowered!

*3:15 a.m.* Wake up, face in a puddle of my own drool. Jelly Bean, screaming. Floor, tilting. Head, thumping. The bloody wine!

## DO SOMETHING FOR YOURSELF

The joys and rewards of parenthood are many, and they get plenty of coverage. Less newsworthy are the sacrifices, trials and heartache. Challenges don't make as good a story as cuddles, but for parents, they are the moments that can make or break us.

To survive, both physically and mentally, it is critical to occasionally put yourself first and do something just for you. It can be as elaborate as a girls' weekend away or as simple as a weekly hobby class, so long as it is just about you.

I struggle to find time to exercise, so for me, a treat is taking out thirty minutes to pound the pavement with the dog, or hide myself away in another room and slip on a Pilates DVD. There is nothing remotely romantic about sweat and Lycra, but it's my time out to recalibrate, refocus, and most importantly BE ALONE!

As parents, sometimes the thing we crave most is some kind of affirmation that we are doing it right. Unfortunately, such affirmation is seldom forthcoming. Our kids aren't going to thank us for putting them to bed on time and making them eat their greens. However, I have developed a system whereby their most important chore each week, for which they get pocket money or TV/iPad hours, is to write me or their dad a letter, telling us about something they have done, their thoughts on something, something they would like to do. Alternatively, they can tell me about their day, with full details and plenty of embellishment. Or they can tell me a story they have made up at bedtime.

This system has multiple purposes, all positive. It forces them to engage with me and their siblings; they have to focus on the events of their day in order to be able to relate it back to me; it gives their imaginations a thorough workout; it gives me a crucial insight into their thoughts and feelings; and it improves their speaking and conversational skills. One positive outcome has been they work harder on their schoolwork, and are prepared to do other chores so they have something good to report on and receive praise for (and, let's face it, rewards). Our children seek our approval and affirmation, and we seek theirs. This system provides both, and there is nothing as sweet as snuggling up with your little one, even when they are not so little, as they strive to entertain you with a story they have concocted themselves. There is a fair chance it will feature fairies, mermaids, Barbies, superheroes, Lego and Minecraft characters, but their vivid imaginations are at work, and nothing is more rewarding than that.

# FRIDAY 13 MARCH

*6:15 a.m.* Dare I even say it? I am almost too scared to even think it lest I somehow blight this rare and wondrous occurrence (it is Friday the 13th after all, and while not naturally superstitious, I certainly suffer from a decent dose of stupidity and suggestibility) but I have to share: it looks like I am almost going to have a night to myself. (I say 'almost' as the twins will be with me, but they cannot yet dart out of my slippery grasp, fresh from the bath, to frolic wet and naked through the dusty, dirty construction site that is my front yard, eluding capture till the weight of caked mud they manage to accrue finally slows them down. Yes, I am talking to you, Princess!)

The Chef is headed away for a two-day cheffing commitment, and with my being 'grounded' (both literally and figuratively) by the twins' youth and my general unwillingness to schlep them around any capital that doesn't offer white beaches, blue seas and a 24/7 nanny service, Minnie is going in my stead for a rare weekend of dad and daughter time. Princess and Tink are being collected at lunchtime for a long-awaited weekend at Nanny Spaghetti's, while Buddy, after an evening of Mum-and-son time (otherwise known as 'hen's teeth' around here) is going suit shopping with his uncle and aunt-to-be tomorrow in preparation for his role as page boy at their upcoming wedding.

So do I plan an evening out? Book a show? Organise dinner with friends? No: I spend two hours over-packing the kids' bags, lest a heatwave and another ice age visit in the same day, compose numerous love notes to Minnie and litter them throughout her clothing, THEN record some trash television shows in preparation, put a good bottle of wine in the chill drawer, purchase a wedge of my favourite cheese (two, actually: a bitey Roquefort and an irresistibly oozy sheeps' milk cheese) and a packet of Tim Tams, and make sure my favourite tracksuit pants are not in the washing machine. I'm not proud to say it, but sometimes an evening alone really has to be an evening alone.

*6:15 p.m.* By 3 p.m., all had been shipped off, leaving only Buddy, the twins and me. In a vain attempt to suck up to my children and assuage the warped guilt I felt at looking forward to some semi-me time, I spent the morning giving in to audacious food requests, packing bags, waving the art-lovers off, watching trains on the bridge on the way to playgroup and pickling enormous cucumbers from the beach house garden in beer (one for the pot, one for me), and succumbing to Buddy's request for post-school hot dogs and curly fries from the kitsch American diner a few blocks from our home (even bought the little bugger a bloody Twinkie!). With the house quiet, I find myself at the fridge door, contemplating a simple dinner for one. The Chef's mum loaded us up with fresh eggs when collecting the girls, and there is ample leftover white vinegar and sugar from my pickling. What's the logical dinner option here? Boiled eggs with a green salad in tangy vinaigrette? No . . . pavlova? Yes! I spend another two hours assembling the stupid thing, then eat half . . . by myself . . . *sigh*.

## SATURDAY 14 MARCH

*11:15 a.m.* Up at 6 for a 7 a.m. supermarket delivery and to feed the twins and tidy the house. With a quiet moment to play with my tiny girls without distraction, I discover Lolly Pop has her two bottom teeth! When did that happen? Where were the tantrums, temperatures and gnashings of tender gums? What a superstar!

I had dragged Buddy out of bed at 8 a.m. so we could catch a 9 a.m. train into the city to attend a 10 a.m. movie (have to love those 10 a.m. kids' film screenings on a Saturday. Pump your progeny full of popcorn and choc tops, then sit back and watch them bounce off the walls like pinballs till they crash at 7 p.m. – it's like a spectator sport!).

Buddy was beside himself with excitement. He flitted about the platform, spouting train facts dredged up from his *Thomas the Tank Engine* phase, and validated his ticket with such ceremony you would think we were catching a one-way express to Disneyland. I had perhaps underestimated the significant weight and functionality difference between manoeuvring single prams and doubles on to trains, but thankfully our train was clearly ferrying a number of participants to a Good Samaritans retreat, as they came out in force to assist me.

As we whizzed into the city, Buddy carefully read out each stop to me, delighted to be putting his newfound skill to such good use. It felt so nice so be out and about, the thick mental cloud cover of discontent which has been hovering over of me of late, like an unpaid bill, slowly dissipated, even if only temporarily.

Upon arrival, like any practical mother,

SHOPPING LIST

Photo album: for all the little moments too easily forgotten

I took the kids for a pre-cinema detour to the nearest supermarket to collect snacks and drinks for about 1/1275th of the cost at the candy bar. Buddy is agog at being allowed chips AND chocolate at 10 a.m., so is more than happy to acquiesce when I force a bottle of water on him. Still bemoaning my pavlova piggery of last night, I had pre-prepared a salad to snack on, but can't resist just one Caramello Koala (ahem, king-size, cough, splutter).

We sit down, and as the opening credits begin, so too do the twins. One squawks, so I pick her up to stop her disturbing anyone then, sensing she is missing out, the other one begins. As I'm bouncing both on my lap, Buddy needs help to open his choccies so one has to return to the pram momentarily, prompting howls of protest. Then the 'shussshh'-ing begins.

It's from high up at the back of the theatre but it's insistent, following hot on the heels of every little squeak from the girls. I can feel the heat rising to my cheeks. Neither is due for a feed so I haven't heated any bottles in preparation. They are both fidgeting, however and the shushing isn't ceasing so I pack them both up, instruct Buddy not to move from his seat, and dash to the candy bar, practically dislocating a shoulder blade in my efforts to look back over my shoulder to ensure Buddy doesn't escape from the cinema.

'Hi!' I burble at the candy bar. 'Just need a hand to heat up a baby bottle?' The young attendant looks at me with such disdain I'm tempted to do a once-over to check for baby puke on my clothing. She spins on her heel and returns with a small cup full of hot tap water. What can I say? 'This ain't gonna cut it, love . . . please, go to that coffee machine and pour me some boiling water in a large cup, one that will actually accommodate the bottle, and while you're there, pour yourself a shot of "Cheer the #+% up, it might not happen."' Instead, I smile, graciously accept the cup and return to the theatre. Once back in my seat, the girls begin again and I have to chug half of the tepid water myself before cramming the bottle in. Jelly Bean went on the boob and I jiggle Lolly Pop (jiggle being a verb exclusive to the realms of baby wrangling and, perhaps, porn) as I wait for the 'hot' (ahem) water to do its magic. A minute later all I have is a cold bottle and a cold half-cup of water. Okay, second dash to the candy bar (and I do mean I actually run) for more tepid bath water. This time I'm served by a young man who immediately pointed out that they do have a microwave, up in the premium section. What?!?

I follow him, negotiating the twin pram around obstacles and through doorways not designed to accommodate it, constantly keeping an eye on the entry to our cinema. The young man disappears into a kitchen area I've no hope of squeezing into. Naturally, the bottle comes back searing hot . . . lucky I have some cold water back at my seat to cool it down!

Suffice to say, I never really got the gist of the film, being up and down through its duration like a frustrated jack-in-the-box. Buddy loved it, though, and managed to cram in a large bag of Twisties AND a large raspberry Fanta before the final credits rolled.

The next stop, naturally enough for any red-blooded boy, is the large department-store toy section, with a quick detour to the chemist for a box of extra-strength paracetamol (for me).

After another hour strolling the city streets, chatting amiably about robots, ghosts and how much he misses his sisters (cue collective: 'Awww!') I treat Buddy to a burger lunch before hooking up with Uncle Top Gun so they can go suit shopping.

Alone but for the sleeping twins on the home-bound train platform, sipping a hot, strong coffee, I marvel at the sensation of having just the two to watch over for a whole night. Relief, relaxation, tranquillity even, flood my body, sparkling through my synapses like glitter through novelty glue. It's only as I've alighted and walked halfway home that I realise I don't have my handbag, and therefore my wallet, keys or phone. Somewhere back there, perhaps on the train, perhaps in the cinema, perhaps the parents' room, or any one of numerous stops in between, the city has claimed it as its own. Bloody hell.

*3:15 a.m.* Suffice to say, managed to get in the house. No landline these days so had to borrow the neighbour's to cancel my credit cards; send a general post alerting everyone I am temporarily phone-less and only available on email. Feeling at a loose end, I resolve to have a dance with myself in the lounge room to nineties hits, before I finally fall asleep, drooling on the couch, only to be woken fifteen minutes ago by Lolly Pop. Come home, family! Your mother doesn't know how to behave when left to her own devices.

# CREATING MEMORIES

As I was waiting on the train platform at 9 a.m., my mother, Nanny Gypsy, called. When I explained where I was, she said, 'How do you do it?' My reply was simply, 'I have to; I am creating memories.'

It's so critical to occasionally go out of your way to help create magic moments your child will remember forever. Those memories of childhood we, as adults, treasure above all else. Mental snapshots of time and place that bring sights, smells and feelings flooding back.

Creating memories with your child doesn't require flying them to Paris to climb the Eiffel Tower (but hey, if you've a ticket going begging, I'm free!) or road trips visiting all the northern theme parks; it just requires making simple plans, following through on them and being entirely present.

It is so easy to 'be there' with your child bodily while really having a deep and meaningful relationship with your mobile device. Put it away and be completely present for your child. Take a short train ride, go for a stroll, watch a favourite program together and make a concerted effort to engage. Ask questions and answer their questions, after actually considering your response. Small gestures have big meanings in the eyes of your little people, and it is these moments they will truly remember and treasure forever.

# CHAPTER

## SATURDAY 21 MARCH

*9 a.m.* Uncle Wing's wedding day is upon us.

You have to love a good wedding; even a mediocre one has its charms, and they invariably end with mildly decrepit relatives of the couple shaking their groove thing to a bit of Spandau Ballet or Bryan Ferry crooning 'Slave to Love', so who is judging?

Weddings mean many things to many people. To the newly wedded, it represents the end of the long, sweet dream that is their engagement. Whereas holding hands before was love, holding hands post-nuptials probably qualifies as self-defence. For the groom's parents, it means gaining a daughter and having to install safety locks everywhere, because if the grandkids to come are anything like their son, danger lurks at every turn. For the bride's parents, they don't so much lose a daughter as gain some serious wardrobe space, as the groom can attest: his walk-in wardrobe has been magically transformed into a walk-in shoebox. For the guests, it represents free food and free booze in exchange for gifts they have no idea whether the couple will ever use but hope they like, and if they don't, hope their pawnbroker will.

Hence why I love a good wedding, and why I've never married myself. Why spoil the fun?

The day has dawned warm and sunny, but first, there are four children to bathe, one to ferry to her netball game, and then three white dresses that need to be donned and delivered to the ceremony, still on their respective owners, without being besmirched by dirt, tomato sauce or blood. Fingers crossed.

We've opted to play it safe and have Buddy get dressed on site. If we can get him the 20-odd metres from the B&B cottages attached to the venue to the actual reception without skinning a knee, wiping grotty hands on his shirt, or tripping on his shoelaces, he can then go for his life.

The Chef's mum and dad have offered to take the members of the tribe who are in the bridal party up to the venue early to be 'bedazzled' by the hair

> **SHOPPING LIST**
>
> *New beginnings*
>
> *A new maternity bra with petite straps that hide effortlessly beneath any frock, rather than revealing dumpy, greying, reinforced boulder-holders at every turn.*
>
> *A pack of those sticky things you put on your heels before donning stilettos; I am not ruining another event because of bloody blisters!*

and make-up professionals hired in for the occasion. I'm secretly thrilled. The thought of trying to get my girls to stay still long enough for me to curl their tresses and crown them with coils of baby's breath was enough to keep me awake at night. In a remarkably cohesive demonstration of how it takes a village to raise a child, Grandma and Grandpa loiter just beyond our driveway till they get the all-clear from me that Tink is taking her nap. Once she is down, they are in and round up the remaining three, ushering them to their waiting vehicle like mountain goats gone AWOL. Tink, though she has the frock and the shoes, is not an official member of the bridal party, and so I thought it best if they slip away while she sleeps to save tears and tantrums later. She is very cute but I'd steer clear of handing her the flower girl mantle at this age; she would be more likely to dump her rose petals unceremoniously and pop the basket on her head before running around the venue beeping like a Dalek than float serenely down the aisle, leaving a cloud of tenderly tossed petals in her wake.

Three down, three to go.

Paragon of physical fitness that he is, The Chef heads out to sweat all over some gym equipment. As I lurch up the stairs with my third basket of folded washing he recommends I have a workout, to 'make me feel better'.

'You think?' I splutter when I finally manage to catch my breath.

With Tink and the twins all snoozing, I make the foolish decision to get ready early. Sure enough, I'm fully dressed and made up an hour later when the babies awake. Post-feed, burping Jelly Bean, the little darling naturally heaves up all over my hair and down my back. Her chuck is so comprehensive I'm forced back into the shower, but alas, the frock cannot be saved. The only option remaining is a black-and-white number, which, given its monochrome palette, is really asking for trouble. Ah well, beggars can't be choosers!

Two hours later, we are all dressed and arrive at the designated 'Functions-R-Us'-type venue with ample time.

As one of the groomsmen, The Chef joins the huddle of testosterone surrounding his now-pacing brother for a fortifying shot of something to warm the cockles and steel the nerves.

Feeling in need of a pick-me-up myself, I order a short black and am savouring it when Tink, deciding she wants a 'cup-ha-tee', launches herself up on to the table and spills the lot, predominantly on her beautiful white dress. I manage to prevent any major stainage but she doesn't help the situation by smearing her espresso-tainted face and hands all over the front of my dress. Quite amazing that she only attacks the white panel on my dress, not the stain-forgiving black bits.

Fifteen minutes later the first guests trickle in; forty-five minutes later the pre-arranged bus from the city unloads its chattering contents, all keen to start on the cold beverages on hand. The groomsmen assemble before the ornate arbour the groom has assembled himself (between being a pilot, completely renovating his home with his own hands, being a semi-professional photographer AND the best cook I've met apart from his brother . . . sorry, ladies. He's taken!) and there is my little man, clutching his little cushion with its precious cargo.

Finally, the majestic strains of the Bridal March heralds the arrival of Princess, chucking petals with the same force you would a cricket ball; Minnie, performing her 'step, together, step, together' with concentrated grace, and the always beautiful bride, looking more radiant than any bridal-beauty cliche could do justice to. This amazing lady, Gemma, or Gem, is just that: a gem, a perfect cut diamond set amidst us cubic zirconias. She is the pinnacle of accomplishment, dedication and unaffected elegance, an incredible role model I am blessed to have in my daughters' lives. Here she comes, smiling fit to outshine the sun.

As vows are exchanged, I am presented with the most magical photo op a mother can ask for. My beautiful children, dressed to the nines: my girls in pristine, flowing white chamois with antique lace-detailed bodices. My son, dapper in his white shirt, navy-blue trousers and bow tie (and true to form, mid-vows, he approached Dad and asked him to tie his shoelace). They huddle together in a clutch of gorgeous heart wrench. Minnie poses with the poise of a seasoned performer, Buddy is hamming it up for the cameras, Princess's floral wreath has come askew on her head and she gives herself a bit of a scratch where the world's eyes best not be looking. Once the deal has been sealed with a lingering kiss, Tink joins the fray, just long enough to steal Princess and Minnie's petal baskets, dumping their contents and standing slightly away from the throng for fear someone may try to retrieve them. I cannot help it, the heady cocktail of emotion and sentiment sweeps me far from all reason and before I know it I'm crying, pawing through my impractically small handbag for tissues. Amazing that this tiny scrap of material accommodates a nappy, wipes, sunscreen, credit card and an emergency muesli bar but I could not remember to pack tissues! But we have discussed my handbag hang-ups already.

With the ceremony complete, I just have to keep holding my stomach in long enough to get through the stand-up pre-dinner drinks, then it will be towering heels off and on with the slip-ons I've squirrelled away in my seemingly bottomless clutch. That's when the real fun begins!

*12:45 a.m.* Midnight has struck and after a very long day and some manic dancing (much to everyone's delight), my beautiful babes have turned into pumpkins. We carefully unload each one directly on to their beds, stripping off shoes, bow ties and headpieces but letting them doze in the rest of their finery.

I wake Lolly Pop for a bottle and a cuddle, before rousing Jelly Bean to relieve my aching chest. Once the babies are back in bed, The Chef and I are quick to slip between the sheets, deliciously anticipating a long sleep-in, when two little figures appear in our doorway, in the form of our eldest and her partner in crime, her younger brother.

'Can we watch our iPads? It's the weekend and we haven't watched them all day!'

Kids! Talk about wringing every minute from the day!

'No! Now get to bed!'

## MONDAY 23 MARCH

*11:23 a.m.* Dinner – why do I even bother? No matter what I put on the table, regardless of how exquisite or simple, complex or basic, there will be a hue and cry, refusals to eat, tantrums and tears, before either they willingly relent and eat, or

SHOPPING LIST

*Vegetables*

I leave said meal on the table until they profess hunger, at which point the only option I'm willing to present is the now-cold, semi-congealed matter glued to the crockery that was once a hot dish. Either way, by hook or by crook, they will eat.

Tuesday is my market day so Monday's meal is never fair of face, more a hodge-podge of whatever is left in the bottom of the chill drawer. Today's mystery box throws up an assortment of root veg, beans and corn, and there are lentils in the pantry, along with tinned beans and stock. Vegetable soup it is.

This particular dish is always divisive. Sometimes they love it, frequently they hate it, purely because the word 'vegetable' is included in the title.

Bread rolls are always a welcome accompaniment, but they are often all the little brats will eat. I need an option that will satisfy their desire for simple carbs, but still ensures they are getting a healthy dose of vitamins.

Time to play in the test kitchen.

After preparing some steamed carrot and steamed pumpkin purees, I fiddle around with a savoury scone mix, adding equal proportions of purée to flour. To the pumpkin mix I add crisped and shredded bacon and grated Cheddar; to the carrot I add mixed seeds, parsley and black pepper. The wet dough is cut into rounds, basted with a little milk and baked for ten minutes in a hot oven, and the end product is gorgeous little circles of brilliant orange (always a hit with kids – it's the same colour as Cheezels and Fanta!) that resemble a fat, crisp-skinned cookie, but are soft and pillowy in the centre. Perfect for soaking up hot soup, and composed of 50 per cent vegetables!

And so, the Soup Penny (trademark pending) is born!

## SOUP PENNIES

225 g self-raising flour
250 ml vegetable purée (eg: peas, pumpkin, carrot, sweet potato)
50 g butter
50 g brown sugar
1 egg
125 ml milk
generous pinch salt
handful of toasted mixed seeds/walnuts/finely chopped herbs/crumbled crispy bacon/chopped ham/grated tasty cheese/crumbled feta/drained tinned salmon

(My faves are a carrot base with parsley and black pepper, and pumpkin with grated cheddar and bacon, and peas with feta and mint)

1.  Preheat oven to 200°C and line a baking tray with grease paper.
2.  Cream butter and sugar.
3.  Stir in purée, adding egg, then half the milk, a little at a time.

4. Sift in the flour and work into a wet dough.
5. Stir in any additional ingredients.
6. Turn out on to a floured surface, roll to 3 cm thickness and cut into rounds.
7. Place rounds evenly on tray, brush with remaining milk.
8. Bake for 15 minutes or until golden brown.

NB: They won't rise as high as traditional scones, but will form crusty little rounds more akin to a puffy dollar, hence the name!

Enjoy dipped in soup, as an accompaniment to salad, stuffed with tuna, egg, or whatever takes your fancy, or just lashed with butter and gobbled up warm.

## FEEDING THE HORDES THROUGH THE AGES: SOME TIPS FROM A SURVIVOR

It never ceases to amaze me how, as parents, our most concerted efforts at good parenting are so frequently thwarted by self-doubt, fear of failure, and a general sense that we just don't know what we are doing. This is never more apparent than at meal times.

Feeding children requires military precision. The food must be nutritionally rich and mindful of intolerances, yet must look and taste appealing enough to ensure it gets eaten. It must land on the table at a time that strikes the perfect balance between when they are hungry and alert and when they are too over-tired and sated on snacks to eat a meal. Finally, once you have finished preparing the bloody thing, catering to all their peculiarities and idiosyncrasies, their likes and dislikes, they must be assisted in actually eating the damn thing. This is not unique to babies and toddlers, new to the arts of mastication and digesting solids; I've been known to spoon-feed a six-year-old if it means their nutritional needs are met and, more importantly, they won't re-emerge from bed at 8 p.m. claiming to be 'starving'.

My brood's reaction to my meals leaves me feeling a failure at least once a day, and when a lovingly, thoughtfully prepared hot meal meets a lukewarm reception, I want to blow my top! Especially when I'm forced to spoon-feed multiple mouths with multiple meals only to have 70 per cent of it spat back at me, the table and even the walls.

The advantage of having so many children, beyond developing excellent reflexes for catching spat-out food before it hits the wall, the carpet, or my couture, is that I've gone through the process enough times to have gleaned a few general tips others might just find useful.

1. Do not disguise food. Grated zucchini hidden in bolognese? Puréed carrot lurking in the sausage rolls? Unless it has a specific purpose or taste profile, don't relegate vegetables to something that must be pulverised and dressed up to be palatable.

   Children must learn to appreciate and enjoy the appearance, flavour and texture of vegetables in their own right, even if it takes a lengthy period of re-offering them to get there. 'Sneaking' nutritious food into their diets only delays the inevitable and enforces habits and phobias which will be harder to break the older they get.

   Give kids a story and teach them about the provenance of food and seasonality. Better still, create a garden of your own! Even if it's just herbs in pots or tomatoes on the balcony. Pique their interest, get kids involved and you will set them up with good eating habits and a healthy respect for food for life.

2. Introducing babies to solids. This is such a contentious issue; some argue that you should feed them early to fight the chance of allergies, others that you should introduce them later for the very same reason. In my experience, babies are ready for solids when *they* are ready. There is no point in forcing them and they will let you know with cues and gestures that are hard to miss. It begins with watching you eat, following the motion of hand to mouth. Next they may show an alertness to the smells of food. Finally, they may start mimicking the movements of chewing.

   When you feel they are ready to begin, LET THEM PLAY WITH THEIR FOOD.

   I know this sounds counterintuitive, but I find spoon-feeding at a very young age pointless. Before they turn one and their molars come in, the facial muscle structure of babies is built only to suck, so when food on a spoon is presented, their tongue goes forward to suckle and any food that makes it into the mouth is promptly pushed out, all over them and all over you. Also, finely puréed food is not an ideal introduction; there is no point in blurring the lines between liquids and solids when they each require a different manner of consumption.

Instead, when they indicate they are ready, ideally when they are old enough to sit up in a high chair, offer them soft solids, such as a portion of mashed boiled potato, mashed avocado, rusks or banana. Things they can grasp with their hands and mimic the hand-to-mouth action, gnaw, but not necessarily consume large amounts of. The end goal is not to initially sate their hunger but to teach them the action of eating. Be extremely conscientious in gauging where your child is at developmentally. If they are simply not ready, EVERY FOOD is a potential choking hazard.

The other wonderful advantage of this method is that if they're allowed to play with their food, they will have skin contact with a variety of foods before they actually ingest them. If an underlying allergy exists, you will be alerted to it by mild irritation,
a rash or just general discomfort, rather than a terrifying race to the emergency department. Also, young children have excellent intuition. If a food makes them itch or causes them discomfort they will not want to touch it again. Win win!

3. Don't sit for hours forcing food down their throats. One thing having many children teaches you is that they will eat when they are hungry; no child will let themselves starve. There are not enough hours in the day to cater to behaviour which, when repeated, teaches them that if they act up and refuse to eat they win your undivided attention. And that old chestnut of putting an uneaten meal aside until they are hungry works a treat if you follow through with it.

4. Involve kids in the cooking; it is absolutely incredible just what kids will eat when they prepare it with their own hands.

Vegetable stir-fry anyone? Princess harvested a bunch of vegies one afternoon, patiently chopped them with her little safety knife, and chose some sauces in which The Chef stir-fried the crop, and she hoovered down the lot!

A favourite 'whole family' dinner activity in our household is to let them each choose a vegetable to harvest or buy, and let them decide how it will be prepared (it will probably involve butter, but a bit of good butter never hurt anyone). Condition is: they must eat it AND whatever veg their siblings choose.

5. This one will be controversial, but good sense dictates that it is right – and deep down, we all know it. Don't give your kids too much processed, packaged food (I know, I know! I can hear your children screeching in protest at the supermarket aisle from here!).

   For time-poor parents navigating rife food allergies, the convenience and ample labelling of packaged foods is undeniable. But so too are the rises in diabetes, childhood obesity, and a loss of appreciation for what real food is and where it comes from.

   I'm not suggesting banning it altogether; we don't want to make such foods taboo, thus heightening their appeal. A party isn't a party without Smarties and Twisties, and heaven help anyone who tries to separate me from an open pack of Tim Tams, but these are 'sometimes' treats that shouldn't be confused with daily lunchbox fillers.

   I'm not suggesting you install an industrial kitchen, but what's a few minutes to slice up carrot sticks? To pop a handful of rice crackers and cubed cheese in a snap-lock bag? To box up last night's leftover pasta with tuna and corn kernels for a tasty, economical lunch? Sometimes the smallest effort yields the greatest rewards.

6. Show your children where food comes from. A backyard veggie patch is ideal but not realistic for everyone. Planter boxes are a terrific, compact option, and even pots, sown with vegetable seeds or seedlings, make an attractive addition to porches or windowsills. If neither of these take your fancy, visit a farm or

even a local nursery. Seeing fresh fruit and vegetables in their natural state, ripe from the tree or field, is illuminating. Even more so when a child has grown them themselves. That first crop of cherry tomatoes is always the sweetest. A carrot, plucked from the ground and given a quick scrub, always has the perfect crunch. An apple, leaves still attached, tucked into the lunchbox the day after it was picked, is utterly irresistible. Making the effort to take your children to buy milk from a small-yield dairy farmer, with the very cows who produced it grazing peacefully in the background, has greater rewards than just a tasty cup of tea. These things teach our children about the importance of whole foods and knowing what they are, where they come from, what time of year they are best to eat, and how to eat in a manner that is not just good for our bellies, but good for the planet.

## FRIDAY 27 MARCH

*6:15 p.m.* It's here. I've been avoiding it for as long as politeness and excuses would allow, but tonight, I'm attending the *Neighbours* thirtieth anniversary celebration.

What this means, essentially, is being confronted by a past I left behind thirteen years ago; that of a girl whose body I inhabited but whom I barely remember, and whose wants, needs and motivations now utterly baffle me.

SHOPPING LIST

*Patience, fashion sense, a pair of strappy killer heels*

Knowing this date was looming, creeping stealthily towards me through the calendar grid, a sensible and warranted reaction would have been to buy a new dress, of course. But of course, I leave it until the very day of the event.

The invite specifies 'cocktail'... crap. Cocktail? For me, that term only has relevance if there's a frosted, salt-rimmed glass involved, or perhaps an olive or maraschino cherry. The closest my frocks come to 'cocktail' are the occasional lurid stains some boast where the dry cleaner didn't do his job.

So, once the house is organised and pre-school kids ensconced with Sal, I'm off to seek some sartorial satisfaction.

My habit of hiding behind bright colours and bold prints (a direct conse-quence of my shyness, actually) has led me to many a fashion faux pas, and so I'm taking The Chef's sage advice and going simple. A well-cut LBD would be just the ticket. Always almost impossible to find, the fashion-forward woman's *Moby Dick*, yet I'm prepared to go the hard yards because only perfection will do.

So I buy the first thing I see . . . and it doesn't even fit.

Party panic got to me again.

So begins the mad dash to find a dressmaker to do the necessary altera-tions on the spot. Miraculously, I find one wily enough to practically sew me into the damn thing. Terrified I won't be able to wrangle the zip back up, I decide to stay in it till the event. Now, in theory this makes perfect sense; in practice it's bloody ridiculous. I can't bend over to paint my exposed toenails, so look like I've dropped a pot of red ink and my feet copped the resultant splatter. I can't feed Jelly Bean, but stick stubbornly to my resolve. She is happy to take a bottle but by the time I get home tonight my swollen chest will probably have busted open the seams of my frock anyway. I'm starving but dare not eat lest I bulge where I do not care to, so one glass of bubbles will probably transform me into a babbling fool, like Cinderella in reverse. I just can't seem to get my make-up right, my hair refuses to sit nicely, the Mickey Mouse band-aids I've secreted under the vicious straps of my unforgiving high heels just won't stay hidden. After sweating over which bloody earrings to wear, I fumble putting them in and snap a post. Noooooooo!

Hang on . . . what's going on here? Then I realise: the prospect of return-ing to the environment and the faces from that time, so long ago, has sent me toppling back, reviving all the silly insecurities and obsessions of youth which so plagued me back then. I look in the mirror, appraising the lines and spots which ain't going anywhere without the kind of touch-ups I will never succumb to. Those same lines and spots signify that I am a woman now, hurtling toward middle age, in a wonderful relationship that has, somehow, survived six kids, no less. I guess there is something in that old notion of wrinkles being a badge of honour, even if I still think it sounds a bit wanky.

And so I held my head high, let it go, and booked my taxi. Admittedly, when it still hadn't arrived fifteen minutes later, I might have hyperventilated just a little. Ditto when The Chef called to say he was running an hour and a half late to meet me. I was a survivor – sewn into a dress, with boobs on the verge of an atomic meltdown, wearing Mickey Mouse band-aids, but a survivor none the less.

*7:45 p.m.* I . . . am . . . an . . . alien . . . freshly come to Earth . . . and I know not what to do!

No, I haven't been hitting the magic mushrooms, nor smoking no peace pipe; I'm just so red-carpet rusty any photo with me in the frame must resemble an advert for discount-store dummies. Hang on, I'm waging a concerted inner war convincing my abdominal muscles to behave, so best make that a constipated discount-store dummy.

Once inside, the nerves subsided, and the impulses of my attention-seeking youth did not take over. I felt no compulsion to chase the cameras, contort myself into entertainment-page-worthy poses (one leg forward, knee softly bent, rotate hips into profile, chest front-on to camera, face slightly tilted to best utilise available light, come-hither smile gently playing on lips, pronounced enough to make clear it is a smile not a grimace, subtle enough not to invoke too many wrinkles), or placing myself strategically in front of the assembled press pack. Instead, I felt light. I engaged with my former castmates, many, having greater stamina than I, still playing those same characters, and chatted amiably about all that has come to pass since my departure. Just as my energy started to flag, my gorgeous man arrived. We did a dutiful round of 'hellos' and 'goodbyes', and slipped away unnoticed for a nightcap. I managed to drag away one of my gorgeous former castmates, now friend and fellow survivor, to join us and when The Chef's incomparable mentor, former boss, and now dear friend, on a flying visit from Europe, appeared out of the rainy night, our little company shared a bottle of red and some fabulous milk ice-cream and chocolate soufflés amid much political opining and laughter.

The evening's true highlight awaited us at home. Six children fast asleep in their beds. I tiptoe in to give each a feather-light kiss, and then drift off myself, suffused with the euphoria of a good night out. Sometimes it is critical to be just you: sassy, independent, carefree you. Mummy-you will be waiting to reclaim you the minute you walk back through the front door, so enjoy the spoils of freedom wherever and whenever they present themselves. A mini-break is as good as a holiday.

*3:15 a.m.* Funny how fast the euphoria wears off once the reality of teething babies kicks back in. Jelly Bean and Lolly Pop take turns to squeak, squall and cry their way through the early hours of the morning. I, meanwhile, buoyed by a few hours stepping out of the domestic routine, find myself toying with the notion of a long-overdue family holiday. The Chef has a few days' work in Queenstown coming up . . . hmmmm, might drag the tribe along on his coat tails, and follow up a few days in the snow with a few days in the sun, somewhere where kids are welcome and the locals will gladly take them off your hands. Gee, that narrows it down. Might have to purchase a sun lamp and holiday at the local crèche!

## THE MANY JOYS OF TEETHING

Getting a new set of gnashers is no fun for anyone, be they a young child with pearly white baby teeth pushing through red, swollen gums, or senior citizens having their tea-stained teeth ripped out before upgrading to a pair of Hollywood Smile dentures. It's a phase; it will pass, but always have on hand:
• Amber beads: do nothing for some kids, work miracles for others.
• Bonjela: store in fridge for soothing, cold application.
• Teething rings, rubbed with Baby Panadol and kept in the freezer.
• Shares in Baby Panadol.

## THURSDAY 2 APRIL

*9:45 a.m.* Holiday obsession growing. Probably gaining urgency because the term draws to a close tomorrow and I'm surrounded by people spouting off about their Easter holiday destinations. We have decided to ship shop down to the little hideaway for two quiet, lazy weeks of R&R. Sal will be taking the whole period off, taking a brief spell to have a long-awaited surgical procedure, so I'm girding my loins for her absence, but am quietly looking forward to the silly nostalgia of Easter egg hunts and unfettered family time. Minnie and Buddy are enrolled in surf camp on the second week, so much fun awaits. I'm also feeling calm, composed and quietly chuffed with myself as I've been slowly stockpiling chocolate treats over the past few weeks, so now I am Easter-ready without having to make any last-minute dashes to the supermarket for poor-quality, foil-wrapped rubbish just to make up the numbers. While it terrifies me, I am also relishing the prospect of being in proximity to all that Easter fare. Hot cross buns? PHWOOOAR! There is something deeply sensual about the caress of melting butter across their fruit-flecked, spicy, tangy, fluffy flanks. Ooh, a good bun has me coming over all Nigella. And chocolate eggs, bunnies, chicks, whatever. There is some undeniable trait in the structural integrity of moulded chocolate

> SHOPPING LIST
>
> Dental floss (fancy kind that is waxed and also fluffy)
>
> Holiday brochures
>
> Fake tan (gotta practise so fake tan looks completely natural when arrive on holiday, then can work on real tan undetected)

that makes it taste so much better than it would in block form. You know it's true. Chocolate eggs are irresistible. Mmm, bring it on.

## FRIDAY 3 APRIL

*10:15 a.m.* Bugger, bugger, bugger. The Chef informed me last night he had invited a 'few' friends down over the Easter break. The actual list gave me hives immediately. Have bought no Easter goodies for any of them, am now forced to scramble about like apocalypse-espousing harridan, trying to gather up

> SHOPPING LIST
>
> Anything remotely egg-shaped wrapped in something approximating decorative foil.

as many Easter-themed chocolate vittles as possible, like a bloody hamster (actually, make that squirrel) desperately collecting acorns before winter. Of course, the quality chocolate providers have nothing left. Nothing for it but to head to the supermarket. Sigh . . .

## EASTER WEEKEND

*11 a.m.* Every man, his dog, his aunt, her dog, the local postman, and the neighbour at the end of the street you have never shared two words with but who once picked up your wheelie bin when it had fallen over on bin day and to whom you now nod on the way from the car to the front door, has visited us in the past week for 'a day or two' and the flood doesn't look like subsiding any time soon. As at Christmas, I have spent most of that time, once again, hiding in the laundry ironing or pretending to do so. My greatest respite comes from indulging in a little intellectual wordplay with you, dearest diary. For me, it seems nothing soothes the anxious beast better than the written word.

Still, a week in and I'm more tired than before the 'holiday' started.

Accordingly, my obsession with taking an actual family holiday, somewhere that has cleaners, cooks and child-minders, and where I am not expected to do any of the above, or change a single piece of bed linen, or wake up knowing there are baying hordes waiting at the refrigerator door to be fed (not including my children), and where I don't have to make small talk endlessly with new faces every few days, has reached fever pitch.

> SHOPPING LIST
>
> A maid
>
> A butler
>
> A personal chef
>
> A year's supply of fresh linen
>
> A good lie-down with a damp face washer across my eyes

Okay, so perhaps I'm being a right cow and have no right to be banging on like this, but when you throw six not yet independent children who still largely need their parents to do everything for them into the equation alongside our guests, phew, the situation is starting to resemble a carelessly loaded moving van with bits of poorly secured furniture threatening to topple off in the middle of a three-lane freeway, shedding bits of loose paper, padding and toiletries at every turn.

Clearly the only solution is to open a bottle of wine before lunch and accept that these dishwasher hands are not gonna heal any time soon. However, there is an actual holiday on the horizon and the promise of that alone is enough to steel my constitution. Must keep moving, the ironing awaits!

*7:10 p.m.* Text message from Sal. Her doctor recommends she take another week off to recover. Oh dear . . .

## SATURDAY 11 APRIL

*3:30 p.m.* Amid the revolving-door chaos of the Easter break, my darling little boy's birthday has almost been lost. With school starting Tuesday, we resolve to leave early on Saturday so we can celebrate his big day back in town. I scrape together what ingredients we have left in the fridge in the hope of throwing together a chocolate cake to mark the occasion.

Cars loaded, we set out only to discover that today there is a huge bike race along most of our route, hence we spend an inordinate amount of time sitting stationary in our vehicles admiring the fluoro race gear of the riders passing us by. Happy birthday, Buddy!

Finally we arrive, many hours after we had planned, and as I flit about unpacking, writing lists and disposing of forgotten perishables, The Chef and the three eldest, perhaps inspired by hours exposed to Lycra-bound riders, have set out to get Buddy a bike for his birthday. Several hours, bike shops, soft drinks and grey hairs later the tribe returns with not one but two mountain bikes, Minnie having somehow sold The Chef on the idea of getting her birthday present early. Not so crazy when I remember I cajoled The Chef into buying me a bike, a beautiful burnt umber vintage specimen, for my birthday, two years ago, and still haven't ridden it once.

The Chef has previously taken the kids for a practice ride on their fancy machines and so, immediately inspired, I announce that I'm taking the troops out to the park for a practice ride too. The Chef nearly falls over when I wheel out my bike, brushing off the cobwebs.

Fifteen minutes later, the kids are now giddily hooning around the padded, grassy safety of the backyard, while I sulk, folding laundry with a bag of frozen corn kernels down the back of my pants, soothing my bruised coccyx. Having wheeled our bikes to the park, me with my gorgeous sunset-orange machine, strutting like a rooster with a barn full of chickens, I'd managed a lap of the park before toppling off, straight on to the backside, grazed bum cheeks, orange paint flying, bike scratched to buggery.

Suffice to say it is now safely back in the cobwebs where it belongs.

> SHOPPING LIST
>
> *Bloody birthday candles . . . how the hell do I not have a single bloody birthday candle in the house?*

## TUESDAY 14 APRIL

*4:30 p.m.* Officially losing my mind . . . Sal! Please! Come back!

Desperately need a break, ready to fling myself on one of those wanky 'mystery flights', even if it means winding up in Adelaide looking at churches – I don't care!

First day back, Minnie and Buddy now have dry-land ski training to add to their growing list of activities (yeah, yeah, I know) which means a 7 a.m. start, then I drop Princess at 8:30. The day slipped by: ballet class for Tink, grocery shopping, put all three littlies down for a nap and made a batch of eyeball cupcakes for Buddy's coming party. At 2:30, I woke and fed the trio, then buckled everyone in to head to the school for pick-up. On track. Turned the key and . . . nothing. Battery dead. Noooooo!

I proceeded to try turning the key in a variety of styles: really quickly, really slowly, quick-then-slooooooow, to no effect.

With five minutes until Princess was due to be collected, and having fumed and beat the dashboard before turning the ignition one last time, I slumped back and suffered a brain freeze. What to do? Call The Chef? And what? Have him collect the kids telepathically from the *Masterchef* set? The neighbour? Nah, her driveway is empty; she's already gone to collect her own brood. Call another mum at the school? Might be a possibility were there just one extra child to collect, but three? And I don't know any mums or dads boasting a minivan, or at least any with spare seats! Get a taxi? How many taxis accommodate seven, including three infant seats and a booster? I could take out all my car seats, install them in a maxicab . . . oh, this is getting ridiculous.

> SHOPPING LIST
>
> *Tranquilliser darts*
>
> *Target practice (must master the art of shooting self in bum as can't do needles)*

I called the school, let them know I was running a wee whisker late, strapped Lolly Pop into one seat of the twin stroller, Tink into the other, slung Jelly Bean into the Baby Bjorn, and trudged up to the school. Now, I know, this would probably be the first option most would come up with when faced with a flat battery. But that would require one ingredient I seem to be running low on these days: logic. And it presented the chance I might sweat, which doesn't sit well with me at the best of times.

Suffice to say, all were collected in a timely manner, and we made the return trip amid much whinging (Minnie), asking of questions (Buddy) and lengthy pauses to investigate bugs, leaf matter, and other people's rubbish (Princess).

Roadside assist was waiting for me upon my return (yay) and I've just discovered that somewhere along the way someone has stepped in doggy doodoo and walked it into the house. Great . . .

*5:30 p.m.* Bath time. Try to implement time-saving measure by bathing four youngest kids all at once. Water everywhere. As I lift out Lolly Pop, Tink lunges for my arm. I twist awkwardly, trying to re-establish my balance with babe in arms, slipping on the wet tiles in the process, and go down, slamming ribs on the lip of the bath as I fall. I kept Lolly Pop upright and safe, but I've hurt my back, badly. Now plan to self-medicate the only way I know how: by falling into a large pack of Tim Tams.

*12:30 a.m.* Can't sleep . . . my back . . . and my digestive system . . . *sigh.*

## THURSDAY 16 APRIL

*2 a.m.* Still no sleep . . . back . . . and rendered sleepless by thought of dragging myself through another day like yesterday, with all six in tow and my back in its current state of dysfunction.

I believe I've hit rock bottom.

I'm exhausted, strung out, borderline insane, and that's all before breakfast. My body aches, my mind aches, my willpower aches. This is ludicrous.

Kids sense I'm doing it tough. Start helping me.

SHOPPING LIST

Shopping? I've no time for shopping! And besides, I don't have enough arms to carry it home with!

NB: Must get a giant 'SOS' symbol, like they have in the desert when they need rescuing. Must fit in the backyard and be highly visible, especially to anyone with child-minding experience.

## FRIDAY 17 APRIL

*3 p.m.* Shoot me. Shoot me now.

Sal's recovery has extended unexpectedly for another two weeks, hence I've been struggling with the return to school and extra-curricular activities solo. The Chef has pitched in where possible, but his commitments at work have been mounting, and with *Masterchef* in finals week he is burning the candle at both ends too. No time to write, dear diary, hands are full juggling children! But I had the little monkeys so gotta keep them balls in the air!

The days alternate between being an endless expanse of chores, stretching out interminably, and flying by in the blink of an eye, just a flurry of breathless hustle and bustle. And today is my big, seven-year-old boy's birthday party.

SHOPPING LIST

*That extra set of hands I've been seeking since 2005.*

*NB: If found, please order double.*

When organising the whole affair weeks ago, in a moment of rationality and clarity, I'd contemplated outsourcing the whole thing. Then of course thought, 'Nah, I've got this covered . . . I'll organise everything, set it all up and make the food. Hey, I've got Sal, my saviour, ready and willing to help, what can go wrong?' Famous last words . . .

Naturally, despite my urging in the direction of a superhero party (read: category boasting lots of widely available party accessories) Buddy decides on a zombie theme . . . in April. Would be all very well and easy as pie come October, with Halloween just around the commercial corner, but not in bloody April. So, of course, the invites had to be hand drawn and printed up, and the party favours carefully sourced and tweaked to fit. (Who am I kidding, I loved every minute!) Accordingly, I've just spent the last four hours sticking zombie paraphernalia to every possible surface, stringing up inflatable ghouls, laying out a 'blood-splattered' plastic tablecloth, and applying 'Warning: Zombies' police tape to the walls.

The Chef again very kindly offered up a room at one of his venues for the party (clever man, it was that or listen to me whinge about how terrible any alternative venue was for the next four months) and offered up his pastry chef (lamb to the slaughter) to design a cake. I had already designed a disembodied eyeball as the invitation, and was planning to make cupcakes along the same lines, so a giant, chocolate sponge-filled eyeball was just the ticket.

In the days leading up to the event, I've transformed into the domestic goddess on crack, flinging myself around the kitchen whipping up ghoulish goodies between school drop-offs and pick-ups while using any opportunity to escape the three tiny tots (hello, Disney junior channel, Foxtel, I love you!) and stuff lolly bags, piñatas and my mouth with all manner of teeth-rotting deliciousness. Yesterday, I'd just pulled a pot of hot honey-joy mix off the stove to fill patty pans when I glanced at the clock to discover it was already 2:45 p.m. Where has the day gone? Between changing nappies, a quick trip to the park to blow off steam, a bit of tidying and laundry, prepping dinner and now making the final party treats, those precious hours between 8:30 and 3 had somehow evaporated, leaving me still in my trackies, hair sticking in greasy strands to my sweaty forehead, having not sat down or managed a bite to eat all day. Instinctively, I ducked into the laundry, away from the prying eyes of little Tink, who was tiring of Peppa Pig in the other room, and shovelled a great wad of the gooey mix into my mouth.

'Ffffff-yaaaaaa-AAAARK!!'

Red-hot, molten sugar-coated cornflakes clung to my tongue and the roof of my mouth, inflicting what felt like third-degree burns as I attempted to spit it out on to the sink while huffing and puffing in a vain attempt to cool what remained adhering.

Alerted by my screeching, Tink tottered over to check out what the heck all the ruckus was about to find me dancing a jig while trying to operate the cold water tap with cornflake-encrusted fingers. She spotted my trail of honey joy mix and promptly started eating it, straight off the floor. Ah well, it was very hot originally; surely that means it's hygienic?

Anyway, I then bundled up the little 'uns and headed off to school pick-up, determined to mime out having developed fast-onset laryngitis. How the heck else was I going to explain not being able to talk?

*4:25 p.m.* Kids collected from school and appropriately zombified (torn-up clothes, talcum powder on the face, purple eyeshadow under the eyes, the odd eyeliner scar and teased hair), we get stuck in a bloody traffic jam.

Going to be late for own party. Fantastic.

*4:40 p.m.* Made it. Guests all assembled and milling about. What secret back streets did they all take? Little boys all in their Halloween finest dragging themselves about, zombie-style. Cute.

*5 p.m.* The Spider-Man I've booked to provide entertainment (they don't see fit to offer Frankenstein for kids' parties, apparently) seems a bit surly. Asks for his 'cash' straight up and has holes in his costume, as a number of the kids point out. Getting the sense he is one of those children's entertainers who hates children.

*5:30 p.m.* Have done a sly Q&A with all parents assembled: this guy is definitely a dud. Hmm.

*5:45 p.m.* Wrap up Spider-Man before he starts on a Shakespearean monologue and settle the kids with hot food.

*6 p.m.* Cake! Hurrah! Buddy has a mild meltdown over the Spider-Man debacle, but rallies at the sight of the giant, fondant-iced eyeball, and the 'oooohs' and 'aaaahs' it evokes from his friends.

*6:10 p.m*: Cake done. Is it only 6:10? What do we do for the next twenty minutes?

*6:15 p.m.* Oh, thank goodness, the piñata! Clearly this is precisely the purpose piñatas were invented for: to fill time with physical exertion as you are winding up a kids' party.

*6:25 p.m.* Piñata popped after much whacking with a broomstick; the kids had a go too. Quite cathartic for me at the end of a long day. Kids all stuffed with lollies, parents stuffed with catering provided by The Chef's fabulous staff, everyone slowly peeling away and heading home.

*6:45 p.m.* With all hands on deck, clean-up is quick and simple. Both grandmothers simultaneously offer to take a few kids next weekend. By my reckoning, that equals a whole weekend with just the twins, The Chef and myself. Priceless . . .

## SUNDAY 26 APRIL

*6:10 a.m.* Why is it that on school mornings, I practically have to lever the children from their beds at 7 a.m. with a hammer and chisel, yet when they can sleep in to their hearts' content come Sunday, they are all up by 6 a.m.? WHY??? Resolve to summarily ignore them. Roll over and pull pillow over head. Bugger off!

*2:15 p.m.* Eventually emerge from bed long enough to have shower. Nanny Spaghetti will be arriving soon, as The Chef and I are headed out for a well-deserved afternoon at the football (I can look forward to it with glee as we have been invited to a corporate box!). The moment I step into that cab (yes, there is a good chance alcohol may be involved) I feel light, carefree, almost giddy with freedom. Oh, why did we have so many munchkins?

Within twenty minutes of arriving I have the phone out, giving anyone who will pay attention a virtual slide show of my proudest parenting moments, to a chorus of cooing and admiration.

Aahhh, yes. That's why I had so many kids.

# TUESDAY 28 APRIL

*5:19 a.m.* Goodness, it's been a while since I've been up diarising my memoirs at this ungodly hour! Both Tink and Jelly Bean woke in the night with fevers. Two sick kids, soon to topple all the others like so many dominoes . . . why didn't we install a bloody quarantine room?

My mind whirs, equating how I can balance out doctors' appointments with school drop-offs and karate class, then remember: Sal is back today. Hallelujah!

*10:23 a.m.* Tidying up the kids' school bag drawer, I find an invitation stuck to the bottom of Princess's library bag. Unlike the standard invites I find in the vicinity of my children's belongings, however, this one does not boast superheroes, fairies or anime figures. Its intricate silver script swirls and curls across classic black vellum. It's a grown-up party invite, to a grown-up party, this Saturday night! It is for the 50th birthday of a good friend of The Chef, a celebration I knew was looming but had pushed to the back of my mind among the other detritus of a busy life, gathering dust and mothballs. Dang! A quick scan of the details reveals . . . no . . . please . . . it can't be! Black tie!!!

SHOPPING LIST

Dry dog food

Bulk buy baby paracetamol

Teeny-tiny thermometer batteries

Bugger. Broke thermometer trying to install teeny-tiny batteries.

New thermometer

Now, as you and I both know, dearest diary, if a dress code meanders beyond 'lounge suit', I develop a nasty rash and start talking gibberish. Black tie?

I think I was born without the 'couture' gene, and frankly, I only ever attend award ceremonies and the like because there is a good chance someone will dress me, someone will feed me, and someone will give me a goody bag at the end.

Hence, I don't actually own anything that qualifies as 'black tie', and have resigned myself to the fact I will need to go and buy a frock. I know this proposition would send shivers of delight up the spines of many women, and more than a few men, but all it gives me is a cold, quaking dread and sweaty armpits. Yep, can't wait to rock into a few boutiques, asking to sample their finery, wild of eye and damp of underarm.

*12:25 p.m.* Oh joy! Rapture! The impossible, the unthinkable, the Ripley's believe-it-or-not has happened. No, the dress code hasn't changed to 'denim', but by some miracle I have found a frock!

With the contents of the school bag drawer tidied, I consulted with Dr Google to help treat my frocklessness. Admittedly, my searches were probably doomed to never get results. Typing in 'pretty dresses' and my postcode merely led me to a children's ballet school and an advertisement for a drag night at a venue around the corner. Good to know.

My second plan of attack was a dress drive-by, which involves just driving around the nearest shopping strip, hoping for the best. As luck would have it, the first street I targeted boasted a Carla Zampatti boutique, and there in the window posed one of the most exquisite samples of couture I have ever laid eyes on. This thing was the stuff of sartorial wet dreams. Electric blue (my favourite shade, as seen in all my best accessories), floor-length, slim-cut with a fetching split up the back, covered bodice terminating in a delicate halter which enclosed the neck then twisted down the back to wrap under the bust, while displaying the shoulders and collar bones (my favourite feature) to full effect.

I actually hit the brakes and very nearly caused a suburban lunchtime pile-up. Road raging to the nearest available car park, I swung into the store and pounced on the manager, breathing raggedly and pointing frantically at the frock and then at myself. Clearly fluent in Over-Excited Shopper, she immediately brought it down from the display, passed it to me, and directed me to the dressing room without saying a thing. Sometimes there is no need for words.

It was perfect; just my size – except too long, too small in the bust, too big in the hips. Details, details.

As she steered me towards the register, the assistant informed me it was the last they had, and they had been going to send it to the online store that very afternoon. This was all very gratifying for me as it really isn't a miracle purchase without the miracle backstory to go with it.

Cradling my gown like a fragile baby bird, I dazedly wandered into the nearest shoe store, and not wanting to tamper with my great run thus far, seized the first pair of shoes that bore some approximation of matching the dress. Again, my size and ON SALE! Clearly destiny had stepped in, taken my hand, and was guiding me through what would go down in history as the most successful shopping experience of my life.

I bundled my precious cargo into the car and in a moment of caution buoyed by exuberance, strapped them into Lolly Pop's capsule. Not wanting to take any chances, we drove immediately to the dressmaker recommended by the sales assistant to have some slight imperfections in my dream dress sorted.

Once pinned in, the promise of the end product gracing the mirror before me, I felt I could finally breathe out, and would have if it hadn't still been so bloody tight. 'Black tie' decoded.

My anxiety faded away and I am now actually looking forward to the night. I feel like some small, long-lost part of myself has been returned to me. For a brief moment, I feel less like Mum, nappy-changer, chauffeur, cook, cleaner and fish wife, and more like Madeleine.

## THURSDAY 30 APRIL

*10:12 a.m.* Get a call from kinder. Panic. Has Princess fallen from something? Had a fit? Broken something? Broken someone??? Teacher 'just' wants to 'chat' after school today. Hmm . . . potentially even worse.

*3:15 p.m.* Once all the other kinder kiddies have been collected and Princess has been installed in the 'home corner', patting the bottom of a baby doll slung over one shoulder, a toy phone tucked under her ear, muttering, 'But when will you be home, babe? Well, what do you wanna have for dinner? Shall I get a pizza?' (cringe), the teacher dons her serious face and gestures for me to sit at a kiddy table. It's kinda hard to keep my own serious face on as I hunker down on the itty-bitty green chair.

'Now, I've called you in as there have been some complaints about some of the language Princess has been using in the classroom.'

Oh no . . . my blood curdles. What has she said? Please, don't let her have regurgitated any of the doozies The

> SHOPPING LIST
>
> An old-fashioned bar of soap, the really gritty, astringent kind, good for washing out mouths
>
> Should I pick up a swear jar?

Chef hurls at the screen while watching an Arsenal match.

'Princess has been saying . . .' (pause for effect) '. . . bum and poo.'

Huh? Bum and poo? Are you serious? I cannot help it, my serious face slips and I crack a cheeky grin. She doesn't respond in kind, so I pick serious face back up off the floor, check for dirt and glitter, and slap it back on.

'I see, well, I will be having a serious conversation with Princess about the language she uses in the classroom.'

'Thank you for being so understanding.'

I gather up my little butterball, who is busy making an elaborate plastic meal, still on the phone relating how 'exhauuuuuusted' she is (double cringe) and make for the door. Just before we exit, I turn.

'Does she use those words in context?' I query.

'Well, yes.'

'Hmm, well, it might be useful to note that Princess here is one of six children, two of them older. If the worst she can come up with is "bum" and "poo" in context, then really, it's some kind of miracle. And if other parents have an issue with that, maybe they need to shed a little of that cotton wool and get themselves a hobby.'

Princess's teacher then bestows on me a broad and very cheeky grin. Yep, she has to do her job, but she totally agrees.

> SHOPPING LIST
>
> New watch – mine must be broken, time is going too fast!

I will encourage Princess to use the word 'bottom' over 'bum', and maybe just say 'I need to go to the toilet.' I mean, what else should a four-year-old be saying? Fecal matter? Excrement? Puh-lease! It's priggishness gone mad! In five years' time I will be wishing the extent of her naughty words was 'bum' and 'poo', especially if she starts supporting Arsenal.

## FRIDAY 1 MAY

**5:10 a.m.** My little twinnies are six months old! They are huge. Lolly Pop has two bottom teeth flashing but still not much hair, while Jelly Bean has a magnificent mane worthy of a ponytail. She is my only brunette. For two originally considered to be 'identical', they are so different. Appearance-wise, they look nothing alike. As different as cats and dogs. In fact, that's quite an apt comparison: Lolly Pop is like a roly-poly puppy: observant, curious, at times a little anxious, and eager for love and attention. Jelly Bean is more of a little kitten, busy, into everything, but at the end of the day much more laid back, she can take you or leave you – whatever! Both now roll happily on to their tummies, heads lifted high, surveying the chaos and destruction all around them. They can't wait to join in.

Jelly Bean has been suffering a temperature and runny nose so her sleep has been quite broken and what one does, the other must follow. Hence we have been nesting on the couch since 4 a.m., a contented if snotty little trio.

I hear the thump thump thump of heavy footfalls just after five, announcing Princess's arrival. Pale gold hair, like gossamer threads, sits bunched up on one side where she has slept on it. She rubs those ice-blue eyes and curls up with us. Twenty minutes later a timid little voice drifts out from the darkened kitchen, 'What are you guys doing?' Buddy totters in, PJs askew, hair tousled, one eye squeezed shut against the lamp light. Without a word, he joins our little huddle, tickling the irresistibly squishy bellies of first Lolly Pop, then Jelly Bean. We sit in companionable silence, watching the first light of dawn thread through the darkness. Moments later, a burst of hiccupping squawks announce that Tink has woken and wants to be released from her cot. Suddenly she bursts into the room clutching lay-lay, followed closely by Minnie who, roused by the rowdy chorus, kindly pulled her out. They too find little nooks to curl into and there we are, which is exactly where The Chef finds us, all fast asleep, an hour later when he wanders downstairs to find out why the house is so quiet at 7 a.m. when usually it's a veritable madhouse.

Having such a large family is cause for chaos more often than not, but in moments like these, it is absolutely priceless.

*9:10 a.m.* Yeah, priceless schmiceless . . . school run complete, I'm more than ready for them to head to Nanny Spaghetti's tomorrow so Mama and Papa can party. Woo hoo! Provided I don't asphyxiate from my dress being too tight, it's guaranteed to be a good night.

## SATURDAY 2 MAY

*7:50 p.m.*
- Hair washed: check.
- Hair sprayed with so much lacquer and styling mousse it looks suitably unwashed: check.

- Fake tan applied: check.
- Nail polish on fingers AND toes: check.
- War paint slapped on with spatula: check.
- Dress fiddled with, fussed over, finally put on: check.
- Dress taken off so a strapless bra, seamless underpants, and Spanx can be applied and those fiddly little straps that attach dress to coat-hanger cut off: check.
- Dress on: check.
- Shoes on: check.
- Shoes off, precautionary band-aids on: check.
- Shoes on: check.
- 'Going out' mini-handbag emptied and re-filled: check.
- Emergency late-night-I've-had-too-much-wine chocolate bar stashed: check.
- Babies fed, changed, gratefully handed to babysitter: check.
- Kids at Grandma's called, told they are loved and wished good night: check.
- Grandma warned not to let nine- or seven-year-old call us before 10 a.m., even if they did see a really interesting show about sharks, or reached Level 6 on *Minecraft*: check.
- Taxi twenty minutes late: check.
- Halfway to destination and realise gift you have sweated over is still on bench: check.
- Return for gift, back in taxi, frightfully late, arrive to find hardly anyone else has arrived: check.
- Survey sea of strange faces, get party stage fright, wanna return home to Tim Tams and Milo, suddenly spot a friend who proceeds to introduce you to everyone while you are plied with fancy deep-fried canapés and bubbly: check.
- Feeling it's gonna be a fabulous night: check.

> ### SHOPPING LIST
>
> *The satisfaction of walking into a room, heaving with beautiful, be-gowned women, and knowing every single one of them is wearing Spanx or Nancy Ganz is something money can't buy.*

## SUNDAY 3 MAY

*1:29 a.m.* Ss-great! Whas all gret. Love eryone. Evyne at there swas gret. Im a bit tiredd. I'm hABBY. I'm a bit sikky. Eschuse me, gott git mTim Tam. Gnight!

*5:57 a.m.* Twins.
Crying.
UuuuurrrGGGGH!

*8:30 a.m.* The Chef's mother sends through some gorgeous photos of Minnie and Buddy riding their bikes, Tink mucking about in a sandpit, Princess smothered in lipstick and frocked up as *Frozen*'s Elsa, clearly belting out her rendition of 'Let It Go' . . . and I go to water.

What the heck is wrong with me?

Here I am, with an opportunity to lie in (albeit with two squirming turnips in the bed too) nursing my sore head, have a disgustingly inappropriate breakfast consisting of carbs and grease, and all I can think of is the four who aren't here to share it with me. Twit.

I'm gonna force myself to enjoy this moment, savour it, take a mental photograph to meditate on when they return home this afternoon and after a few hours of chaos, I'm feeling ready to swiftly send them back again.

> SHOPPING LIST
>
> Souvlaki
>
> Pack salt and vinegar chips
>
> Chocolate Big M
>
> Iced doughnut of some description
>
> *Urgh . . . groan*

# CHAPTER

# WEDNESDAY 6 MAY

*6:11 a.m.* Last night The Chef got on a plane.

He has a few days of commitments in Sydney, returning Friday night, then jetting off Saturday for the European cruise we were to be working on together.

I'm feeling shattered. So low it's an effort to drag my head off the pillow.

I've accepted this is what it is, and have mapped out my days with many a lovely distraction. I'm having coffee with some school mums this morning, lunch with a gorgeous friend, plan to make Mars bar slice with Princess and Tink before school pick-up, and this afternoon we are all heading to the south side to see my mother's new apartment. The rest of the week is busy: I've booked in writing sessions, am proposing a radio segment to some producers, have a meeting regarding a role in a new web series, and there are school events culminating in Mother's Day on Sunday. The kids are very excited about the little creations they have been putting together for me at school, and The Chef secreted an envelope into each of their bedrooms with $5 and instructions to buy me something I would like, not something *they* want from the Mother's Day stall. Sweet. Also, there are plans afoot for a big family lunch on Mother's Day itself at a local restaurant. I've got a couple of cake recipes I'm looking forward to trying out for some post-lunch coffee and dessert back here . . . but The Chef won't be here for any of it.

I miss him already.

It is part of his job description these days to travel widely and frequently. I have grown quite accustomed to it. Last year, he was on the road for more than 200 days of the 365, writing, reviewing, promoting. I was up to my neck filming *Fat Tony* at the time, and work proved a wonderful distraction from his absence. Now, however, being at home with all our babies, day in, day out, I see bits of him everywhere, but he is not here.

He has made a concerted effort of late to be home more. At first, it cramped my style, and at times I resented that he was here but was shooting

SHOPPING LIST

Distractions

Time-fillers

Tim Tams . . . feeling so rubbish don't think even Tim Tams can save me now.

off emails rather than changing nappies. A funny harmony emerged, however, and I relished the subtle security of just knowing he was around. It allowed me greater freedoms too. If The Chef was tapping away in his study, I could sneak out to school pick-up unencumbered, leaving Tink, Lolly Pop and Jelly Bean to nap in my absence. I could shoot around the corner for milk without having to load up the people mover; I could slip in a coffee with another mum post-drop-off without bored little fingers dipping in the sugar bowl and using the cafe's generous provision of crayons to draw on the walls.

Yes, I have the wonderful Sal at hand, but she is not here all day, every day, and there are limits.

And I just miss him.

Yesterday, I kept busy. I made a roast, which between keeping Princess and Tink occupied by having them chop soft veggies with their plastic knives, and tending to the twins, took all afternoon. After dinner, baths, and a bedtime story, the little girls went to bed, followed swiftly by the twins, while Minnie, Buddy and I watched the first episode of *Masterchef* over ice-cream and hot chocolates, hoping for a glimpse of Dad. There he was in the closing moments. Just makes me miss him more.

If truth be told, I'm bloody jealous too. He's about to cruise, in unparalleled luxury, between some of the most exquisite ports in the world. I'm about to spend that time changing nappies, mashing potato, and separating the white wash from the colours . . . *sigh*.

My mood remains deep, dark and unapologetically self-indulgent, like chocolate sauce.

Need . . . a . . . holiday . . .

*5:46 p.m.* What does any self-respecting gal do when she's feeling out of sorts, out of luck, and maybe out of her mind?

She dresses up. A little effort goes a long way, and a bit of slap on the face, a squirt of expensive scent, and ditching the old duds for your Sunday best can lend a certain sartorial swagger, a spring to your step; can really ice your cake, so to speak. Not that I'm espousing going on a depressed dessert binge – not in your good clothes, anyway.

So, feeling shite with a capital CRAP today, I trawled through my wardrobe and dusted off a few pieces that make me feel a bit special. A lovely marle grey sleeveless dress The Chef picked up for me in Hong Kong was cinched in with a wide, strappy leather belt, black leggings and, in a shout out to my misspent youth, a pair of ridiculous, knee-high lace-up boots, with heels so towering you can virtually see the curve of the earth. Basically, I looked like Princess Leia on hormone therapy.

Anyway, out I tottered, first to drop-off, then to coffee. Raced home to tidy, play with the girls and make a batch of the promised Mars Bar slice (phwoooooooar!) before scuttling off to a local cafe for a dose of girly gossip with a friend over salad and cake, just like a veritable social butterfly.

Slipping in a quick grocery shop post-lunch, I find myself limping back to the car afterwards, feeling as if I had spent a sizeable portion of my day en pointe. Was I performing *Swan Lake* in street wear, or was I just wearing ludicrously high, torturous heels for no discernible reason? Chafing at my own folly, I peeled the boots off just to ensure I could safely drive my car to school for pick-up. Somehow, released from their bindings, my poor feet did some serious swelling, so much so that when I got to the school, I could not get my boots back on. (See where I am going with this?)

Yep, with no better solution readily presenting itself I just had to take off the socks (hole in one toe, naturally) and collect my children barefoot.

Sure, it was raining, and the bare feet in no way corresponded with the rest of my ensemble, but I figured if I didn't make a big deal of it, why should anyone else? So I didn't mention it, and strolled in there as if it was the most natural thing in the world to pair naked feet with Hong Kong couture and my good earrings. Every eye in the school yard went to my tootsies with their shamefully chipped slather of black polish, but no-one said a word either. Stalemate. So I just collected my portion of children and got outta there.

Stuff it, it's nearly Mother's Day so I'm celebrating early, stripping it back and keeping it real. If a girl can't lose her shoes after a sugar-infused girly lunch and a modest glass of bubbly, she just isn't trying.

## FRIDAY 8 MAY

*9 a.m.* I've just left the kinder room, almost stumbling into various inanimate objects through my tears. Princess's little class have just presented their Mother's Day breakfast, with an assortment of pastries, fruit, coffee, beautiful and painstakingly threaded bracelets and glorious handmade crowns. The celebration ended with some beautiful songs they had practised just for us, followed by long kisses and cuddles. Princess so enjoyed the novelty of having Mama to herself, she cried when I had to leave, begging me to stay and play with her at the fairy table. My little darling, so independent and forthright, but still so much my baby, my little girl. Before I had the twins, I was actually anxious, wondering how I could find enough love for all of them. The answer was quite simple: your heart just keeps expanding, each new little

> SHOPPING LIST
>
> *Chest extension. No, I'm not having a boob job, but my ribs can't possibly contain my heart; it's so full of love it's bursting.*

one finding their own nook, making up part of the whole and filling it with such powerful adoration and overwhelming devotion, you can't imagine how that spot was ever empty before. Mothering this little tribe has given me a big responsibility, a big love, a big life. Should I ever require a chest X-ray, I'm pretty certain the sonographer would find that, thanks to my current circumstances I, like Pharlap, and every other parent, carer, aunt, uncle, and friend, have developed a super-size heart.

## SATURDAY 9 MAY

*8:36 a.m.* The Chef returned last night and will be gone again this afternoon. The children are all in some state of illness, be it the dry cough on the other side of a bad cold, or the fully fledged snot-clotted fevered glory of a winter flu. It's Mother's Day tomorrow, but alas, with several members of the extended family also down and out with seasonal colds, all plans of a get-together have gone awry.

So I'm contemplating yet another Mother's Day flying solo, this my first with six children.

Accordingly, I've decided we are going to bunker down, shut all the curtains and blinds, and watch movies all day in our pyjamas. I've ordered a grocery delivery online to ensure we genuinely have no reason to leave the house, and made the unprecedented and frankly controversial decision to pre-order lunch for the kids on Monday so my Mother's Day, if devoid of a fancy

> SHOPPING LIST
>
> *A freezer-worth of ready-made meals*
>
> *3 loaves bread (freezer)*
>
> *2 bottles long-life milk*
>
> *Hydraulic lift for my crappy mood*

breakfast in bed, will not be interrupted by my usual obsessive-compulsive preparations for school.

## SUNDAY 10 MAY

*1:05 a.m.* Princess is up, coughing, spluttering. Poor little cherub, she coughed so hard she has vomited in her bed and all over herself. I strip her off along with the bed, as quietly as possible so as not to wake Tink, give her a quick dip in a warm bath, administer medicine, and tuck her into my bed. Literally moments later, Jelly Bean starts coughing, which wakes Lolly Pop,

SHOPPING LIST

250 g gratitude

100 g responsibility

200 g patience

2 tbs humour

1 tbs tickles

Large pinch 'stop whinging'

Cuddle and kiss for 45 minutes or till sufficiently loved up.

and now they are both wailing. I bring them in, give them a quick change and a feed, and am returning Lolly Pop to bed when little Jelly Bean, full of phlegm, starts coughing again. I dash back in time to see her hurling, in a manner fit to rival *The Exorcist*, all over herself, the bed and poor Princess. Bloody hell!

Right. Strip Princess again and put her in one of my T-shirts, strip Jelly Bean, strip my bed and remake as swiftly as possible, redress Jelly Bean and attempt a half-feed, before being a terrible mother and popping her in her bouncer downstairs in front of some cartoons. I'm scared if I lay her flat in bed she will have another coughing episode and choke. By the time I'm loading the wealth of soiled garments into the washing machine I'm in tears, sucking in oxygen between huge, wrenching sobs that set up an ache in my ribcage equal to the ache deep in my being, in some spiritual nerve centre that is blaring out a message behind my eyes in neon lights: 'I don't wanna do this any more, I don't wanna play mum!' Fury and guilt and desperation compete for prime position, whirling through me, each in turn making me feel progressively worse. I dissolve into a puddle on the cold laundry tiles and indulge in the wracking sobs till they resolve into mere hiccups, then sniffs, then silence. Just the steady thump thump thump of bedding being churned through spin mode.

Happy bloody Mother's Day.

I slink back to bed, certain my resentment of this situation will send any attempt at sleep packing. I testily toss beneath the covers, nerves humming, and nearly jump through the roof when I feel a tiny, featherlight touch against my back. It's Princess; I'd forgotten she was there. In her sleep, she has gently curled herself behind me, instinctively seeking warmth and comfort. I delicately roll to face her, soft strands of silky hair stroking her cheeks, rosebud mouth pursed in a Cupid's bow, both hands clutched beneath her cheek like a Disney princess in repose. Love, pure and unadulterated, swells up to my chin like a balloon inflating, so rapid and with such force it hurts. I'm immediately compelled to check on the rest of my babies. Tink is curled, bum up, atop her lay-lay, impish little face soft and angelic in sleep, snuggled deeply in the soft fabric. Buddy is lying across his bed, legs dangling out one side, head slumped over the other, a pile of Lego lurking under the covers, evidence of his industry before sleep settled in. I gently correct his position and tuck him in with a kiss, to be rewarded with a slurred 'love you'. Lolly Pop lies with hands up in classic baby 'it's a stick-up' pose, still clutching her soft puppy dog toy, her dummy abandoned, long black lashes tickling those perfectly rounded baby cheeks.

Downstairs, Jelly Bean is snuggled in her bouncer. I bundle her up and she reflexively curls into me, fluffy mop of brunette tresses snuggled into my neck. When I lay her in her cradle her tiny hands grasp for me, rapidly opening and closing before she too assumes the stick-up position and drifts back to sleep. Minnie looks like a mermaid, sunbathing on a pink-elephant-printed beach. She is stretched out full length, her arms modestly crossed over her belly, golden hair flared out about her head in a sweeping arc. I return her covers with a kiss on the forehead, to which she smiles, fluttering her lashes briefly before sleep reclaims her.

As I return to bed I'm so infused with love, dear diary, I just have to get it out on paper. Lately I've spent a good deal of time railing against the limitations imposed on me by motherhood, the freedoms curtailed by these little people. Well, no more: today it ends. My Mother's Day resolution is to accept what cannot be changed, and start focusing on the good, not the bad. Look at all the precious little lives that have been entrusted to my care, all the tiny people I have the honour of calling my own. It's time to be grateful for the miracle that is motherhood, and the gift I have been given six times over. Grateful for the broken sleep, the rejected meals, the spontaneous cuddles, the devotion in their eyes when they look at me. It is precious, it is a gift, the power of which cannot be underestimated.

*8:09 a.m.* Best Mother's Day gift EVER! My online shopping order arrived ON TIME, and they gave me some chocolate-coated, pop-corny, pretzelly, caramel stuff FOR FREE! Woo hoo! The day is looking up already!

*10:23 a.m.* Roll up, roll up! See it here, folks! Four words you will never see appear in any peer-reviewed and approved parenting manual: ICE-CREAM CAKE FOR BREAKFAST. That, folks, is Mother's Day, freestyle.

*11:23 p.m.* The perfect day, diary, the perrrrrr-fect day. Whenever the kids grumbled, or asked for something, I pulled out the It Is Mother's Day, card, and immediately the whining stopped, they sorted it out themselves, or in the case of the younger ones, asked a bigger sibling to help them. A beautiful sight to behold.

I enjoyed quite a haul of gifts; my brood must have stripped the Mother's Day stall at school bare! Amid the handmade cards and painstakingly decorated gift paper were five cellophane-wrapped soap bars, four lavender bags, three magnetised shopping lists, two 'World's Greatest Mum' mugs and a partridge in a pear tree.

Together we made a gloriously messy, gooey chocolate cake, ate whatever mysterious foods we could find lurking in the cupboard and stayed in our PJs most of the day, dressing only briefly to pop out and see my mum.

Minnie, Buddy and I watched *Masterchef* over tea and cake, and now I'm sitting up in bed. Tapping away, I'm absurdly grateful to Jelly Bean for this morning's escapade. Without her vomiting everywhere, I would not be experiencing the singular joy of slipping between freshly laundered sheets. That's what Mother's Day is all about: celebrating the small pleasures.

## THE HONEST MOTHER'S DAY WISHLIST

Do you want to give your mum the perfect gift? Show her how much she means to you? Let her know she is the perfect mum?

Well, give her a day of not being a mum, at all, not even once.

The ultimate way to celebrate motherhood is to give mums a moment away from it. The idea is to give Mum a chance to see her role objectively for a day. See all she does, see how much it means to you all, and appreciate how much she enjoys being Mum, hence returning to that role renewed and reinvigorated. Just don't make the departure from day-to-day life too alluring – Mum may never come back! Here is a list of suggestions.

1.  Let Mum wake in her own time, rather than to alarm clocks, schedules and wailing children. This may involve creating a complicated network of buffers, running serious interference, distractions and bribing the children, but the sheer luxury of being able to wake when she feels ready (personally, I cannot even remember what that sensation is like; it's like a desert oasis to me, tantalisingly close but just out of reach) will be such a gift, you will accrue some serious brownie points for that alone.

2.  DO make breakfast in bed for her; just keep it simple, light and likely to cause minimal mess downstairs, because while she is grinning her way through charcoal toast and coffee that could strip paint, all she is thinking about is the clean-up. It is a Mother's Day tradition, however: one that must be undertaken to give Mum that tingly feeling of being adored and give her bragging rights tomorrow at school drop-off.

3.  Now take her out for an actual breakfast. Do not allow her to sneak in a bowl of muesli (unless of course that is what SHE truly wants). Just remember this is her day, NO mummy duties.

4.  Don't give her flowers, or if you do, put a little note in her card explaining that YOU will trim them, arrange them in a vase, monitor their decline, remove drooping stems and clean up dropped pollen, finally binning them and washing the vase when the time comes.

5.  Chocolates: only a fool wouldn't give chocolates on Mother's Day. Give two boxes, one that she can do the polite Mum thing with and share, and one she can scoff alone with a glass of red in front of a box set of *Breaking Bad*.

6.  A box set of *Breaking Bad*, or a box set of *Downton Abbey*, or a box set of David Attenborough's *Life of Bugs*, whatever. So long as she gets to watch it in peace with a box of chocolates, a self-respecting mum will watch anything.

7. This is the hard bit: send her out into the world. Make her a lunch booking for somewhere she likes, or even better, let her choose it herself in advance, with a guest of her choice (absolutely cannot be a family member beyond her own mother, even if she insists, as she is just being polite again), give her a credit card and send her on her way, with instructions to buy herself something nice while she is out. We mums all love the photo frame sets, the perfumes, the vacuum cleaners, the novelty tea towels, the soaps wrapped in cellophane, the 'WORLD'S BEST MUM' mugs, and the books on subjects we have no interest in, will never have an interest in, and have never indicated we have an interest in, but which you probably picked up as part of a 'two for the price of one' deal in the Boxing Day sales, but an opportunity to actually buy ourselves something, with an open credit card in our hot little hands, is the ultimate gift bar none (except for perhaps our very first macaroni necklace).

8. Now this is the one that shows true love and devotion: post-lunch, before she has the chance to toddle home, still buzzing from too much bubbly, send her off for a night in a hotel, BY HERSELF. This sounds indulgent, counterintuitive and downright risky, but that's precisely what every mum needs now and then: a bit of risk to blow out those cobwebs. It doesn't have to be expensive, just somewhere nice to relax, have a glass of wine and watch a movie in bed, alone. Yes, we love our families, but one of motherhood's chief laments is the utter obliteration of 'me time'. Time alone every now and then is not an indulgence, it's a very real need; just a brief sojourn to have your body, mind and soul to yourself is priceless. It doesn't necessarily need to be a night away – maybe just a day at a spa, a day rock-climbing, a day SHOPPING! Whatever floats your mum's individual boat. Once she's had a decent sleep-in, maybe a dip in the pool, and enjoyed a quiet continental breakfast, there is a good chance you will wake to find Mum back home in high spirits, raring to go. If not, well, maybe you weren't treating her right in the first place!

9. If you want to eschew the commerciality of the day, why not give a gift that keeps on giving: a week's worth of ready-made gourmet meals, catered to her tastes, delivered to her door?

10. Set up an online grocery delivery account with one of the major supermarkets, or even a small gourmet grocer, and organise the first month of deliveries.

11. A month's worth of garden maintenance.

12. A cleaner for a month, or a year, or a lifetime. Go the extra mile and organise for her to be out of the house for the first clean, then personally take the cleaner through how she likes things done. The utter delight your mum will exhibit (once she gets over the shock of thinking a burglar broke in and decided to do a bit of tidying) will be a joy to behold. Perhaps make a point of taking her out for a walk/lunch/movie at the time the cleaner is booked, otherwise she'll end up doing what mums do best: cleaning the house so it's nice and tidy for when the cleaners arrive (mothers: we are our own worst enemy).

13. Best gift of all: hugs, kisses and telling Mum how much you love her. It's the thing we rejoice in most when our children are small and we are the centre of their universe. It is something our babies grow out of too soon, and it is the thing we miss the most: being kissed, being held, being demonstrably loved. Look Mum in the eye and tell her you love her. Not just on Mother's Day, but every day. You are her greatest achievement, her pride, her joy. Let her know she is yours too.

## MONDAY 11 MAY

*7:04 a.m.* TV isn't working. No discernible reason, just isn't working. Life as we know it could possibly be over.

*4:10 p.m.* TV fixed, hallelujah! Okay, back to life as we know it.

> SHOPPING LIST
>
> Horse and bloody cart
>
> Instruction manual on converting to Amish

## TUESDAY 12 MAY

*9:55 a.m.* Drat! Drat! DOUBLE DRAT!

I'm enjoying a simple play in the park with Tink, remarkable only for how deceptively dry the slide looked till she slipped down it and clearly collected a full night's rain residue in the seat of her trackie dacks, when, while I'm fiddling with my phone, a calendar alert springs up blurting that I have a casting at 10:30!!!!

> SHOPPING LIST
>
> Brown paper bag... need, panicking ...can't... breathe!

Crappity crap crap CRAP!

How did I forget?

Oh, that's right, it's Tuesday, otherwise known as 'Gee, I'd rather stick a blunt pencil in my eye than get out of bed today day.'

See, Minnie and Buddy have 7 a.m. dry skiing lessons (yes, you read it right, dry skiing lessons, who knew?) which means the troops have to be mobilised at 6 a.m., and if I want to finesse my personal hygiene with a shower or some such luxury then I have to get up at 5 a.m. I do the first round of drop-offs then scoot home to collect Princess to drop her off, then, if I haven't had the wherewithal to drag Tink along, I have to return home again to collect her and take her to toddler sports at 9 a.m. Can't I just have an unanaesthetised root canal, please?

So here we are, having a post-toddler-sport park play, and now I've got a meeting in thirty-five minutes where I'm obligated to impress producers with my razor-sharp wit, my unfettered drive and my smouldering charisma, all in a grotty tracksuit with a bit of stubborn peanut butter still clinging to one lapel, a bare face, and still-damp hair yanked into a lop-sided ponytail.

I'm not a rough diamond, brimming with potential; I'm one of those charcoal beads you chuck on the barbie, and I'm brimming with cold coffee, the children's toast leftovers, and a sleeveful of used tissues.

That's show business.

There is nothing for it but to attend the meeting as I am. I would be doubling my journey if I dropped Tink home then headed there, and I simply haven't the time, so she is now officially part of the package. Maybe I could use her as a prop?

There has been no time for the usual angst-ridden lead-up to an audition: the primping, the preening, the fretting, the practising, the merry-go-round of potential outfits. There has been no opportunity for make-up applied too audaciously then removed, then more make-up applied too sparingly so beefed up at the last minute, only to arrive at the studio and see myself under the alien glare of a different light in the bathroom and end up scrubbing at my face with a bit of wet toilet paper. Basically, I've saved myself a whole morning usually wasted on stomach-churning, nausea-inducing, nail-biting nervousness, so even if I don't get the job it's gotta be a win for my spiritual growth – and my nails. The nerves will come, however, because work is important to me. This acting caper is a bucking bronco I've been riding since childhood. It can be harsh and unforgiving, make you question your sanity, and is notoriously not family-friendly, but I love it; it is in my blood, and despite forays into other creative pursuits, I cannot escape the singular thrill of performance.

I want to return to work.

Yes, it has to be the right project.

Yes, my family is my priority so the job has to be malleable enough to fit in with my kiddy commitments.

Yes, the hours have to be more forgiving than they have been on past shoots.

Yes, I have to be very clear with the producers about how all of the above has to be respected in order for me to perform at my best.

Hence there is a very good chance all the pieces will not fall together, especially given the grotty tracksuit, but what if this is that perfect job? Oh, the joy, to have a hefty script clutched in my hands. To have a meaty character to break down, build up, create a back story for, plot an emotional journey for, give a voice to. Oh, to emerge from the make-up department, transformed and not recognising myself beneath the result of their labours. Oh, to sip that first cup of coffee in the green room and finish it while it is still hot.

And so, this casting has to be about personality, because the only other thing I have to offer them right now is a Cinderella colouring set and a package of baby wipes. Wish me luck, diary, wish me luck.

*2:15 p.m.* Stuffed it, for shizz . . .

Tootling towards the production office where we were to meet, I slipped in a sneaky double espresso, just to give me a little pep-up and ensure I was capable of stringing two words together, and proceeded to paint my nails at each red light (so shoot me, there had to be some concession to femininity amid the grotty-tracksuit make-uplessness).

Arriving, I ushered Tink in ahead of me, and the producers, spotting small child in tow, immediately recommended we reconvene at a cafe next door (fair call too, they had pastel upholstery to consider; cafes always tend to be more user-friendly when it comes to two-year-olds). Seated, Tink kindly provided with a strap-in high chair (no escape) and coloured pencils (wipe-off-able) and coffee delivered, we began 'the chat'.

Halfway through said coffee, I felt the oddest sensation. Having never partaken in illicit pharmaceuticals I can't describe an exact verisimilitude, but I'm tipping this is what a seasoned user would call a rush. That third coffee had tipped me over some existentialist cliff and now I was flying! Motor-mouth in overdrive, I started punching out some snappy one-liners, all well received, which quickly transformed to a verbal stream of consciousness, quickly devolving to verbal diarrhoea, and finally to virtual gibberish. The amusement on their faces was soon replaced with confusion, bewilderment, then fascination, as if they were observing some strange new exotic creature – all except one dude with a beard and sleeve tatts who looked on, nodding in a knowing manner which suggested he might pull me aside later to find out where he could score.

I attempted some yoga-like deep breathing in an attempt to quell the madness, but all that fresh oxygen in the bloodstream seemed to exacerbate the hysteria, which multiplied, slamming my synapses and frying my vocabulary. Soon, I was answering their questions with monosybillic grunts, too scared to actually give an opinion lest my caffeine-scrambled brain trotted out some dissertation on the finer points of yurt-construction in modern-day Mongolia. Feeling my composure slipping, I quickly excused myself, citing a suspicious odour emanating from Tink, and yanked her out of the high chair, ferrying us both to the bathroom quick smart. Safely ensconced in the disabled users' cubicle, I splashed my face with water and felt panicky tears pooling somewhere behind my eyes. Job hopes jettisoned.

Pathetic.

Then a tiny hand slipped into mine.

'Awwwright, Mama?'

My darling little girl. Impish little face upturned, a clutch of pencils still in her hand, staring at me, all concern.

'Yes, I'm all right, sweetie.'

She smiles, that cheeky little dimple dancing over one cheek. I kneel down for a cuddle and feel my mind settling. I take the time to check her still-dry nappy and by the time we emerge I am suitably composed. The meeting wraps up soon after, and I don't think I managed to impress them with my swift recovery of the use of the English language. But in the bigger picture, it really doesn't matter. What's one job when I've got this little fairy dancing alongside me?

As I'm strapping her back in the car, I realise she still has the pencils. Contemplate returning to the cafe, but can see the producers still huddled at the table within. Oh well, at least we scored something from the morning's exertions!

Thankfully, there isn't time to dwell on it anyway. There is still shopping to be done, a casserole to be made, naps to be had, and kids needing to be collected and deposited at home with Sal so I can take Minnie up the mountain for a horse-riding lesson.

See? I'm too busy to have a job anyway.

*5.45 p.m.* Traffic! Both still damp from exposure to rain and hail in 6°C conditions, and covered with a liberal coating of mud, Minnie and I are eating our way through a crusty French stick as we sit, stuck in peak-hour traffic. We misjudged our departure time and now face the full brunt of every other sucker also on the road trying to get home.

It's been like this for an hour and forty-five minutes now, but who is counting?

We chew on our bread, Minnie with the contented air of a yogi at peace with the world, having had her horse fix, me with increasing agitation, rehashing the morning's events, vowing never to touch any caffeinated products again (that would include chocolate, and especially Tim Tams, so we know that ain't gonna happen).

'It was a stupid job anyway,' I reassure myself. It was a week's work, big deal. I've bigger fish to fry, more traffic hazards to avoid, and more laundry to fold . . . *sigh*.

## WEDNESDAY 13 MAY

*2 p.m.* It's been one of those days. Struggling through the butcher's, my pram wheel catches on a stand of shortbreads (shortbreads in a butcher? Wha—? Clearly the manager is going for 'boutique deli', but is only succeeding in being a wanker) and suddenly I'm wedged, blocking the flow of people traffic, awkwardly unable to manoeuvre my way out single-handedly. Three customers squeeze past me; not one offers to help. It's as if they cannot even see me; I'm just an oversized, inanimate object coming between them and a selection of marinated chicken fillets. I know some women think the world revolves around them once they become mothers, but that's not the case here – this is just a human being needing a little assistance from another human being.

> SHOPPING LIST
>
> Fluorescent work-out gear
>
> Loudspeaker
>
> A flashing neon sign 'I'm still here!'
> As clearly I'm invisible.

I manage an overdue catch-up with an old friend over lunch. Mother to five, all quite a bit older than mine. She is a picture of elegance and good humour. She has been in the trenches and come out on the other side (almost; still a few years of digging to go) with good grace and enviable composure. We rant on about the lot of the modern-day mother, bemoaning our lost liberty, till our chardonnay glasses are drained. My gorgeous friend has returned to work, just a handful of days a week, but enough to elevate the pall of unrelenting slavery that can be full-time motherhood. She looks happier and more fulfilled than I remember in a long time. She openly admits that on the days she works, surrounded by adults, eating lunch uninterrupted, leaving the lunchbox construction to someone else, are like a holiday, and she returns home refreshed and unapologetic. Yep, I'm jealous.

It was a stupid job, Madeleine, you gave a bad audition, get over it.

## FRIDAY 15 MAY

*10:19 a.m.* I got the job.

> SHOPPING LIST
>
> Wha–? Sorry, huh?
>
> Say that again?

## SATURDAY 16 MAY

*5:56 a.m.* Can't sleep; get up. So much to plan. My week of work starts in three weeks' time, and I need to set up structures, organise timetables, check the long-term weather forecast . . . and learn the bloody script!

The reality of what a juggle this wondrous week of work presents is only now hitting home. Is it perhaps tarnishing the prospect of returning to work a little? Yep. However, I'm relieved knowing this is such a short break (I mean job), like a practice run for when I invariably do return to longer-term work – if I'm not sent to an institution first (and it's not The Ponds Institute I'm talking about here). This particular job pays a pittance, but is one of those crucial gigs which will lead to more work, is in an area I've never worked in so presents an opportunity to learn, and, quite frankly, these days every little bit helps, right? Everyone is aspirational. For the first time in over a year, I feel like I'm making a contribution. Yes, I know I keep the ship afloat, even if the decks are imperfectly scrubbed and the sails could do with a good soak and spin cycle, but it is nice to know I'm squirrelling a little aside towards the kids' winter coats, or paying a term of karate lessons, or making a dent in the small fortune required to take six ratbags and ratbags-in-training on holiday. It's a nice feeling.

And who am I kidding? For a whole week I will get to eat breakfast sitting down AND drink a whole cup of coffee while it's hot AND have conversations with adults that don't revolve around sleeping schedules, snotty noses and toilet training. Heck, I'll pay them!

## MONDAY 18 MAY

*9:12 a.m.* It's Monday and school has started, yet my children are all still in their pyjamas, fast asleep in bed, at the beach house, while I brew a second

> SHOPPING LIST
>
> Polaroid camera – I need to take photos of how the kids like their lunchboxes put together, how they like their sandwiches cut, what treats to include and when, how to assemble a ham and cheese Salada to Buddy's specifications, the correct mix of berries for Minnie's fruit snack, the exact consistency and temperature of the macaroni cheese before it goes into Princess's thermos, the correct ratio of sultanas to oats in the cookies I make for Tink's playgroup, and stick them up on every available surface. The composition and content of your child's lunchbox can mean the difference between a good day at school and Armeggedon.

cup of coffee to take back to bed myself. I am sooooo naughty!

With The Chef away, when a tradesperson informed us he needed access to the property to go through the jobs yet to be completed on what must be the most excruciatingly long build in history, my hand shot up. And rather than being practical and scooting down straight after drop-off to meet with him, then returning in time for pick-up, I opt to schlep the whole catastrophe (that being my favourite new collective noun for my tribe: 'a catastrophe of children') down to our hideaway the day before to stay for a night. Now I'm here, I'm thinking I might stretch it out to two. I have the ultimate respect for my children's education, but it has been a rough few weeks between illness, Dad's absence, and the whole catastrophe being dragged from pillar to post, so I don't feel particularly guilty about giving them a day off.

Of course, we arrive to find the heating system is kaput, so the entire house is stone cold. I spent two hours scabbing about for dry kindling and attempting to chop rain-soaked wood, before finally getting a couple of fires roaring. It tided us over for the night, but the twins woke at 4:30 a.m. with little fingers and toes like tiny icicles, their button noses red and shiny. There is something bracing about waking to genuine cold in this era of temperature-controlled living. Even as the mercury dips outside, many of us maintain a toasty-warm Bahamas climate within our homes, cruising about in Hawaiian shirts.

A change of scenery was just what the doctor ordered. I had spent the entire weekend driving myself nuts over preparations for my upcoming week of work. No matter where I looked, everything needed to be re-organised, diarised, alphabetised or sterilised. I needed an escape, although sadly one cannot escape one's own head so even now I'm collating lists of phone numbers of people I can call in should Sal need support, lists of grocery items for the

---

SHOPPING LIST

Shopping list

1 week temporary:

* Personal assistant

* Personal chef

* Personal trainer

* Personal stylist

* Personal cleaner

* Personal ironer

* Personality transplant: crikey, if I get everything done for me, I think I might need a new one.

---

simple meals I plan to have stocked in the freezer to cover that week, and lists of what I need to do to get myself camera-ready (naturally, exercise doesn't get a look-in, just eyebrow plucking, fake-tan application, and a bit of toenail pruning).

Why am I so anxious? It's a one-week job, with just two or three days of rehearsals, and I'm sweating, if not bullets, then at least very firm play-doh.

Princess emerges, rubbing sleepy eyes. Somewhere between her bedtime story and dawn she has had some reason to take off her PJs, as they are now on backwards.

'Hey Mum, in Egyptian Egypt [Princess's interpretation of Ancient Egypt] there was alotta kings, wasn't there?'

'Yes, sweetie.'

'And the bestest king was King Kardashian, wasn't it?'

'Okay . . . and what made King Kardashian so special?'

'Oh, King Kardashian was just the king with the weally fat butt.'

Oh dear; what can you say to that?

Maybe that's why my brief sojourn working is prompting such angst. What if in that week I miss one of Princess's famous clangers? Or Jelly Bean finally catches up and sprouts a tooth? Or crawls? Or my laid-back little darling, Lolly Pop, actually moves? (Some might bandy about terms like 'sloth'; I just think she is a deep thinker.) Tink might crack counting to ten, or Princess might lose her divine lisp. Who will carefully go through Buddy's reader with him? Who will guide Minnie through the curly questions in her homework?

It is all these tiny gems amid the general chaos of each day that make parenting so rewarding and, let's be honest, bearable. It is these little gems we miss the most when we can't be there to share them. I realise now why I am so nervous about stepping away for five minutes. It's not so much that I will miss them, which of course I will. The truth is I am worried they won't miss me.

## TUESDAY 19 MAY

*11:47 a.m.* Spoon-feeding pumpkin to the twins. Lolly Pop is lapping it up, Jelly Bean spitting it out. Feel the spoon connect with something hard as I attempt to rescue some of the orange purée her little tongue forces back out of her mouth. Jelly Bean has finally caught up with her sister and grown two tiny pearly whites while I wasn't looking. My heart bounds up with joy

SHOPPING LIST

Flour

Water

Paper shreds

(Is that the recipe for paper mâché?
These kids are growing too fast;
figure if I smother them with a few
layers and let it harden, might be able
to halt their growth just a bit.)

and pride, then swiftly rebounds with a heavy thunk!, plummeting to the floor.

Please tell me, diary, how is it possible to simultaneously feel so proud of your child's milestone, yet so heartbroken knowing that with every one reached, your baby is growing away from you? Is it normal to mourn the fact that with each passing day, my children are less mine, and more the world's?

## SATURDAY 23 MAY

*6:20 a.m.* I tried, diary, I really tried.

I know I promised nothing but bright, positive thinking, a glass-half-full approach to life and mothering, and a zen-like calm sprinkled with a wry, tongue-in-cheek levity when it comes to coping with life's little challenges, but I'm stuffed. Well and truly stuffed. Turducken-stuffed.

I wanna fake it till I make it but the final goalpost keeps shifting.

It just doesn't end.

I know, diary, I know. One day soon my little tribe will start peeling away from me, building lives where I no longer play a starring role. I understand that; it terrifies me, but there are some mornings, like this one, where I have gone to bed utterly spent, and it then seems like I've no more than blinked my eyes before it has started all over again.

I'm having erotic fantasies about sitting in bed and having a coffee.

I'm having erotic fantasies about sleeping past 6 a.m.

I'm having erotic fantasies about having the time to have erotic fantasies.

I'm running on empty. And I fear that if something doesn't give soon, I won't be good for anything or anyone.

SHOPPING LIST

1/2 cup sugar-coating

1 cup saccharine

1 bag marshmallow

Whipped cream

Mix to a paste, and use to liberally
smother your true feelings, sweeten
your mood, and give your real thoughts
a crackling candy crunch

The only options for doing that are a return to work OR a fabulous holiday, OR both.

The Chef is finally on the last leg of his trip, and when I 'Face-timed' him before passing out last night, he commented that I looked spent. He, meanwhile, looked sun-kissed and relaxed after another day on the open seas. I know he is working his guts out but why does he have to look so damned refreshed? Using that as leverage, I pushed for a commitment on that holiday to Fiji we had discussed but which hadn't gone anywhere. Being the loving husband he is he immediately agreed, admitting that as I hadn't mentioned it for a while he thought I had lost interest. Here I was thinking precisely the same thing of him. Gotta love marital communication!

Despite the late hour, before I collapsed, comatose once I hit the pillow, I shot out an email to our travel agent, who on more than one occasion has managed to work utter miracles for us. Such is my desperation, I push for the impossible: two adults, six kids, Fiji, during the June school holidays. If anyone can make it happen, it is him.

## MONDAY 25 MAY

*2:35 p.m.* Hallelujah! Despite yesterday being a Sunday, our trusty agent came back with a myriad of options by early evening. I've highlighted my favourites and forwarded them to The Chef to get his thoughts, then plan to lock it in ASAP.

Feeling celebratory, and with The Chef due home, I thought, why not be very very naughty, take the kids out of school an hour early and have a late lunch at our bistro in the city? I had some documents to drop by the office anyway so felt justified in taking a slight detour, slipping and falling mouth first on to two delicious courses with a matched glass of white.

> SHOPPING LIST
>
> Wine
>
> Wine glasses (ours are all dirty, haven't the strength to wash them)

Just to make life more manageable, my understandably fatigued nanny is now working a four-day week (crikey, if I could reduce my hours in this madhouse, I would too!) and this happens to be one of those days she is footloose and fancy-free. Accordingly, I was up at sparrow's fart to get the house organised and the kids up, dressed, fed and off to school. I made my usual trek to their individual classrooms with Tink and Lolly Pop in the twin stroller, Jelly Bean strapped to my chest and Minnie, Buddy and Princess following along in my wake, much to the amusement of other parents and general onlookers.

Three down, three to go.

We head to Tink's sports activity, where I feed the twins, then scoot home so the twins can nap. I do a load of washing, prepare tomorrow's lunchboxes and start a special dinner. I'm feeling adventurous and am going to try to convince the brood that the mash I'm serving alongside the lamb stew is potato when in actual fact it is cauliflower and celeriac. Cooked off in stock alongside sautéed onions, and finished with butter and a dash of milk, it is absolutely heavenly to the adult palate. Whether my finicky children agree remains to be seen.

Chores done, I wake the twins, dress them in pretty little outfits and put my tiny princess in a sparkly dress, much to her delight. We head back to the school, and between assembling and collapsing the pram, collecting school bags and other assorted paraphernalia, and hunting down my children at their various classes, forty-five minutes later we are back home and the eldest two are out of their uniforms and into nice outfits.

Finally we arrive at the car park next to the bistro. I can already taste something fabulous cooked in oodles of butter and that first crackling hit of a half-glass of fine champagne. I have three out and assembled when I realise . . . where is my bloody pram?

Scrolling back through my debris-scattered short-term memory, I can picture precisely where I dumped it on the driveway to allow Princess and Buddy out of their seats, and in the frenzy to get away, failed to put it back in. Damn!

Do I just turn around and go home? Do I waste a precious hour and strain my children's already tenuous patience by going back to retrieve it and return? Bugger it. We are having lunch NOW, period.

# TEN-AND-A-BIT TIPS ON HOW TO HERD THE KIDS TO THE TROUGH WITH NO BLOODY STROLLER

1. Keep those who are able to walk trapped in the car until the minute you are ready to go. Unloading will be a slow process and you want to avoid any opportunity for bored munchkins to wander off, probably into oncoming traffic.
2. Don your Baby Bjorn. If you haven't brought it with you, you clearly need to get out more often, and are now stuffed, so just give up and go home via the drive-through (both the fast food and bottle shop variety).
3. Once the Baby Bjorn is in place, take two safety pins (every self-respecting mother, having faced the last-minute 'But today is the Easter Bonnet Parade/Book Week dress-up day/dress as a character from the olden days' proclamation at school drop-off, or dealt with a child who has managed to rip a hole in the seat of their shorts getting out of the car, will have a ready supply of safety pins in their handbag for last-minute costume creation or garment mending). With these safety pins, pin one end of your two-year-old's favourite blanky/teddy/rag to the scruff of their shirt, and the other to your sleeve. They are now effectively bound to you.
4. Put one baby in the Baby Bjorn. Jiggle them to one side, slightly off-centre.
5. Sling nappy bag/handbag/snack bags over your shoulders.
6. Position the other baby on your hip, to the side, where there is marginally more room.
7. Release the other children.
8. Instruct said children to each grab hold of one of the many dangly bits on the Baby Bjorn and don't let go!
9. Shuffle carefully to your destination.
10. If your phone rings, DON'T ATTEMPT TO ANSWER IT! It will just be some telemarketer who wants to waste your time and will invariably tip the balance, causing complete collapse of your carefully orchestrated operation.

11. Once at your destination, request banquette seating, so you can lay the babies down as you attempt to shovel food into the mouths of the other children, or at least get some food into their mouths as opposed to on the floor, on their clothes, and in your hair.

## Part ii: How to survive the meal without electronic aides, hired help, or a circus performer

1. Bring electronic aides.
2. Bring hired help.
3. Bring circus performers.
4. Pay someone to pretend to be one or all of the above. (Young wait staff can pull off some incredible YouTube-clip reconstructions when you wave $20 under their noses.)
5. If all of the above prove elusive, pencils and blank paper are always well received.
6. Play Illustrated Twenty Questions, in which each person in turn has to draw a picture, and as they do so the rest of the table has twenty guesses in which to guess what they are drawing. (Yes, this is a total rip-off of Mr Squiggle, but he is currently off air, so trademark be damned!)
7. Read them a story between/during courses if you can juggle it.
8. Play 'taste test' whereby they must each take a mouthful of their dish and nominate what they taste OR what that mouthful tastes/feels like, in a manner not unlike wine tasting. This keeps mine occupied for ages, with the run-on effect that they actually eat.
9. Order a bottle of wine, drink until you forget the kids are there.
10. Hire yourself a circus performer.
11. Hire yourself two, and sell a few kids to the circus in exchange.

# CHAPTER

## SATURDAY 30 MAY

*7:15 a.m.* I awake, glance at the time on my phone and lurch out of bed panicking we will be late for school. The sudden chill sharpens my senses and I realise it is Saturday, we are at the beach house, and it is bloody freezing!

With gratitude thick enough to slice, I slip back into the warm embrace of the covers, luxuriating in a few more stolen moments of slumber till the tribe rouses . . . but I can't sleep.

The thought of only having Sal four days a week rolls around my head like so many marbles, skittering from nerve ending to nerve ending, twanging my synapses, leaving me anxious and short of breath. I bunch the warm doona hard against my face, inhaling recycled warm air till the panic subsides.

> SHOPPING LIST
>
> Halloween make-up (I keep finding myself assuming a pose not unlike Edvard Munch's 'The Scream', so might as well make the most of it)
>
> Escape hatch, ejector seat, large hole I can disappear into at will – basically, anything that will allow me to escape my current situation as quickly as possible.

But then it steals in again, clamping down hard on my throat and revving my heart up to levels that leave my head spinning.

We had planned a weekend jaunt to the hideaway while The Chef was still away, and now I feel it has been ruined because, obsessive-compulsive worrier that I am, I will spend the whole weekend fretting about what impact this new development will have on us all. Do I need to interview for a new nanny on the sly, while my perfect nanny is still in my home, but struggling? Do I need to lighten her load and take more responsibility on myself? But I never have time to sit down as it is, and the times when I am out of the house, invariably auditioning, running errands for the business, or doing the household shop, are what keep my sanity intact.

Princess wanders in, hair tousled and nightgown askew. I put my fingers to my lips, gesture that Daddy is still sleeping, and pull up my side of the covers to her. She slips in, grateful to be escaping the cold. The chill down here at the beach is bracing, life-affirming, invigorating. But it still doesn't change the fact that when you first slip out of a warm bed in thin nightwear, it is bloody cold!

'What's for dinner?' she whispers.

'Umm, we were going to roast a chicken.'

She sticks her tongue out and twists her face in a comical display of disgust.

'I don't want it, I don't wanna eat animals.'

'Why is that?'

'Cos I love animals, they are so cute and fluffy.'

'I see; so what would you like instead, pumpkin soup?'

'No.'

'Tomato pasta?'

'No.'

'Well, what then?'

'Just something not made of animals . . . I'll have meatballs.'

Oh, the innocence of youth. Maybe being forced to be home more isn't such a bad thing. At least I will be guaranteed a front-row seat to more of Princess's famous clangers.

## SUNDAY 31 MAY

*4:19 a.m.* Jelly Bean and I are huddled together in the lounge, soaking up the circle of heat radiated by a tiny electric heater, doing its darnedest to hold back the oppressive, blanketing chill that is winter on Victoria's southern shores.

Tomorrow, my tiny munchkins will be seven months old.

SHOPPING LIST

*Birthday candles. Why do I never have any birthday candles? They generally come in boxes of twelve and my brood are all still aged in the single digits, so where are the leftovers?*

Where did that time go?

A quick tally of the twins' achievements at seven months:

- Rolling on to tummies: check. Jelly Bean happily rolls back again, Lolly Pop has a tendency to roll herself into a nook or cranny from which she cannot roll back and, already exhibiting a fear of heights, gets stuck there in a head-upright position and cries.
- Curiosity: double check! Lolly Pop has amazing hand-eye coordination, and anything she can grasp is drawn in close for a detailed examination. Jelly Bean, on the other hand, is a born explorer. She adopts a scooting style not unlike upside-down breaststroke, and I invariably discover her wedged beneath tables, under cabinets and stuck in corners, crying out

only when she is unable to scoot any further.
- Bottom teeth: check.
- Gnawing the heck out of anything they can lay their hands on, hence indicating that more teeth are soon to follow: check.
- Immunisations: up to date with no ill effects, beyond Mummy being reduced to a nervous wreck in the lead-up to the actual inoculation because watching her babies cry makes her cry and then, as though she has been given an impromptu therapy session, she cannot stop, and needs to be heartily consoled by the doctor while the twins look on, bemused expressions on their chubby faces, embarrassed by their mother already.
- Healthy weight gain: check – they are veritable butter balls.
- Solid foods: check. As I've mentioned earlier, at this age I'm more interested in them handling food and experiencing texture and flavour rather than forcing it down their throats with a spoon, so their clothes are enjoying heartier feeds than the twins themselves, but they are making the connection and bringing the food to their mouths all the time now, and enjoying it with gusto.
- Smiling and laughing: check and check.
- Feeding: Lolly Pop has been a bottle girl for months now; Jelly Bean only takes one or two breastfeeds now, morning and night, but both look at me with such adoration, such rapture, such love, it is all I can do to not want to just swallow them whole!

They each feel different in my arms, unique. Lolly Pop strong, sturdier, softer, so curious about the world but only from within the safe circle of Mummy's embrace. Jelly Bean is squirmier; she curls up snugly beneath the curve of my chin, then attempts to launch her pudgy little body at any passing noise or glowing screen. Both adore their big brother and sisters, and love playful interaction with them all. However, I frequently see a moment of doubt cloud their expressions whenever Tink arrives on the scene, as she has a tendency to love them a little too hard. But it is my voice they both instinctively look toward, my form their enormous blue eyes follow relentlessly across the room. Both arch upwards from their bouncer toward me when I approach, wanting to be picked up, cuddled and treasured. How honoured am I, to have all these little people to love and be loved by? How special to be the centre of their universes, if only for such a fleeting moment. I am tethered by their love, their dependence on me. I have my moments of fighting against these ties that bind me, but I am so very conscious of how quickly these years, days, minutes will pass. Give me strength, diary, the strength to hold them fast, keep them safe, and give them all the love they need so they too can face the world knowing that if all else fails, Mum will always be there.

## TWELVE SYMPTOMS OF MATERNIS EXTREMIS OR 'EXTREME MOTHERHOOD'

1. Finding yourself rocking a basket of groceries in the supermarket aisle, or jigging a trolley at the checkout as if it is a stroller bearing a restless toddler.
2. You practically live in sportswear, not because there is any danger of you setting foot in a gym, but because Lycra is easy to sponge down. It also tends to hold in wobbly bits, and at least looks like a step up from a tracksuit.
3. You go shopping precisely because you have nothing in your wardrobe beyond Lycra and trackies. Three hours later you depart with a bootful of 'essentials' for the kids and nothing for yourself.
4. As if on auto-pilot, even the most innocent department store visit always winds up in the children's wear section, and even though your offspring may all be finally toilet-trained, safely at school, able to tie their own shoelaces and you have off-loaded the entire contents of the nursery on eBay, the mere sight of a onesie sets your ovaries singing like a nightingale, and your mind wondering if the car will fit just one more baby seat.
5. You wake at 2 a.m. with palpitations because there is no fresh bread for lunchboxes, OR
6. You wake at 3 a.m. with palpitations because you forgot to defrost something for tonight's dinner, OR
7. You wake at 4 a.m. with palpitations because you are concerned you are not getting enough sleep, OR
8. You wake at 5 a.m. with palpitations fearing something is wrong because you haven't woken with palpitations ALL NIGHT!
9. You invariably cook one meal for the munchkins and one for

yourself and any other adults in the household, but then eat the scraps from their plates as you clear up, then can't eat your meal anyway.

10. You find yourself, at 11 a.m., once the chaos of the morning routine has subsided, absently eating Froot Loops straight from the box.

11. You have, at least once, woken in fright, dressed, brushed your teeth, woken and dressed the kids, fed them breakfast, packed lunches, loaded school bags, opened the front door, marvelled at how dark it is this morning, checked your watch, and discovered it is 1 a.m.

12. You have, at least ten times, woken in fright, then proceeded to wander about the house, moving from room to room, checking they are still breathing, for no reason other than that your love for them is so enormous, so all-consuming and so complete, you would give everything and anything just to be sure they are safe. Congratulations, you are officially an Extreme Mother.

# THURSDAY 4 JUNE

*9:54 a.m.* I've done it. I've gone out, done my homework and started interviewing for a second babysitter for my catastrophe of children.

SHOPPING LIST

Mary Poppins

Yes, it seems excessive, but looking into my crystal ball, I know I will not always be able to fill the gaps on those days Sal is no longer working. What if a job comes up? A last minute voice-over? If someone gets sick? What then? Can I clone myself? Split myself clean down the middle to be in two places at once?

The two people I've interviewed so far were just wrong. I'm not sure if I'm being too picky but holding anyone up to the standard of Sal's ability will leave any potential candidate wanting. This process is painful, emotional, deeply personal, tiresome and sometimes demoralising. Yet it is one you cannot take any shortcuts on, because after all, the people you are vetting will be the caretakers of your most precious possession: your children.

# FRIDAY 5 JUNE

*10:13 a.m.* I've found her! Her name is Halle (yep, as in Hallelujah), she is young, vibrant, clever, solicitous, joyful, studious, flexible

(schedule-wise; I didn't ask her favourite yoga pose) and considerate. She ticks all the boxes, said all the right things, and she starts Friday. Yippee!

Let's hope she doesn't take one look at my brood and run.

---

## FINDING MARY POPPINS: TICKING ALL THE BOXES

The task of finding carers for your little people, be they nannies, babysitters, daycare centres or schools, is one fraught with fear and uncertainty. It is possible to find your Mary Poppins, however, without risking your sanity.

Here is a checklist I've formulated over the years.

1. Be specific. Before you even tap 'excellent babysitter' into Google, discuss exactly what you are looking for with your partner AND children.
2. Figure out your budget.
3. What days or hours do you require help: is it a full-time proposition? Mornings? Evenings? Two days a week or five? Weekends?
4. Will they need a car, and if so will it need to fit your brood?
5. Are you in a position to let them use your car if necessary, and can you add their name to your car insurance policy?
6. What duties do you require them to fulfil? Just child-minding or some house-keeping and cooking too?
7. Would you consider an au pair? Would you have room to accommodate one?

Now for some tips:

• Word of mouth: priceless. Make sure to ask families with a similar dynamic to your own – a sparkling reference for a nanny from a family with one child may not hold water if you have four children. Also, talk to families with older children – they may be able to recommend some excellent people they have used, or you could strike gold and find a nanny/babysitter who is leaving a family because they are no longer needed.

- Where word of mouth fails you, nanny agencies more than fill the gap. You will not be able to negotiate on price, and agency nannies and sitters are expensive, but all the legwork regarding background checks has been done for you, all candidates are fully trained and accredited with important qualifications such as first aid, and agencies can find people who cater specifically to your needs.
- Make sure you hold an interview with potential employees without the children. This is an opportunity for you to have a frank, detailed conversation with them about precisely what you expect and what is required in the job. Holding such a conversation is practically impossible with infants crying, toddlers destroying soft furnishings, children hanging from curtain rails demanding food, or sullen teens lurking in the background, undermining the pastel-hued portrait you are painting of your family with their insistence that they are old enough to take care of themselves. (Cut to: every crazed party scene from every bad American teen flick ever made.)
- Be clear and firm from Day One about their duties. You do yourself and your kids a disservice if you try to slip in sly 'extra duties' after the fact. Be honest and upfront about what you need, be realistic about how much you can ask of them and keep in mind how much you are paying them. If what you ask is too much for the candidate in front of you, that person is not right for you and your family. Better to know now than later. The last thing you want is having someone who resents you caring for your little people, and perhaps neglecting your children in order to get all the other duties you request completed.
- Dont be afraid of being forthright in your requests: this person will be caring for your precious children, and they will spend most days inside your home. They have to be the right one.
- Be specific about how you want your children raised. It is so important that your carer's perspective on discipline, morals, and principles corresponds with your own.
- As a devoted 'lister' I cannot over-emphasise how critical a well-thought-out and drawn-up list can be to the smooth running of your household

in your absence. Note down the milestones of each day particular to your family such as nap times, meal times, bath times, favourite activities and numbers for important contacts, along with a copy of each child's school schedule and extra-curricular activities schedule, so your new sitter can help prepare your children for their day ahead of time. Go the extra step and note down where certain favoured toys are kept, what your routine is with the washing and cleaning (should they have a quiet moment, you are not paying them to sit on the couch with their feet up), and have a grocery list available that they can add to as you run out of certain items. I have attached a small chalkboard to an unobtrusive area in the kitchen for just this purpose.

• Once your bases are covered, organise for them to work a few days while you are actually there. This helps your children adjust as they come to view the interloper as Mummy's or Daddy's friend. It also gives your nanny the opportunity to better understand the flow of your household and how you like things to be done. Finally, you get a perspective on how this person interacts with your brood and whether they are the right fit.

As daunting as finding the right person to help care for your little ones can seem, it is not impossible provided you make a plan and stick to it.

## TUESDAY 9 JUNE

*6:36 p.m.* I'M OVER MY CHILDREN!!! Is that wrong? I've entertained them all long weekend. Now I cannot watch the news (all the TVs have been taken up with 'TV time' for individual age groups), I cannot eat dinner until the twins go down (the same dinner summarily rejected by the munchkins who can consume solids, despite it taking three hours to prepare, and which is now coagulating in the pan), and the twins will neither sleep nor feed (too over-stimulated by the chaos playing out around them). I'm snookered.

Princess is using forbidden textas to draw on flimsy paper which goes straight through to stain the marble bench. Tink is throwing a whopper tantrum because the new My Little Pony electric toothbrush I bought for her today, which she has left vibrating since she received it, has been turned off in an

## for week of filming

## Must do
Eyelashes tinted
Re-growth coloured
Legs waxed
Spray tan
Pedicure
Manicure
Prepare and freeze: soups, pies, stews, bread, biscuits (suck-up gift to crew
for when I fluff lines cause I'm so over-tired, and when I'm late to set because
the builders have paved behind my car and it takes me an extra fifteen minutes to
manoeuvre it out)
Spend quality time with my children.

## Must buy
Nice underwear
Healthy, nutritious snacks
Inspiring home decorating magazines
Language tapes (must use down time on set to do something useful, like learn French)
1kg bag of patience.

## What I will realistically manage to get done
None of the above BUT if I can trim my toenails and remove the
three-month-old polish I've been topping up, bleach my old undies, grab a can
of dry shampoo (cuts down on need to frequently wash tresses AND kinda
hides re-growth), cook-off and freeze 2 kg mince to be re-imagined as a variety
of meals (hello, bolognaise, tacos, pies, stews), and buy a couple of massive
bags of Freddo frogs for the crew AND to assuage my guilt at neglecting
my children, I will still be ahead.

## What I must remember when nerves/guilt get the better of me
I love meeting new people
I love my job
I love my children

effort to save a little battery life, so she is now smashing and throwing every-thing within arm's length. Minnie, bless her, has sought refuge in her bedroom, but still hasn't even glanced at her homework journal. Buddy, who called in from the school sick bay at 10 a.m. with a 'stomach ache' but who proclaimed himself 'starving' the moment he arrived home and has been feasting ever since, has just devoured dessert and is now lounging in my bedroom. The Chef, despite a full day's work, is now slaving over endless emails, and I'm reduced to watching *Dora the Explorer* from a distance, having tripped and fallen upon a wedge of smelly cheese and an open pack of water crackers.

*Sigh*.

Also, our plans for a dinner out on Saturday night have fallen flat as we cannot find a sitter (at least, not one who is happy to wrangle six kids).

*Sigh*.

Once again, I'm left feeling a failure. I'm a terrible mother. All I want is to fall into bed and pull the covers over my head, but even that is tainted by the knowledge that once morning comes and I have to pull the covers off, it all begins again. There's no joy today, no sassy upshot to put a positive spin on it all, no cutesy anecdote to salve the day's frustrations. Just fatigue, anger and shame – mothers' little secrets. We all have them. Lurking behind the proud smiles as we slog through another soccer training session on a freezing, muddy sideline. Or clean out the rotting remnants of lunchbox rejects from the bottom of school bags. Or drag ourselves through another shopping trip with three screaming, whirling dervishes in tow.

This is motherhood.

Damn, it's hard.

The acting job begins tomorrow. It is going to feel like a holiday.

# WEDNESDAY 10 JUNE

*3:09 a.m.* Buddy tumbles into my room, skittish as a pollie accused of rorting, a fever raging through his little body, hallucinating about bottles of milk and aliens.

Crap, he really is sick.

I hoist him up, dispense children's Nurofen (the secret fever-slayer) and carry him to his bed. Shaking, he begs me to sleep with him. Naturally I acquiesce, guilt at my rantings earlier in the evening clawing at my throat. My poor little man.

The Chef pops his head in, all concern. I shoo him away with orders to get some sleep while I take the midnight watch over our son.

> SHOPPING LIST
>
> *Apologies for each of my children*

**4:43 a.m.** Buddy rouses, famished with that hunger unique to a fever, and we tiptoe downstairs for cornflakes and cartoons with the volume low. Finally he nods off again, as do I, beside him on the couch.

**5:54 a.m.** Wake with a crick in my neck and gingerly begin preparations for the day, my head held stiffly to one side until my twisted muscles relax. Buddy's temperature is on the rise again, fever unbroken . . . bloody hell. First day of work and I will have to call in sick!

I cannot leave a sick little boy at home . . . can I?

**7:35 a.m.** Sal bustles in, tuts over Buddy, admonishes me for being ridiculous about wanting to stay home, and virtually thrusts me out the door, more than aware of how important it is for me to rejoin the workforce, however briefly. Okay, off to work then.

**5:17 p.m.** I'm in shock. The day has flown like a flock of startled seagulls. I've consumed those promised coffees, hot, as fantasised. I had lunch unmolested by munchkins. No-one asked to eat from my plate and my clothing remained splatter-free. I played with adults, had actual conversations on topics ranging from children (of course) to politics, holiday destinations, music, great cafe breakfasts and the state of our industry, without needing to pause even once for a nappy change or to pack a lunchbox. I wore nice clothes and nice make-up, all compliments of someone else.

Now finished, I can relax in the green room, poring over a trashy magazine, while I wait for a taxi to ferry me home.

I loved it.

But I am exhausted.

And beneath the buoyant nervous energy and adrenaline rush was the steady tug of missing my children, the lurking guilt I felt at leaving my little man at home sick, and the mild anxiety of contemplating how on earth I would catch up on doing all those little bits and pieces around the house that only I would obsess over. If I am honest, I get more pleasure waxing lyrical about my day on the page with you, diary, my old friend, than I do actually being at work. Writing, it feels, is becoming my guilty pleasure. If I could somehow reconfigure my day job to be writing, I might actually feel complete!

How the heck do parents put all these feelings in perspective? How do you reconcile them with the fact that we, as parents, often need to return to work, be it to secure the household finances, or just to secure our sanity?

All day, I worried that my catastrophe of children were missing me.

All day, I worried even more that they hadn't even noticed I was gone.

## HOW TO BE A PART OF YOUR CHILDREN'S DAY, EVEN WHEN YOU ARE NOT THERE

It is the little gestures that send the most love. Even if you are not always there to pick them up from school, play in the park, or read a bedtime story, there are small things you can do to make your children feel your presence and your love. A little can go a long way.

• Lay out clothes and anything they may need for the next day the night before.

• Pop a little note with a happy thought for the day in their lunchbox, in the pocket of their sports uniform, where you keep their toothbrushes, or in their pencil case.

• Ask them to keep a diary of their days so you can go through them together when you get home.

• Write them letters and have them write you letters in return. This may sound twee but it's a wonderful way of keeping in touch with each other, and you can often learn a lot more about their thoughts and feelings when related to you through their eyes than if you are there in person.

• Read to them when you get home; it may be the last thing you feel like, but it forges such important bonds.

• Play. Fifteen minutes of uninterrupted play each day can more than make up for twelve hours' absence. Leave the washing, the dishes can wait, the ironing won't get any more wrinkled for being ignored till tomorrow. When we finally shuffle off this mortal coil it is not the housework we didn't do we will regret most, it is the time wasted letting meaningless mundane chores overtake family time and letting our careers dominate our days. Ten minutes of nightly story time, five minutes of wrestling on the couch, fifteen minutes building a Lego fortress, twenty minutes discussing the day's events over dinner. These are the moments that make for the most wonderful memories.

## THURSDAY 11 JUNE

*5:02 a.m.* Wake, lurch out of bed, grab for the clothes I've been laying out each evening so I can quickly dress and get to the set without waking anyone, and find myself grasping at thin air.

Where are the clothes?

Why didn't I lay any out?

Who moved them?

Oooooh, hang on, I didn't lay any out as the job is finished.

Relief suffuses my body, like a warm flood racing through my system and tingling at my fingertips. Back under the covers! I had been pining to escape back into the world of sets, make-up vans, hot coffees and lines half-learned before needing to be performed, so am mildly shocked that I feel so ebullient about not having to go in to work today. But I guess at the end of the day, a job is a job, and the joys of slipping back into a warm bed beat out a dawn commute mid-winter any day.

I'm feeling deeply grateful to The Chef for the long, hard hours he puts in, and has been putting in since he was fifteen, that enable us to live as we do. It is an indescribable luxury to be able to choose if and when I work, one that is only possible because any

> SHOPPING LIST
>
> *Personalised T-shirt:*
>
> *'Yes, I have six children.'*
>
> *'Yes, they are all mine.'*
>
> *'Yes, they all came out of my body.'*
>
> *'Yes, really.'*
>
> *'Yes, twins in there too.'*
>
> *'Yes, they all have the same father.'*
>
> *'Yes, we have a television.'*
>
> *'Yes, we know how to use it.'*

salary I earn, while always helpful, will not cause undue hardship if it is not coming in every week. It is a long time since I have had to work just to get by, subsisting and supporting others on whatever income I can glean from my wonderful but not always consistent line of work. I now work not so much to support my household but to escape them, and that is the truth!

The Chef's sacrifices guarantee my freedoms. I think it's time to start respecting that a little more, tighten the belt, and stop bemoaning my lot. Time to focus on being the best wife and mother I can be and stop feeling ashamed by those labels. They don't necessarily define me, but they are testament to the many things I do well to keep this leaky boat afloat.

## FRIDAY 12 JUNE

*2 p.m.* Quiet morning; kids all unusually helpful. Funny that. Mid-term, I'd have an easier time pouring wet concrete into their uniforms than I do getting them dressed, fed and out the door, but when the last day before holidays rolls around, they are all awake at sparrow's fart and are bending over backwards to help me. Go figure!

Sensing the coming deluge that will be taking six brats on holiday, I bundle up Tink and the twins to trundle down to the local markets for 'Kiddy Friday', otherwise known as the day of the week when the market proprietors wheel out a batch of large, uninterested 'baby farm animals', and stage a batch of large, uninterested 'children's performers' (I've displayed more passion and vigour scrubbing out a toilet bowl) all in the name of extorting another $5 from weary parents at the end of another long week. However, Tink loves it, and it is better that I let her cut loose breaking out some dance moves in a market food court and trying to hug a clearly irritated goat than have her running around the house like an off-kilter whirling dervish.

Once I'm installed in a plastic chair (a bit sticky, but it is best not to focus on such things) within the market courtyard, lukewarm latte in hand, Tink clapping her hands, the twins wriggling in time to the strains of 'Hot potato', it is really rather pleasant.

Once the festivities wrap up, the twins quiet and Tink covered

SHOPPING LIST

Spare set of jumper leads . . . if the events of today are ever repeated, I may need them on hand to re-start my heart in papier mâché from the craft corner, it's time to make a quick nappy change pit stop, then onwards to home.

Naturally, when I manage to manoeuvre my travelling road show into the public toilets, the baby change cubicle is engaged. We wait and wait and wait. With Tink starting to fidget and the usually sanguine twins beginning to fret, I knock on the door, before a stallholder, on her way to spend a penny of her own, pauses to inform me that cubicle is under repair.

Bloody hell.

Following the friendly stallholder's directions, we wend our way to the other side of the market to the second public toilet. This one is only male and female. I cannot fit my 'wide load' pram through the door and there is nowhere to change the babies bar the grotty tiled floors. No thanks …

There is really nothing for it but to find a fast-food shop and make hypo-critical use of their toilets while abstaining from their 'cuisine'. The nearest temple of sugar, trans fats and deep-frying is one as famous for the lure of its kids' meals as it is for the amount of sugar in its burger buns. Knowing the potential here for Tink to go bananas and throw an epic tantrum when she realises where we are and all that targeted marketing begins to work its evil magic on her, I upload 'YouTube: Princess Kinder surprise eggs being unwrapped' (it's a phenomenon) and hand it to her while sheepishly approaching the counter and purchasing a bottle of water as a small conces-sion so I'm not just blatantly using their facilities without providing custom.

Thank goodness they have a disabled users' toilet with changing table. Inside, with Jelly Bean fresh as a daisy, and Lolly Pop mid-wet wipe, I notice Tink loitering by the door, momentarily distracted from the phone, eyeing my movements. I resume the nappy change and, quick as a flash, she has unlocked the door and is gone. Bloody hell! I'm paralysed by a moment of indecision, tempted to head straight out after her, but opt to secure the nappy, strapping Lolly Pop back in the pram without refastening the buttons of her bunny suit. Inside the restaurant, there is no sign of Tink. I scout the perimeter, calling her name, knowing deep down that should she be within earshot, this would all be some great game to her and she would be unlikely to respond. I ask the lethargic sixteen-year-old at the counter if they saw where the tiny little blonde girl with a Peppa Pig backpack clutching an iPhone might have headed, to be met with a shrug. Fan-bloody-tastic. I start asking patrons, all deep in their burgers and fries, aware that my voice is rapidly scaling up the octaves, a sure sign that hysteria will soon follow. No-one has seen her. One kindly gentleman offers to help. I have to put aside the automatic reaction of questioning his motives and gratefully accept his assistance. Another gentleman offers to mind the twins while I look, but, as genuine as I am sure the offer is, it would be pushing my trust too far. So with pram in tow, I make another round of the restaurant floor before heading for the doors. Outside, a busy pedestrian thoroughfare and traffic-clogged main road await. My baby girl is out there somewhere. So tiny, with just her Peppa Pig backpack, lay-lay, and my phone for protection. And it's not like she can call for help. To her, the device's sum worth is that it allows her to watch people unwrap surprise eggs.

Looking at the nameless faces, the packed stores, the crowded footpath, panic settles in my gut and my knees turn to water, threatening to drop me. What do I do? Stay here in case she makes her way back? Call the police? Run screaming through the streets? Visions of Madeleine McCann's angel face, and that of every other tiny child lost in limbo, sear my eyes. I blink, desperately seeking rational thought. But time and again my mind meanders back to my daughter's tiny little body, her halting smile, her dancing dimple, her shiny blonde hair in a pink-ribboned ponytail. So soft, sweet, and innocent. A perfect target for any depraved individual intent on taking what is not theirs and destroying lives in pursuit of their own despicable desires. Hysteria floods through my system, ice-cold, chilling, jolting me into a shambling run. 'Tink!' I scream, head swivelling side to side, 'TINK!' My repeated cries dissolve into shrieks.

As the traffic lights change, I bolt and am mid-way across the road when a man yelling out 'Ma'am!' halts me. I spin on my heel. The kindly gentleman who earlier offered his help is standing at the entry to the restaurant, beckoning me back with a wave. I scamper back to his side, and he points within, to the flight of stairs I had missed earlier, clearly leading to an upstairs seating area, but currently occupied by the sixteen-year-old girl from the counter, now animatedly discussing whatever is playing on the phone in the hand of a tiny little blonde girl with a Peppa Pig backpack and a stained blankie. Tink.

Relief — warm, soft, tender — wraps its arms around me and sucks the air from my lungs. I'm tempted to faint but instead stumble forward, falling upon Tink with a flood of kisses. Do I reprimand her? Scream, cry, gnash my teeth? No, I bundle her up, thank everyone profusely, and buy her a bloody kids' meal.

I really need a holiday . . .

# SUNDAY 14 JUNE

*5:36 a.m.* I seriously feel like I'm living large, *Entourage*-style.

The Chef and I had organised lunch with friends, at another friend's restaurant which just happens to be in Sydney. After spending a week trying to bend our combined schedules around our commitments and those of our children (our friends have five older children, taking the grand total to eleven) then make them fit within commercial flight times that would allow us to get up there in the morning and back by evening, our gorgeous friend texted: 'Let's just take the private plane.'

Ooohhhhh, yeaaaaaah! Two words guaranteed to bring on a state of bliss almost tantric in its power: Private Plane.

Who knew they had such an exotic, hypnotic, slightly erotic effect? Instant karma on the tarmac; Viagra with velocity.

And so, before you could say, 'Why yes, I will have another glass of Cristal,' there we were, strutting across the tarmac, being greeted by our personal pilot and sipping steaming lattes. Literally ten seconds after buckling up, we were in the air.

> SHOPPING LIST
>
> Grills
>
> Bling
>
> Greenbacks
>
> Pumped-up kicks
>
> Killer wheels
>
> Hoes
>
> (Putting together gear to keep my entourage happy, but looking at it, it looks like a farmhand's Bunnings shopping list)

I actually counted.

I don't think I will ever be able to queue for a revolting public toilet aboard a commercial airline ever again.

An hour later, we are navigating suburban Sydney back streets, thrumming with Saturday-morning activity. No security checks, no baggage carousels, no taxis.

Midway through a sumptuous lunch, a few fine vintages already imbibed, we were talking shop, and naturally the conversation turned to when they could expect to see me return to the screen. I found myself responding with limp enthusiasm, and suddenly realised that day might never come – and if it doesn't, I won't mind. Shock! Horror!

As we waxed lyrical about entertaining pastimes, I suddenly found myself talking animatedly about my love of writing. Here I was, enthusing about writers whose work I enjoy and expounding with unbridled, mildly inebriated rapture on the unparalleled joy of having someone read and enjoy my own words. My sweet friend paused, and held me with a look more sober than a judge delivering an unpopular verdict.

'If you love it, why don't you do it?'

'What? Write? Ha! Write what? And about what?'

'I dunno . . . write a book about what you know?'

'Well, that will be bloody short. A pamphlet on making lunchboxes?'

'Maybe – it's a start!'

Her words, like a cold, hard slap, stunned me. She issued a challenge and in doing so exposed a desire I had locked away in my heart of hearts years before. It stopped me short, cleared away the vino-induced fog, and set my heart beating like a dieter's catching a whiff of hot chips.

Madeleine West, author. I like the sound of that.

Once home, with the family tucked in bed, my mind was racing, ideas ricocheting off the walls, evaporating or summarily dismissed before having a chance to take hold.

Write about what I know . . . What do I know?

I'm a jobbing actor so I am a jack of many trades, master of none.

And I'm a mother of many, so I'm a mean multi-tasker, but does that make for an inspiring read?

Hmm. Mother of many.

I'm no expert at the mothering game but I've got six of the little drunk midgets so I must have gleaned some knowledge along the way. And where better to find inspiration than in the minutiae of dealing with the trials and tribulations parenthood throws up every day?

And where better to mine the everyday than between the pages of a religiously kept personal journal?

Dearest diary, this could be the beginning of a beautiful friendship . . . .

## FRIDAY 19 JUNE

*11:12 a.m.* Head in hands, heart in mouth, I've spent the week dividing my time between two tasks: preparing for our much-needed, much-longed-for family holiday, and collating, editing and transforming my diary entries from the past year into a tasty little sampler of the book I hope to write. It's essentially an anti-parenting guide. Anti-much of the useless advice spouted by many parenting 'bibles' at the expense of the perfectly suitable set of instincts we all have and need to listen to better. A tongue-in-cheek look at the wonderful, frustrating, hilarious, heart-breaking world of parenting, and a rather black, comedic look at my first seven months as a mother of six. Not just how it happened, but how I've survived to tell the tale.

SHOPPING LIST

*Pens*

*Paper*

*Laptop*

*Smoking jacket with patches on the elbows*

*A new career*

*Shares in flying pigs, cause if I can pull this off, fairytales really do come true.*

This morning I've sent said sample to a reputable, respectable publisher, one whom I admire. At this early stage, I would just love some feedback, some gentle constructive criticism, and a little bit of advice. To say I'm nervous would be like saying a lava-bath might be a bit warm. I'm terrified, elated, apprehensive, but also rather proud of the fact that I've taken a chance, taken a risk to attempt something I've dreamed of for a long time. Even if it comes to nothing, at least I will have no regrets. And thankfully, a certain four-year-old wet the bed this morning, then filled her wet sheets with her clean clothing in an attempt to disguise it, so I've mountains of laundry to keep me busy.

Keep smiling, Madeleine, keep smiling!

*6:09 p.m.* I've heard nothing. I know it sounds absurd but I'd imagined I would have heard something by now – even if it was just the ping of an email from some surly assistant confirming my work had been received, limply assuring me that some editor's underling would glance at it dubiously once they had finished fawning over their vegan, paleo, raw-food wrap and pruning their raffish designer beard.

Oh, the agony! I've made a fool of myself, I just know it! How presumptuous of me, to assume anyone would be remotely interested in anything I have to say anyway.

How embarrassing. Harrumph! Best forget about it all and move forward as quickly as possible.

Feeling a little fragile, a little battered by the whole ego-bruising affair and the imagined criticisms I will soon have to weather (in my own mind),

I have packed up the car once more to head to our little hideaway before our much-anticipated trip to both the snow and the sun.

Just writing those words makes me realise how very privileged I am to live as I do. Being able to jet off overseas with six smiling cherubs in tow (providing they have been bought off with toys, games and foodstuffs of the junky persuasion) is a rare and wonderful treat few are able to enjoy. And spending the week before we jet off lolling about in a secret little nook on a whim? Once again, a pleasure I would never have even dreamed of as that headstrong teenager who left her blue-collar home seeking the bright lights and big city. I should be thankful! Not moping about because I've thrown out a line in the uncharted waters of a potential new career and haven't had any nibbles.

Regardless, the truth is this: I know now how much I enjoy writing. I would really like to pursue this as a profession, and the fine art of motherhood is what I know best. But most importantly, writing is something I will still take pleasure in, whether it becomes a burgeoning new career or not. If all turns to nappy-filler, I'm sure I can amply occupy my days writing surly letters to the complaints departments of numerous toy manufacturers, junk-food producers and national newspapers, so I'll get my creative fix regardless.

But right now, I need to source some serious beachwear and skiwear.*

*Guess what? I've never seen real snow!

## FINDING YOUR FIRE:
## MAKING YOUR WORK WORK FOR YOU

Every day we teach our children to dream big, follow their passion, chase what they love and never give up, then we lurch off to the train station for another nine-hour day at the grindstone, hating every minute but staying put because it pays the bills.

The best role model our children have for life is us, and so we have an obligation to model those qualities we try so hard to nurture in them: ambition, drive, self-respect, willpower and the endurance to strive to be the best version of themselves they can be.

Finding and doing a job that makes you happy is a privilege, but one that is not impossible if you are prepared to work hard, take risks and think outside the box.

First, ask yourself: what makes you happy? Is there a hobby or a skill you take pride and joy in practising? Travelling, exercise, animals, caring for children, cooking, gardening, fiddling with machinery, putting together great outfits? Are you gifted at packing suitcases or skilled at putting together children's bedrooms? Have you a knack for finding great storage solutions in your busy home or are you terrific at growing herbs in a tiny city apartment? Do you have friends begging you for your healthy muffin recipes or are your kids' parties the envy of the playground? Are you constantly in demand to organise school functions or do you always know how to locate the perfect costumes for school productions? Whatever you can think of, it can be made into a business with a little bit of savvy and a lot of determination.

Look at ways of making that skill work for you. This often comes down to nothing more than identifying areas where that skill could be applied, and where there exists a hole in the market. For example, do you love to paint but are not prepared to live in a garret chewing your beret? Rather than limiting your oeuvre to creating pretty canvases, identify where your skill might have a practical application. Think about approaching local businesses offering your services to design picture walls, decorate menu boards, reinvigorate their store frontage. Pick up some local design courses. Purchase a batch of inexpensive backpacks, customise them with a bit of puffy paint and glitter, and take them along to local markets or school fetes.

When you start to invest time in doing something you love, and that you know you are good at, it has a positive effect on every aspect of your life. It makes you feel good about yourself, so you work harder. The harder you work the better the results. Good results make you believe in yourself more. Believing in yourself allows you to take greater risks, which opens you up to greater opportunities. Perhaps most importantly, doing something that fulfils you makes you happy, which makes those around you happy, and so the circle continues.

I've told you my life motto before: don't make excuses, make it happen. Ultimately, it is we who chart our own destinies, and our behaviours offer a template to our children for how to live a healthy, wealthy, happy life. The only thing shying away from risk promises is that you will be left behind, because people do not seek out those who won't take a chance. It's pretty hard to be a part of the action when you always have an excuse not to.

If there is something you love, take a chance on it. Your children will respect you, you will respect yourself, and at the end of the day, nothing gambled, nothing gained. We are in the workforce a long time; it might as well be doing something you find fulfilling. If that means taking a pay cut now, then get creative to fill the gaps until you become more established. Being hungry makes you work harder to get yourself where you want to be.

A life well lived is a life without regrets.

## SATURDAY 20 JUNE

SHOPPING LIST

Slats

Wetties

Thermals

Slickers

Joeys

Fleecies

(Suggested list of ski gear I need to buy . . . can someone please tell me what the hell this stuff is?)

## MONDAY 22 JULY

*9:08 a.m.* I'm contemplating my still-empty inbox (save a few missives from Rebel Sport, Target and the Greens) when my agent calls, all aflutter. 'Okay, it's last-minute, but we need you to put down a test for this faaaaaabulous

SHOPPING LIST

Lights

Cameras

ACTION!

new American show, shooting out of America. It's terrific! You would be perfect for it! Need to do a standard American accent. Did I mention it is American?'

'Yep, several times! Sounds good, when do you need it by?'

'Good! Great! Umm, it is a quick turnaround, so to get it back to America . . . I'd need it now.'

'What?'

Bloody hell.

I shower, slap on a little make-up and attempt to tame my hair. I need a reader, a cameraman, decent lighting; I have the nanny, a stylish but utterly useless low-wattage lamp and six little darlings.

Bloody hell.

After thirty minutes of script study and numerous attempts to get the three smallest into bed, I surrender and plop them in the study with a *Sleeping Beauty* DVD. Princess has been given the 'special textas' (so special, once applied to soft furnishings they are impossible to remove) and is happily drawing away at the bench. Buddy is building a lego fort. Minnie is my designated reader (she can read! Really, what more do I need?) and Sal will be behind the camera (or iPhone; beggars can't be choosers).

First take: we start out smoothly then Minnie loses her place in the script, starts to giggle and it proves infectious. Sal starts, which sets the camera jiggling, then I erupt too. 'Cut!'

Second take: babies start to howl in the background as Tink has decided that the most comfortable way to view the movie is lying across her twin sisters. 'Cut!'

Third take: almost get through the scene when Princess dashes into shot to show me her art, along with her ink-covered hands, face and shirt. 'Cut!'

Fourth take: action is called, Buddy appears. 'Yum! Where's the bacon?' 'Cut!'

Fifth take: I'm so busy awaiting the next interruption, I forget my lines. 'Cut!'

Sixth take: I'm on the last paragraph! Then . . . the babies bawl, Princess screams out 'Shut up!', Buddy pops up in the background: 'Mum, I would really like some bacon', and ding dong! One of the builders pops his head around the front door: 'Madeleine, we need you to move your car.' MJ goes berserk at the intrusion, which makes Minnie laugh and knock over the apple juice in an empty wine bottle I've been using as a prop, spilling its contents all over the table, the only copy I have of the script, and herself.

'Okay! I surrender!'

However, I have managed to get out the last line and exit the scene. At that precise moment the battery on my phone carks it. Do I have the strength to wait ten minutes and try again?

Quite frankly, no. I have one semi-usable take. Yes, it features a cast of unwelcome extras but this is my life. Once my phone revives I send the single, precious scene to my agent with a small note attached:

'Dear producers: thank you for taking the time to view and consider my audition. Yes, it is imperfect, yes there are interruptions, spillages, unwritten walk-on roles, and a soundtrack that does little to enhance the action. However, if you view my work and feel it shows even one iota of ability, and might just be appropriate for your production, then imagine what I would be capable of on an actual set!

'Warm regards, Madeleine (aka: the crazy lady with all the kids).'

Scene sent, I am spent, suffused with the simple satisfaction of having done my best. But I don't think I will need to be applying for an American working visa any time soon.

SHOPPING LIST

Two packing lists:
warm weather list
cold weather list

Clothing lists:
boys clothing list (short)
girls clothing list (long)
baby clothing list
dressing up list
dressing down list
shoes list
hats list

Toiletries list

Nappy change list

Snack list

List list

Schindler's list

Listlessness list

It's official: I have Listeria
(lister's hysteria)

## FRIDAY 26 JUNE

*9:18 a.m.* At last! The school holidays are upon us. Sleep-ins, no lunchboxes to pack, no uniforms to press, no small children to drag bodily from their beds to dress while they slump, only semi-conscious, against the nearest firm surface – typically my shoulder.

Also no emails regarding my attempt at stringing a few words together (urgh! Have I embarrassed myself?), and no word from my agent on any recent auditions.

Right, I'm taking a stand and severing the ties that bind me to electronic communication. Yes, I'm leaving my iPad at home! Our long-awaited family holiday is finally upon us, and I am not going to let anything spoil it. Five days of snowy Queenstown, ten in sunny Fiji. Just one more hurdle to surmount: we leave Monday morning and I still haven't packed. Where do I begin?

### A GUIDE THROUGH THE DELIGHTS OF PARENTAL PACKING

Where to begin? Okay, a week out from your trip, write a detailed list of everything you think you might need.

Now find a low-traffic area in your home – the corner of a bedroom will suffice.

Pull out everything on that list and put it in a pile in your selected spot.

Leave it for a day to mature (ie: determine what you actually need. No, you will not require a pressed shirt 'just in case' or the novelty coffee machine that plugs in to the car, or snow boots, unless you are actually skiing, in which case go ahead).

Now, divide that pile in half, and put one half back away. BE RUTHLESS! You will only ever use half of what you think you will need.

Pack the remaining half immediately. There is your base.

Check off everything in that case on your list. If there are any glaring voids, collect and pack.

Throughout the week you can add to the case, but you must subtract something from the case in turn.

The day before you leave, if your case is looking empty, you are permitted to add a few items BUT the wiser route is to leave some space as you will invariably end up picking up some touristy paraphernalia, and there is great joy in being able to fit said tat in the one suitcase for the trip home.

Finally, before you close the lid, ensure everyone's bedtime attire is on the top for ease of access, along with anything you may need quickly or in the event of an emergency (medicines, nappies, Tim Tams).

## Creating your list

To begin, you need to answer some basic questions:

1. Is your destination a warm or cold climate?
2. Will your holiday comprise activity (hiking, skiing, scuba diving) or just copious amounts of lying by a pool? Ensure your list reflects your intentions.
3. What do you need to accommodate the specific age group(s) of your child(ren)?

Babies: nappy-changing equipment, blankets, bottles. Sterilising bags. Formula. (Sealed into an airtight bag and labelled, this is easier to carry than in tins.) Portable cot. Teething ointment. Nappy rash cream. Soft toys with squeakers/bells. Baby paracetamol.

Toddlers: nappy stuff and toddler milk/snacks/bottles. Comforter (blanket or favourite toy) pencils and paper, Play-Doh for plane/train trips, paracetamol, sunscreen, hat, band-aids, mosquito repellent, bathing costume and rashy vest (those fabulous light watersports tops that protect against rash and sunburn) or thermal undergarment, waterproof jacket or suit and tracksuits or large onesies. One 'going out' outfit, shoes that can be adapted to a variety of situations (nice sandals, lightweight runners), gumboots if necessary. Flotation vest: these are virtually impossible to get in small sizes once you arrive.

Children up to twelve: any of the above, where applicable. Electronic devices. I know you aspire to a distraction-free vacation, but by a few days in, you will be thanking me. Don't beat yourself up about it, just put some hard and fast restrictions on usage and everyone will be happy. Ask this age group to help you pack what they need. Yes, you will have to do some serious culling, but they will come up with some very useful suggestions.

Teens: basically just up-end the laundry basket into a suitcase and hope for the best. Nothing you do will be right anyway, all the clothes you choose will be hideous, and the last thing they want is to be seen in public with you, BUT if you allow them some degree of autonomy and freedom, let them think they are making the decisions, don't insist they sever the mobile phone to which they are joined at the hip, and don't foist too much 'family time' on them, you might all just have a good time! If they continue to complain, let them know that unless they want to pay their own way washing dishes or travelling in the baggage hold, they better lose the 'tude!

Finally, you need to amass a veritable medicine cabinet as it can be very difficult to obtain necessary medications while away. Ensure any prescription items are accompanied by the actual script so you don't run into any trouble at Customs.
   Some suggested must-haves:
- children's paracetamol
- children's ibuprofen
- antihistamines
- rehydration salts in dissolvable tablet form
- hand sanitiser
- Imodium (just in case)
- antiseptic cream
- band-aids
- sterile wipes (just a handful, most chemists or even your doctor's office should be happy to give you a few)
- children's toothpaste (in case what is on hand doesn't suit their tastes and the nightly brush becomes a water torture)
- a sheet of worming tablets (again, just in case. If they suddenly develop an outbreak while away at some far-flung resort, it can be nigh-on impossible to find Combantrin, and you will spend every night and morning dealing with a very uncomfortable little incubator.)

Naturally, your own first-aid kit should reflect the specific needs of your family, and be tailored to suit the destination. If you are hitting the Gold Coast theme parks, you need take nothing but a heaving bank balance and an indulgent, if slightly pained, smile. But if you are trekking through Nepal, I would be up-ending the entire bathroom cupboard into a rucksack and leaving everything else behind bar some very thick socks!

Bon voyage!

# CHAPTER

# TUESDAY 30 JUNE

*1:47 a.m.* They are still awake. I hear them begin to murmur . . . voices rise . . . giggles . . . a light switch is flicked . . . a door jam creaks . . . and they are up again.

Bloody hell!

Despite almost twenty-four hours of wakefulness, the four eldest of the tribe are still swinging from the chandeliers and stripping the paint from the walls of our accommodation in Queenstown. And please don't attempt to soothe my rattled nerves with excuses of jet lag and time zones. A three-and-

> SHOPPING LIST
>
> *1 kg bag mixed lollies (if I let the kids hoover up the lot, that should be enough to put them in a sugar-induced stupor, right? Or at least keep them occupied for thirty minutes . . . right?)*

a-half-hour flight and mere two-hour time difference cannot possibly justify the degree of hysteria playing out before me.

This is insanity.

This is depravity.

This is travelling with children.

How did I forget the full horror so soon?

When the lady behind the check-in desk for our low-cost carrier refused to let me use her 50-cent Bic pen to write my name on a baggage label, on that grounds that 'It's my pen, I can't lend it to you', perhaps I should have seen it as a sign, a foretelling of things to come, rather than just a hostess with the actual hosting skills of an empty ice-cube tray.

When the same Lovely Lisa told us she had just given our pre-booked seats away (despite us having paid a fee to guarantee we would all be in one row) because 'first in first served', even though we were on time, perhaps we should have seen the folly in attempting to cross international borders with a bevy of bawling babes in tow, rather than just being confused as to how an airline can ask you to pay a fee to secure seating then give said seating away on a whim anyway, or as Lisa would say, 'Because I don't like your tone.'

Finally, when we almost missed our flight battling our way through Customs with our tribe of stragglers because Life-of-the-Party Lisa decided we couldn't have the express passes our travel agent had bent over backward to organise because she didn't give them to passengers boarding A320 aircraft, perhaps we should have taken this as a sign and headed home right then and there, rather than trying to grasp why a commercial airline would front its customer service with staff boasting all the people skills of a rabid bulldog.

But noooo, we kept the faith, through a forty-five-deep Customs queue, through a mad dash from one end of the airport to the other (only to discover our flight was delayed but no-one had bothered to call it, thereby scuttling what would have been a perfectly good opportunity to grab a much-needed coffee), through the endless whingeing of tired, bored children, through begging other patrons on an over-stuffed flight to swap seats with us so we could sit together, through stale trolley sandwiches, through there being only three Smartie cookies available for four famished brats, through overheated babies' bottles and nappies leaking on to laps, and a two-year-old's eardrum-twisting tantrums, we kept the faith that a wonderful, restful, relaxing family holiday is possible.

Needing to vent a little frustration lest it poison the whole holiday, in the thirty precious minutes I snatched while the older kids were temporarily occupied by overpriced entertainment packages and rubbish food and the twins were dozing clutched to our chests, I made use of the one media device my children hadn't snatched, my iPhone, and typed out a little missive outlining our experience, sending it directly to our travel agent upon landing, with the direction to 'spread it far and wide'. Tell me, dear diary, if you think I've been too harsh:

*Dear BlackStellar Airlines,*

*It is with more than disappointment that I write regarding our BlackStellar experience of Monday 29 June; it is with downright disgust.*

*As a couple travelling to Queenstown from Melbourne with six young children, including infant twins, we took the extra precaution of pre-paying a booking charge for our seats to guarantee we were seated together.*

*Upon check-in, we were told by Lisa that our seats had been handed to another family; a family that had not paid to guarantee seats, but who wanted to sit together so 'first in first served'.*

*Interesting.*

*Our travel agent was assured we would receive express passes to make passing through Customs with six children under nine just a little more manageable. Thank goodness we had Lisa on hand to bring us down to earth, informing us BlackStellar was not permitted to hand out these passes to passengers boarding* on A320s (?) and we simply were not important enough to warrant an exception. Clearly affronted by our distress at juggling six kids while trying to untangle the BlackStellar red tape we found ourselves ensnared in, 'Likeable Lisa' called in her manager, Stacey, who reiterated the policy and again refused to assist us with the seating issue, stating that just because you pay money to hold a seat, BlackStellar doesn't actually have to hold it for you! So in lay terms, BlackStellar offers a service which you are asked to pay for, then may refuse to provide that service depending on who happens to be on the check-in counter that day and what mood they happen to be in.

Good to know.

Stacey then summarily dismissed us, swanning off to terrorise other customers with her incomparable people skills. Yet another sparkling example of the true public face of BlackStellar: where the staff's distaste for dealing with actual people is only matched by their delight in wielding unwarranted power.

This was perfectly illustrated moments later when another staff member, recognising me as an actor, paused to talk to our children and hearing of our plight, promptly reached behind the counter and handed us a bundle of those previously inaccessible express passes.

A miracle!

Is that the basis upon which BlackStellar determines how they meet their customers' needs? You are no-one unless of course you are SOMEONE?

The whole debacle cost us a full hour. We almost missed our flight as a result, making an already volatile situation positively explosive. Our children's much-anticipated and previously organised breakfast in the airline lounge had to be abandoned, and we boarded hungry, dispirited and thoroughly disillusioned.

To add insult to injury, when I, with a baby strapped to my chest, juggling another in my arms, asked Lisa – shining example of customer service that she is – if I could use her pen to label a bag, Lisa refused with these words:

'It's my pen, I can't lend it to you.'

Lisa: I was merely asking to borrow your 50-cent Bic, not your first-born child, and I wasn't planning to abscond with the thing! Our frustration felt justified when even her sidekick at the desk confided she felt Loveable Lisa's handling of the situation was inexcusable.

We understand that dealing with the public can be an onerous task, but when that is your job, a career YOU have chosen, it is your responsibility to carry that job out with respect and courtesy for your customers.

What we cannot understand is why a company such as BlackStellar, built *upon a reputation for friendly customer service, retain staff with the compassion of an ice cube tray, and the people skills of a brick wall.*

*Of course, BlackStellar never asked us to attempt to fly overseas with six small children in tow, and we understand that. We just hope that BlackStellar understands that in future all eight of our full-fare tickets will go with another carrier, never BlackStellar ever again, and we will actively persuade everyone we know to do likewise.*

*Regards,*
*Me and The Chef*

And now . . . Buddy is screeching about his iPad charger not working, Tink has escaped her cot and is unravelling every roll of toilet paper in the house, Princess appears to have had a bit of an accident in her PJs and is now stalking about the lounge with no pants on, and Minnie is screaming above the cacophony for them to all be quiet so she can sleep.

Only the twins, whose shared port-a-cot I had the wisdom of shoving into a roomy walk-in robe, are sleeping blissfully, but not before having graced three separate outfits each with puréed pumpkin and baby puke.

In four hours it will be dawn. Look out, Queenstown: Team Catastrophe has arrived. You won't know what has hit you.

## AIR TRAVEL WITH CHILDREN: YOU ARE CLEARLY INSANE, SO HERE ARE SOME TIPS ON CONTAINING THE INSANITY

Be it long-haul or a mere hop, skip, jump over a border, air travel with children, particularly those under eight, will always be somewhat nightmarish. Whether or not the entire flight is one long nightmare depends entirely on how well you prepare before you even set foot in the departure lounge.

1. Before the trip, take the time to explain to your children that they are about to embark on a very special journey, full of wonderful and amazing things, but in order for everyone to enjoy themselves, they must be on their very best behaviour.

That means listening to all instructions given by yourself and the cabin staff, speaking quietly, and respecting their fellow travellers.

2. Checking in can be lengthy and onerous for even the most patient child. Keep them entertained by playing a game my children love: 'Guess the destination'. Have them each choose a passing traveller and guess where that person is going to or even coming from.

3. Put together what I call a 'Sack of Distractions'. This is a bag, preferably a large, resealable plastic bag or container (so they can see the contents and therefore are not tempted to rummage around, spilling most of it on the floor, in their seat and on the poor guy in 18R who had no idea he would be spending a prolonged period trapped next to a semi-trained monkey at the start of his holiday) filled with goodies you know they will love, and more importantly, will keep them distracted for the duration of the trip.

**Some simple rules for the Sack of Distractions:**

- No one item should cost more than $2 (everything should ultimately be disposable; you don't want to be stuck dragging it around for the duration of your holiday once it has served its purpose in getting you there with your sanity intact). Hence, visit discount stores, large chain department stores, craft warehouses and newsagents when putting your haul together.
- Include only one treat of a food nature, eg a lollipop, bag of crackers or chocolate bar.
- Only hand out the Sack once the plane has stabilised and the seatbelt light is turned off.
- Control the Sack. Only allow your child to pull out and play with one item at a time, and each item must be played with for at least ten minutes before moving on to the next. Otherwise your child will invariably empty the entire contents on to their tray table, muck about with the lot, and be whining that they are bored again within the hour.
- The Sack must be put away at meal times, only to be returned once they have finished eating.

- Suggested Sack fillers: Play-Doh with some simple tools (a must: keeps kids occupied and reasonably clean).
- Packets of pencils, preferably the wind-up variety that don't require sharpening, and small drawing pads. Ask them to draw what they see out the window, what they imagine their destination will be like, or to design a postcard for their grandparents or friends. Avoid textas, markers, or crayons. It is much harder for wandering fingers to graffiti the plane's interior with a simple pencil than it is with any of the above.
- Packets of stickers.
- Pack of cards.
- Rubik's cube or other hand-held puzzle (avoid picture puzzles, as bumped tray tables, turbulence or a critical piece disappearing somewhere on a full plane all have the potential to ignite a political incident).
  For older children, let them assist you in assembling their Sack so there is no risk of rejection and it is something they will look forward to. Many airlines offer children a soft toy or a stationery pack, but these are guaranteed to keep them entertained for all of ten minutes. Never underestimate the power of a homemade Sack of Distractions.

4. If you do not have the time or the wherewithal to create a Sack of Distractions, there is always the iPad. Most airlines now offer them as part of entertainment packages which can be pre-purchased, but the advantage of taking your own is you can download games and sites which will appeal to your child (and which you have ultimately condoned) before the flight, and hopefully keep them distracted from take-off to touch-down.

5. Pack some basic medications in your hand luggage: children's paracetamol, sore-throat lozenges, band-aids and nappy rash cream. Airline staff cannot provide these items in flight, and there is nothing more miserable than a child with a fever on a long-haul flight.

6. Ply children with water. Air travel is dehydrating and children are more prone to dehydration than adults simply because they are less likely to drink water before they feel thirsty. At meal

times, let them have juice as a treat, but ensure it is only water they consume in between by offering it frequently. Yes, this may entail several visits to the bathroom, but occasionally having to stretch their legs is a small price to pay to avoid the misery of a dehydrated, constipated child at the other end of your journey.

7.  Put aside an activity they can do after alighting from the aircraft. This is a great time for a Rubik's cube or the like – something that can be manipulated while standing and doesn't require a table or many bits and pieces. A lengthy plane ride is torturous enough for small, easily bored children, let alone a lengthy Customs queue followed by a drive, boat trip, or another flight to your final destination.

8.  Pack some hydration salts for yourself. Every trip is a good trip if it ends with champagne; you just want to ensure you can recover in time to actually enjoy the final destination.

Happy travels!

# FRIDAY 3 JULY

*5:12 p.m.* Queenstown: breath-taking one day, bloody freezing the next.

My goodness, I don't think I'm exaggerating when I say this place boasts some of the most spectacular scenery on earth. From the sky, this city is a veritable patchwork of sparkling blue ribbons intersecting rippling mountain ranges iced with generous dustings of ivory snow, flanked by pristine lakes, mirrors upon which the endless sky admires its own reflection.

The last three days have sped by in a flurry of snow, chapped lips, fatigue (The Chef blames the altitude, I blame pinot), and clomping around like a demented wildebeest shod in ski boots, lugging a ludicrous amount of gear, just for a few precious moments of gliding gracefully through the pristine powder. I've discovered I can actually ski! Who knew? Far from hurtling down the mountain side, gathering ice in my wake, quickly developing into a mammoth snowball slamming into an unsuspecting family of Swiss people who have paused for a yodel on the slopes, I have taken to the rhythmic gliding of the sport like a seasoned pro – well, maybe a slightly geriatric pro,

SHOPPING LIST

*Camera man*

*Sound recordist*

*Grip*

*Light rigger*

*Any actors lying around? (Though I can probably just ask the wait staff at any local restaurant and I will find a few – been there, done that!)*

with a bung knee and weak bladder, but pretty well all the same!

Hence, the past few days have evaporated like so many snowflakes on your tongue, a whirlwind of hitting the slopes, pizza before open fires, gasping at the proximity to those immaculate, white-capped ranges and imbibing much excellent local wine with friends new and old . . . until today.

An innocent email from my agent has slammed me fair into panic mode.

An audition, for a role I really really really want, due by Monday.

The role seems to be a hybrid of a number of roles I've played with aplomb. Clever, empowered, wily – and a stripper (of course!). Her storyline is rich and bountiful, her 'emotional journey' (please excuse me while I go all method on you) deep and satisfying.

I want this role – want it BADLY!

It has been such a long time since a proffered role has made me transcend my general apathy, so long since a work opportunity has infused me with energy and inspiration based purely on its content (as opposed to simply giving me an opportunity to escape the house) that my hunger for this role, my determination to capture it, make it my own and breathe life into it takes me by surprise.

But how on earth do I put down a decent audition holed up in holiday accommodation on the side of a snowy mountain, with a catastrophe of children and a grumpy chef?

My agent offers to put her feelers out, certain she can dig up a contact in Queenstown who will be willing to assist in this, my hour in need. Until then, I have what feels like a million lines to memorise, and more importantly, what am I going to wear? Are there strippers who ply their trade in thermals and woolly ski socks? This might be a greater challenge than I initially anticipated.

# SUNDAY 5 JULY

*10:16 a.m.* What a bloody nightmare.

After a farewell dinner with friends, accompanied by the obligatory bottle of wine (or five) Friday night blurred into Saturday morning as I tossed and turned, flitting between grasping for deep, dreamless sleep and moments of stark lucidity. Time and again I hauled myself from bed to dissect lines, digging for hidden meanings and alternative interpretations. I ransacked my neatly packed suitcase seeking appropriate costume fodder which simply wasn't there. T-shirt and jeans it is.

SHOPPING LIST

*Anti-distress-ants*

Saturday dawned hazy and muddled, much like the state of my mind. An available Queenstown-based actor hadn't materialised (Peter Jackson must be in town) so there was nothing for it but to drag The Chef from bed while the children slept and attempt to record the audition yet again on my phone.

The results were dismal.

Yes, dim, sultry mood lighting is a must in any quality hotel, but what I needed was stark, brilliant wattage to blow out my wrinkles and dazzle my eyes. All the Vaseline-smeared lenses in Hollywood wouldn't be enough to have plumped out the hollows in my cheeks and tightened the bags under my eyes the bland lighting gave me.

Despite his most valiant efforts, holding a camera while reciting unfamiliar lines was too much of a juggling act for The Chef, leading to the scene looking as if it was taking place during a mild earthquake.

My ensemble of blah white shirt coupled with grey thermal pants certainly didn't scream stripper material.

Playing back my favourite take, I discover that, unbeknownst to me, Tink had made a silent cameo, wandering into the back of the shot toting the stuffed kiwi bird toy a bewitched sales assistant had pressed upon her at the ski field's crèche yesterday. Her appearance is swiftly followed with a guest role by Princess, who ducked in, walloped Tink, snatched the kiwi and disappeared, Tink hot on her heels.

Stuff it, it will just have to do.

At the end of the day, I did my darnedest, and there was no time for regrets or endless retakes as we had a plane to catch. It was with that in mind that I consoled myself when finally I pressed 'send', shooting the screen test, with all my hopes attached, out into the cyber-ether, to wing its way to the producer's laptop and hopefully to an acting gig I truly, madly, deeply wanted.

Knowing only too well that I will spend the next few weeks obsessively checking my sources of electronic media, hoping for the results of my test to come through, I make the decision to switch everything off.

Job done, I gathered up our scattered belongings, stuffed them into suitcases, then gathered up my scattered children and tempted as I was to stuff them in suitcases, merely stuffed them back into their winter woollies and hightailed it to the airport. It was time to get our travelling sideshow on the road again.

Fiji, here we come!

*1:23 p.m.* 'Whoa! Bit warmer here, isn't it?' opined a fellow traveller as we finally exited the plane, officially exchanging the land of the long white cloud for the land of the Long Island iced tea – or at least, that was my intention.

'Congratulations,' I muttered under my breath, 'another expert in the bleeding obvious!'

Please forgive my narkiness, dearest diary, it's been a very long three hours, and email withdrawal is already kicking in. The sight of my iPhone trundling along the conveyor belt at security sets my fingers itching. As I boot up my iPad to converse with you, dearest diary, the desire to swipe over to the 'Mail' icon is almost unbearable, urging my fingers to tap in. What harm is one little glimpse? Where is the danger in innocently flicking through a few missives? Touching base with the home crowd? Letting our friends and family know we are safe and well?

Oh, shut up, Madeleine!

I remind myself that these are just trite excuses to torture myself with the audition waiting game, and that once I open that Pandora's box I will not have the willpower to close it.

It's the principle of the thing. We are on holiday. It is time to relax. There is no relaxation in constantly logging in to everyday working life.

This time needs to be less about my compulsions and more about my family.

As we step into the arrivals hall, escaping the sterile chill of artificially conditioned air, the humidity wraps around our thermal-clad bodies like a clammy octopus, moistening our clothing to cling-film texture and just as uncomfortable.

Gotta love the tropics!

Luggage collected, Customs cleared ('Anything to declare?' 'Umm, only that Princess is bored, Minnie is hungry, Buddy is having Minecraft withdrawals, and Lolly Pop is concealing a weapon of mass destruction in her nappy') and it's on to the domestics departures for the short flight to our island resort. Princess insists on rolling about on the floor, as she has done in every terminal we have entered since Melbourne, and somehow manages to gather a large wad of used chewing gum in her hair. I didn't close one of the sachets of formula I used to make a bottle for Jelly Bean mid-flight, so its contents have now circulated throughout my carry-on luggage and, mixed with the humidity, matured into a claggy, crusty, mucky mess. Everyone is sweating profusely. There is nary a bottle of water or decent snack in sight, and if we don't get the children into a pool soon, there is a good chance at least one of them may spontaneously combust.

The tiny plane ferrying us to the island is called, finally, and as we step on to the tarmac to board, it starts to rain.

Gotta love the tropics!

## MONDAY 6 JULY

7:15 a.m. Rain
9:20 a.m. Rain.
11:56 a.m. Rain.
2:19 p.m. Rain.
4:09 p.m. Rain.
7:27 p.m. Rain.
11:46 p.m. Rain.

SHOPPING LIST

Raincoat (who would have known I should pack one for Fiji!?)

## TUESDAY 7 JULY

6:35 a.m. Rain . . . and cold!
7:58 a.m. Rain . . . and muggy.
10:13 a.m. A brief parting of the low-hanging clouds has us out on jet skis. I tentatively follow The Chef well offshore. Rain, harder than ever, pelting my

face, stinging my eyes. Can barely see. Return sheepishly to shore. Back to the room and straight into a pot of what is supposedly coffee. The sun peeps out teasingly, so I dump Minnie, Buddy, Princess and a vest-clad Tink into the pool. Naturally the rain begins again moments later.

'Have fun!' I demand, as they stand shivering in the shallows, squinting against the pelting droplets.

Gotta love the tropics!

## WEDNESDAY 8 JULY

*6:17 a.m.* I wake, swallowing razor blades, in a murky pool of The Chef's sweat.

During the night, we have both been struck down by some horrid lurgy (The Chef significantly worse, thank you again Mr Flu Shot) leaving us weak, sore, irritable and feverish. Basically unable to have any fun whatsoever.

Hut-bound and with nothing to do, the urge to check that

> SHOPPING LIST
>
> Strepsils
>
> Hot lemon and honey tea
>
> Rum
>
> Self-pity (extra large serve, please)

surely mounting pile of unseen emails becomes a mild obsession. I slap it down, force myself out of bed and hustle the children back into the pool outside our hut. As they splash away their shivers, I curl into a tight ball on a damp sun lounge.

Bloody hell.

Time to call in what is perhaps one of the most famed aspects of any trip to Fiji: the babysitters.

From the moment Titi and Eleanoa arrive, calling 'Bhula! Bhula' at the entry to our villa, I know we are on to something good. They immediately tackle all the children in greeting cuddles and swoop up the babies. From now until the time we leave, the twins are destined never to touch the floor. With the kids engaged in hair braiding, paper aeroplane manufacture and playing in the pool, I retreat to the sun lounge, feeling more spoilt than I have in a long time.

Ahhhh, an afternoon of dedicated idleness . . .

Emails? Nup. Don't need to check them. I feel a strange certainty creeping into my bones that everything will work out.

From inside the villa, I can hear Princess performing her famed duck impersonation, the twins squawking in response and Minnie and Buddy fighting. Hmm. As I drift off, I contemplate whether there was ever an island by the name of 'Lunacy', peopled by a community of Lunatics. If so, my lot should be entitled to immediate citizenship.

## SATURDAY 11 JULY

*3:25 p.m.* Oh, diary! This is living on a whole other level!

I woke this morning to pure white dawn light glinting off waves gently teased by warm offshore breezes. The clash of blues as the reef dipped down into deeper water was dazzling.

SHOPPING LIST

*Reality check ... this is all too good to be true!*

The Chef and I were both shocked to discover that suddenly we both felt human! Refreshed and reinvigorated, I sat down and spent an hour mapping out schedules for babysitters, extracurricular activities and family time to work around my coming return to employment. The result is terrifying.

I feel a shift in my core, a lurch of the heart contemplating how tough this will be on the kids. I will barely see the twins. By the time production wraps up they will be walking . . . but I want this job, right? It's what I need. I love the role. It's perfect for me, and I need to do something for myself. I glance at their tiny faces, so angelic in repose, and am struck by how frequently the words 'I' and 'me' peppered the previous paragraph.

Ah well, can't question destiny!

But this holiday is all about the here and now. With that in mind, The Chef dragged the kids out of bed, I slathered them in sunscreen, and we hit the beach.

The pristine main pools of the resort lay before us in all their holiday brochure perfection. We dipped and wove between waterfalls and rock features. Splashing, laughing, gasping when we hit a cold spot, looking suspiciously at the ever-smirking Princess when we encountered warm patches. Photo opportunities exhausted, the beach beckoned.

Sandcastles are erected to much acclaim, then smashed (by Tink) to much wailing and gnashing of teeth. I can already envision her taking up a career in town planning. Minnie transforms Princess into a sand mermaid, at which point Princess declares she is staying there and living as a mermaid forever. That declaration is swiftly reversed when a kindly waiter approaches offering ice-cream lollipops. I see the kids blink in bewilderment. 'Ice-cream at 10 a.m.? Is this heaven or what?!'

Ice confections consumed (to the usual ratio of 40 per cent in the belly, 60 per cent in hair, on faces and over bathing suits), and the babies tucked up in the arms of Titi and Eleanoa, The Chef rustles up a couple of jet skis (again, gotta love the tropics!) and we take a family tour of the island. I take Minnie; Buddy and Princess are lucky enough to hitch rides with our guides, Tom and Joe, while The Chef draws the short straw with Tink. I say draws the short straw because true to form, after five minutes of panicked clutching at the controls, she dozes off, and The Chef spends the remainder of the hour juggling a sleeping child while trying to keep up with the guides.

The resort we have the privilege of staying in takes up only around 20 per cent of the emerald island it occupies, and our tour lifts the veil on the raw, ravishing beauty of the great expanse of untouched, unblemished nature just beyond our doorstep. Wild goats, vanilla vines, mud crabs big enough to take your hand off, incredible birdlife and an abundance of wild fruits greet our every turn. Reefs, bays and quays dip in and out, boasting every conceivable shade of blue, while the full rainbow spectrum plays out beneath our feet as reef fish dart between the shoals. We return breathless, my children red-cheeked and grinning, the girls' Fiji braids dangling in their eyes, Buddy bragging that he spotted a turtle and a shark, Tink fast asleep in Daddy's arm, snuggled down into her too-big life vest.

As we trundle back up the sand for a beachside lunch before a laze on the sun lounges while the kids totter off for a movie and craft at the kids' club, I feel happiness brimming; everything seems so perfect. Yes, I must admit that I am loath to spoil the delicate balance of this little tableaux with my looming return to work but it is a job I really want, or at least the younger, career-savvier me would have wanted, and isn't that what will make me happier? Regaining a little of my former ambition, my thirst, my hunger, my savoir faire? A little of my independence? Perhaps . . .

Truth be told, these days I am at my most fulfilled just trading titbits and turns of phrase with you, diary old friend; writing seems to meet my need to be creative and in tune with my muse most comprehensively. But I want to be a role model for my children, I want to show them that anything is possible, that they can have it all. An insistent little voice somewhere deep inside of me, which I cannot quiet, keeps pointing out, however, that long days on set feeling guilty that I am not with my children, followed by all-too-brief spells at home trying to get everything done and fretting I am doing a bad job at work because I am so rundown, doesn't really feel like 'having it all' – but I haven't quite figured out how making witty observations within the safe confines of my diary can be converted into a career progression, so it is best to stick to what I know.

It is going to be fantastic, it really is.

I cannot wait, truly.

But right now, it's time to work on that long-overdue tan, and imbibe as many tropical cocktails as the kids' club operating hours will permit (hey, there is fruit juice in there, it must be good for me!).

The Chef is dozing when normally he would be dashing off to another commitment, Minnie has headed off for a horse ride on the beach while her siblings cover themselves and every available surface in craft glue and glitter. The twins are being cosseted and coo-ed over by the island fairy godmothers, the sun is shining and my bikini is full of sand. All signs of another perfect day in paradise.

## TUESDAY 14 JULY

*11:12 a.m.* Another perfect day, another mild headache brought on by sun, surf, and perhaps the odd cocktail (90 per cent tropical juice, I promise). But have you ever noticed that, for some reason, the day after the night before is never quite so torturous when you are on holiday?

All this relaxation has made me anxious to start getting things organised for the upheaval to come. And so, with numerous coffees imbibed, I get back to thinking through how this will all work out, arranging schedules and so on. I know I will not be able to relax until I have at least organised the babysitters; I can't bear the thought of jumping off the

SHOPPING LIST

Baby formula (Yep, ran out)

Codeine (Panadol just ain't cutting it)

Tim Tams (temperate climates just don't agree with chocolate *whimper*!!!)

plane and straight into chaos. So it is time to dust off the iPad.

The new job is, in all probability, looming over me now so I log on to send an email to my beloved kid-wranglers back home with my plans. Wading through the backlog of junk emails that have accumulated in my online absence, I almost overlook a missive from my agent. With my finger lingering over the envelope icon, poised to open, I pause momentarily to take in the sight of my tousle-headed tribe, freshly risen and fighting over pancakes. It's probably just a message about scheduling a costume fitting; we only have one more day here, it can wait. My family can't.

## THURSDAY 16 JULY

*6:19 p.m.* Arrived at the airport. Needed to confirm baby cots on board had been paid for. Opened email, immediately spotted my agent's missive. Whoops, had completely forgotten about it. Find the relevant message from our travel rep then flick back to the one from my agent.

'The producers have finally been in touch, and they have decided to go with another actor . . .' The rest of the message blurs, a blend of well-intentioned plati-

SHOPPING LIST

*My bed*

*My pillow*

*My doona cover*

*My pride*

tudes promising my audition was exceptional and they love my work, not the right fit blah blah blah, all of which just compounds my confusion and further provokes my devastation. It all equals the same: the job is not mine, all certainly is out the window. Self-doubt creeps in as the first signs of a brewing migraine cloud my vision and crowd my thoughts.

I make my way on to the plane and settle the children on autopilot. Six hours of hell to endure. Just get me home . . .

## MONDAY 20 JULY

*11:06 a.m.* My harbour in the storm, the little hideaway. I woke early. Refreshed, calm, I watched the day dawn quietly, contemplating the fragile tendrils of hazy light threading through the trees, growing stronger by the minute till the stage was lit and the birds began their show in praise of the coming day. Red sky morning, clouds tinted a brilliant cherry-pink. Seems even the heavens are blushing in sincere condolence.

I headed out into the chill, feeling cleansed, purified, soothed by the bracing cold, to collect sticks and bark for a fire to warm the house. Every time a fearful thought clawed at my chest, I breathed deeply. Washing it away with a rush of crisp, enlivening air, the perfume of damp soil, the sting of winter in my nose and on my tongue.

SHOPPING LIST

A fresh start

A new beginning

A bright, exciting chapter

(Yes, but can someone please tell me where the heck to start?)

The little people emerged, one by one, from the warmth of their beds. Shuffling out into the cold kitchen, warming their tiny hands at the crackling fire.

The simple grace of their youth, amid the calm, gentle setting of this domestic scene, gives me strength.

With breakfast cleared away, I braced myself to check my long-neglected emails, anticipating there might be something lurking within the binary code, beamed in from cyberspace, that I might not want to see. What I find steals my breath.

A brief, buzzing, buoyant correspondence from Penguin.

They loved my excerpt.

They love the subject, the tone, the voice.

They want to offer me a book deal . . .

Bloody hell!

Gonna need your help here, my dearest diary, keeper of milestones, secrets and various indiscretions. How on earth will I retrace this journey to becoming mother to six under eight, when most days I struggle to remember my own name?

Okay, here goes.

In the beginning . . .

# CHAPTER

'How the heck did you let this happen?' You might be smiling, telling me how wonderful big families are. But what you are really thinking is written all over your face. How do I know? Have I untold psychic powers? Some mystical ability to plumb your subconscious depths? No, it's just that I see the same question on people's faces every day, many times a day. I see it reflected in my own eyes when I catch my reflection in the microwave oven door as I heat a bottle at 3 a.m. for one wailing infant while the other gnaws impatiently through my nightgown. (Who am I kidding? The chances of my having had time to change into a nightgown are zero to none, so the poor little tacker is probably trying to suck her supper through yesterday's T-shirt.)

There is no simple answer to that question. Circumstances led us here; I was vaguely aware of the challenges to come from the first, but looking back, was completely blind to both how impossible and how incredible the reality would prove.

Six children under eight . . .

My love for my babies is suffocating, smothering; it brings me to my knees and cuts me to the quick. My love for my babies is also affirming, uplifting, rewarding, it has expanded my horizons in every possible direction, opened my eyes to worlds within worlds, and 'Madeleine: Mother' is the best possible me I can ever hope to be.

Kids: you can't live with them, you can't live without them. I find myself frequently trying to escape the little monkeys, but truly cannot fathom a single moment without them around. Sure, limits have been placed on my freedom by having children and meeting their every need, but I also feel my life expanding, growing bigger, gaining greater meaning with each step they take, each new word they learn, each new challenge they meet. And now, thanks entirely to the fact that I have begotten six little bundles of trial and tribulation, I have triumphed, attaining the one role I always secretly coveted but considered well beyond my reach: Writer.

On some days, motherhood transforms me into a smug, inflexible harridan. On others I'm a valiant, fearless warrior. I can be a snarling tiger ready to pounce and a benign superhero, with only the power of empathy.

And that is the conundrum, the epiphany, the riddle, wrapped in a rhyme, wrapped in an enigma wrapped in a Tim Tam packet that is parenthood.

## A little prayer for parents (on very busy days)

*Bless the little children,*
*Watch over as they play.*
*Please fill their lives with much joy*
*And happiness every day.*

*Bless his rowdy laughter,*
*Bless her halting lisp.*
*Bless her daily tantrum,*
*Bless his refusal to be kissed.*

*Cherish each day as they grow from babes*
*To young ladies, little men.*
*Each night they lie in the arms of sleep,*
*Like angels fallen from heaven.*

*Remind me of their innocence,*
*For time so swiftly flies.*
*Let them play in make-believe*
*Untouched by deceit and lies.*

*Bless the ready smiles, the willing hands*
*That slip eagerly into mine,*
*With a kind of adoration*
*That might not stand the test of time.*

*For life brings so much to discover,*
*And fresh heartache every day.*
*Too soon the tea sets are empty,*
*The trains and trucks are packed away.*

*So bless the little children*
*For their eyes that cannot see*
*The evils in this wicked world,*
*And the flaws to be found in me.*

*Bless their quiet acceptance*
*Of things I cannot explain.*
*Bless the trust in those teary eyes*
*As I struggle to ease their pain.*

*Bless those little arms that reach for me*
*When they get a fright,*
*And the timid voice that calls my name*
*In the middle of the night.*

*Guide them in their little trials*
*And triumphs every day,*
*And let them know I love them*
*More than words can say.*

# EPILOGUE

*2 a.m.* A shrill wail pierces the soft folds of sleep enveloping me. A second shrieking squealer makes it a pre-dawn duet. As I struggle to untangle my feet from the twisted sheets a third voice, higher pitched, adds a glass-shattering soprano; I feel the whole house quivering to this company of wavering cries ricocheting off the walls in unison.

A quick inspection reveals the cause: Princess, Tink and Jelly Bean have all managed to wet their beds, as if by some psychic pact, some cosmic connection among sisters. Clearly Minnie and Lolly Pop missed that email. Buddy wasn't even on the mailing list.

*2:05 a.m.* Three screaming kiddies, three soaked mattresses, three sets of saturated bedding in need of replacement.

Bloody kids . . . wouldn't have them any other way.

# ACKNOWLEDGEMENTS

I would never have had the opportunity to even contemplate sweating over who to thank for helping make this book a reality were it not for:

The magnificent folk at Penguin Random House. Darling Julie Gibbs, thank you for seeing the potential hidden away amid my rambling, and believing that rambling might just have an audience. Katrina O'Brien, thank you for bringing structure to my chaos, and giving me a swift kick in the schedule when needed. Jocelyn Hungerford, thank you for having the nerve to correct an actor's interpretation of Shakespeare. Alissa Dinallo, thank you for the playful cover design. Thank you too to Rob, Earl and the whole shoot team for wonderful kidwrangling and beautiful pics.

The gorgeous grandparents, without whom my various forays into employment would never have been possible, and for loving my little people with all their hearts, and then some.

Kristy and Jess, whose invaluable assistance keeps this show on the road.

Tracy, David, Teresa, and Paul, for their indefatigable good humour when it comes to humouring my whims.

All the parents, whose joyous laughter with every triumph, whose unfettered tears with every trial, and whose weary smiles at every school drop-off, inspired me to write with the same honesty they so selflessly shared with me.

And finally, my shaggy chef and our catastrophe of children ... kids, you are my favourite people in the world. You have made your mum the happiest person on earth simply because, everyday, she gets to be your mum.

My love, thank you for the life we are building together, for believing in me, and telling me straight when I am not fulfilling my potential. The version of me I see reflected in your eyes is the best me I can possibly be, and makes me want to be even better.